FOOD&

Wine
Guide
2012

by the Editors of Food & Wine and Mary G. Burnham

WINE GUIDE 2012

editor in chief **DANA COWIN**

executive wine editor **RAY ISLE**

deputy editor **CHRISTINE QUINLAN**

art director **COURTNEY WADDELL ECKERSLEY**

designer **MICHELLE LEONG**

volume editor **KRISTEN WOLFE BIELER**

associate wine editor **MEGAN KRIGBAUM**

chief copy editor **CHRIS SWIAC**

copy editors **AMY K. HUGHES, LISA LEVENTER, ANNE O'CONNOR**

tastings coordinator **ANNE ZIMMERMAN**

tastings coordinator intern **KRYSTAL CONOVER**

wine inventory management **SAN FRANCISCO WINE CENTER**

chief researcher **JANICE HUANG**

researchers **CARY BECKWITH, TOM HOLTON, TIMOTHY KIM, ERIN LAVERTY, TOMÁS MARTÍN, ELLEN MCCURTIN, KAITLYN PIRIE, PAOLA SINGER**

indexer **ANDREA CHESMAN**

digital coordinator **JOHN KERN**

design concept **PLEASURE / KEVIN BRAINARD & RAUL AGUILA**

cover photography **ANTONIS ACHILLEOS**

produced for FOOD & WINE magazine by
gonzalez defino, ny / gonzalezdefino.com

principals **JOSEPH GONZALEZ, PERRI DEFINO**

AMERICAN EXPRESS PUBLISHING CORPORATION

president/ceo **ED KELLY**

chief marketing officer & president, digital media **MARK V. STANICH**

senior vice president/chief financial officer **PAUL B. FRANCIS**

vice presidents/general managers **FRANK BLAND, KEITH STROHMEIER**

vice president, books & products/publisher **MARSHALL COREY**

director, book programs **BRUCE SPANIER**

senior marketing manager, branded books **ERIC LUCIE**

assistant marketing manager **STACY MALLIS**

director of fulfillment & premium value **PHIL BLACK**

manager of customer experience & product development **CHARLES GRAVER**

director of finance **THOMAS NOONAN**

associate business manager **UMA MAHABIR**

operations director (prepress) **ROSALIE ABATEMARCO SAMAT**

operations director (manufacturing) **ANTHONY WHITE**

ISSN 1522-001X
Manufactured in the United States of America.

FOOD&WINE
BOOKS
American Express Publishing Corporation, New York

FOOD&WINE

Wine
Guide

2012

FRANCE
ITALY
SPAIN
PORTUGAL
GERMANY
AUSTRIA
GREECE
UNITED STATES
AUSTRALIA
NEW ZEALAND
ARGENTINA
CHILE
SOUTH AFRICA

Contents /Wine Guide

2012

Foreword

FOOD & WINE's 14th annual edition of the Wine Guide has a big ambition: to be the simplest, smartest, most user-friendly wine book you can buy. To accomplish this, the magazine's editors, together with San Francisco–based writer Mary G. Burnham, have focused on 500 pivotal wineries in the world's key wine regions—the wineries you can count on to produce sensational bottles no matter the grape, no matter the price. You can find their wines in almost any good store, and every kind of wine they make is worth buying. Still, we've gone ahead and included over 1,000 benchmark bottles that define each producer's style, as well as the best deals and stealth stars in their portfolios. We've also included trend updates from around the globe, a wine-and-food pairing primer and a dictionary of common wine terms. We're confident that you'll find this book to be a clear, concise and supremely easy-to-use resource.

Dana Cowin
Dana Cowin
Editor in Chief
FOOD & WINE

Ray Isle
Ray Isle
Executive Wine Editor
FOOD & WINE

KEY TO SYMBOLS

TYPE OF WINE

● **RED**

● **ROSÉ**

○ **WHITE**

PRICE

$$$$ **OVER $60**

$$$ **$30+ TO $60**

$$ **$15+ TO $30**

$ **$15 AND UNDER**

FOR MORE EXPERT WINE-BUYING ADVICE

Join the F&W community at *foodandwine.com*

🅱 Follow us *@fandw*

🅵 Become a fan at *facebook.com/foodandwine*

Wine
Tasting Guide

Anyone can taste wine, but it helps to know what to look for and how the pros go about it. Tasting wine is like any other acquired skill: The more you practice, the better you become. Most of us possess all the tools we need to taste wine. Our tastebuds can detect sweet, salty, bitter and sour sensations, plus umami, the savory flavor found in mushrooms and meat. And our noses can differentiate among hundreds of aromas. The most important thing to learn is how to pay attention to the wine in your glass. Here are a few tips to help get your palate into tasting shape.

SET THE MOOD Use a clear, stemmed glass that is comfortable to hold. A basic Bordeaux-shaped glass works well for reds and whites. Choose a well-lit place that's relatively odor-neutral, and avoid wearing perfume or scented lotion.

SET THE SCENE Pour just enough wine in the glass so it barely reaches the widest part of the bowl. This way you'll have room to swirl the wine without spilling it.

CHECK THE COLOR A light color generally indicates a light-bodied wine; a darker color, a fuller-bodied wine. Also, white wines deepen in color with age; reds get lighter and take on an orangish or even brown hue. If you've poured more than one wine, compare the colors and guess which wine will taste more concentrated. Young wines that appear brown may be the result of poor winemaking or storage.

SWIRL & SNIFF Hold the glass by its stem and swirl it gently to release the wine's aromas. Sniff. What do you smell? Sniff again. Do you smell fruit? What sort? The wine might evoke herbs, flowers, spices, vanilla or wood. Some wines smell like bell pepper, leather, roasted meat or even manure. Don't worry about cataloguing every aroma. Just articulate what you smell. Sharing your impressions will help you learn and remember. Noxious smells like sulfur or must might dissipate with air. If the wine smells bad, give it a few minutes and swirl the glass to bring more contact with oxygen. If the wine still has an unappealing odor, move on to another one. If a wine smells like wet, moldy cork or cardboard, it may be corked, meaning it has been infected by an unpleasant-smelling compound called TCA that can be found in corks. TCA is harmless, but it makes wine taste bad. If it's hard to describe what you're smelling, try comparing two wines side-by-side—the contrast can be very helpful.

SIP & SWISH Sip the wine and swish it around in your mouth. Try to suck air into your mouth while wine is still in it (this takes practice). This allows the wine to release more aromas. How does it feel? Does it coat your mouth? Is it light, prickly and refreshing? Does it taste bitter or sweet? Does it recall specific fruits or spices? Smell again. Does it smell like it tastes? Do you like it? There are no wrong answers.

TO SPIT OR SWALLOW? If you're tasting more than a couple of wines at one sitting and want to be able to detect as much as possible from every glass (and remember your impressions the next day), it's important to spit. After the wine leaves your mouth, notice how long its flavors linger—that's called its finish.

TASTE IN CONTEXT In a horizontal tasting, you sample a range of wines that are alike in all but one way. This could be a group of wines from the same region and vintage, but made by different producers, or a group of wines from the same producer, same grape and same vintage, but from different vineyards. Comparing the differences among such similar wines will expand your knowledge. In a vertical tasting, you sample the same wine from the same producer made in different years. It's a great demonstration of how vintage can make a difference, as well as how age can change a wine's look and taste.

Wine / Terms

You won't find much fussy wine jargon in this guide, but some of the terms commonly used to describe the taste of wine might be unfamiliar or used in an unfamiliar way. References in tasting notes to flavors and textures other than "grape" are meant to serve as analogies: All the wines in this guide are made from grapes, but grapes have the ability to suggest the flavors of other fruits, herbs or minerals. Here's a mini glossary to help you become comfortable with the language of wine.

ACIDITY The tart, tangy or zesty sensations in wine. Ideally, acidity brightens a wine's flavors as a squeeze of lemon brightens fish. Wines lacking acidity taste "flabby."

APPELLATION An officially designated winegrowing region. The term is used mostly in France and the U.S. In Europe, a wine's appellation usually reflects not only where it's from but also aspects of how it's made, such as vineyard yields and aging.

BALANCE The harmony between acidity, tannin, alcohol and sweetness in a wine.

BIODYNAMICS An organic, sustainable approach to farming that takes into account a farm's total environment, including surrounding ecosystems and astronomical considerations, such as the phases of the moon.

BODY How heavy or thick a wine feels in the mouth. Full-bodied or heavy wines are often described as "big."

CORKED Wines that taste like wet cork or newspaper are said to be corked. The cause is trichloroanisole (TCA), a contaminant sometimes transmitted by cork.

CRISP A term used to describe wines that are high in acidity.

CRU In France, a grade of vineyard (such as *grand cru* or *premier cru*), winery (such as Bordeaux's *cru bourgeois*) or village (in Beaujolais). Also used unofficially in Italy's Piedmont region to refer to top Barolo vineyards.

CUVÉE A batch of wine. A cuvée can be from a single barrel or tank (*cuve* in French), or a blend of different lots of wine. A Champagne house's top bottling is called a *tête de cuvée*.

DRY A wine without perceptible sweetness. A dry wine, however, can have powerful fruit flavors. *Off-dry* describes a wine that has a touch of sweetness.

EARTHY An earthy wine evokes flavors such as mushrooms, leather, damp straw or even manure.

FILTER/FINE Processes used to remove sediment or particulates from a wine to enhance its clarity.

FINISH The length of time a wine's flavors linger on the palate. A long finish is the hallmark of a more complex wine.

FRUITY A wine with an abundance of fruit flavors is described as fruity. Such wines may give the impression of sweetness, even though they're not actually sweet.

HERBACEOUS Calling a wine herbaceous or herbal can be positive or negative. Wines that evoke herb flavors can be delicious. Wines with green pepper flavors are less than ideal, and are also referred to as vegetal.

LEES The sediment (including dead yeast cells) left over after a wine's fermentation. Aging a wine on its lees (*sur lie* in French) gives wine nutty flavors and a creamy texture.

MINERAL Flavors that (theoretically) reflect the minerals found in the soil in which the grapes were grown. The terms *steely*, *flinty* and *chalky* are also used to describe these flavors.

NÉGOCIANT In wine terms, a *négociant* (French for "merchant") is someone who buys grapes, grape juice or finished wines in order to blend, bottle and sell wine under his or her own label.

NOSE How a wine smells; its bouquet or aroma.

OAKY Wines that transmit the flavors of the oak barrels in which they were aged. Some oak can impart toast flavors.

OXIDIZED Wines that have a tarnished quality due to exposure to air are said to be oxidized. When intended, as in the case of sherry (see p. 275), oxidation can add fascinating dimensions to a wine. Otherwise, it can make a wine taste unappealing.

PALATE The flavors, textures and other sensations a wine gives in the mouth. The term *mid-palate* refers to the way these characteristics evolve with time in the mouth.

POWERFUL Wine that is full of flavor, tannin and/or alcohol.

RUSTIC Wine that is a bit rough, though often charming.

TANNIN A component of grape skins, seeds and stems, tannin is most commonly found in red wines. It imparts a puckery sensation similar to oversteeped tea. Tannin also gives a wine its structure and enables some wines to age well.

TERROIR A French term that refers to the particular attributes a wine acquires from the specific environment of a vineyard— i.e., the climate, soil type, elevation and aspect.

Wine

Buying Guide

Knowing where and how to shop for wine makes discovering great wines easy and even fun, no matter where you live or what your budget. Take advantage of these tips to shop smarter.

IN SHOPS

SCOPE OUT THE SHOPS Visit local wine shops and determine which ones have the most helpful salespeople, the best selection and the lowest prices. Ask about case discounts, and whether mixing and matching a case is allowed. Expect at least a 10 percent discount; some stores will offer more. These days, many retailers are increasing their discounts and offering one-liter bottles and three-liter wine boxes that deliver more wine for the money. Finally, pay attention to store temperature: The warmer the store, the more likely the wines are to have problems.

ASK QUESTIONS Most wine-savvy salespeople are eager to share their knowledge and recommend some of their favorite wines. Let them know your likes, your budget and anything else that might help them select a wine you'll love.

BECOME A REGULAR The better the store's salespeople know you, the better they can suggest wines that will please you. Take the time to report back on wines they've suggested—it will pay off in future recommendations.

GET ON THE LIST Top wine shops often alert interested customers to special sales, hard-to-find wines or great deals in advance. Ask to get on their e-mail lists.

ONLINE

KNOW YOUR OPTIONS Take advantage of the Internet to easily find the wine you want and get the best price on it. The two most common ways to buy wine online are via online retailers or directly from wineries. Retailers may offer bulk discounts if you buy a case and shipping discounts if you spend a certain amount. Wineries don't often discount, but their wines can be impossible to find elsewhere. A great advantage of online shopping is price comparison: Websites like Wine-Searcher.com allow you to compare prices at retailers around the world.

BE WILLING TO ACT FAST Some of the steepest discounts on prestigious or hard-to-find wines are offered via so-called "flash sales" at sites such as WineAccess.com, WinesTilSoldOut.com and Lot18.com. Announced by e-mail, sales typically last just a day or two, and the best deals might sell out in under an hour.

KNOW THE RULES The difference between browsing for wine online and actually purchasing it has everything to do with where you live and how "liberal" your state is about interstate wine shipments. The laws governing direct-to-consumer interstate shipments differ from state to state. If you're considering buying wine from an out-of-state vendor, find out first whether it can ship to your state.

KNOW THE WEATHER If you're ordering wine online when it's hot outside, it's worth paying for express delivery: A week spent roasting in the back of a delivery truck risks turning your prized case of Pinot into plonk. Some retailers and wineries offer free storage during the summer months; they'll hold purchased wine until the weather cools and you give the OK to ship.

IN RESTAURANTS

CHECK OUT THE LIST Many restaurants post their wine list online or are happy to e-mail it upon request. Scoping out the wine menu in advance dramatically increases your odds of picking the right wine for your meal. For starters, if the selection looks poor, you can ask about the restaurant's corkage policy and perhaps bring your own bottle instead. A mediocre list might be limited in selection, have a disproportionate number of wines from one producer, fail to specify vintages or carry old vintages of wines meant to be drunk young and fresh. When faced with a bad wine list, order the least expensive bottle that you recognize as being reasonably good.

On the other hand, if the list is comprehensive, you can spend all the time you like perusing it in advance, rather than boring your dining companions while you pore over it at the table. You'll have plenty of time to spot bargains (or overpriced bottles) and to set an ordering strategy based on the list's strengths and your own preferences.

ASK QUESTIONS Treat the wine list as you would a food menu. You should ask how the Bordeaux tastes in comparison to the California Cabernet as readily as you'd ask about the difference between two fish dishes. Ask to speak to the wine director, if there is one. Then, tell that person the type of wine you're look-ing for—the price range, the flavor profile—as well as the dishes you will be having. If you want to indicate a price range without announcing the amount to the table, point to a bottle on the list that costs about what you want to spend and explain that you are considering something like it. And if you're unsure how to describe the flavors you're looking for, name a favorite producer who makes wine in a style you like. With this information, the wine director should be able to recommend several options.

TASTE THE WINE When the bottle arrives, make sure it's exactly what you ordered—check the vintage, the producer and the blend or variety. If it's not, speak up. You may be presented with the cork. Ignore it. Instead, sniff the wine in your glass. If it smells like sulfur, cabbage or skunk, tell your server that you think the wine might be flawed and request a second opinion from the wine director or the manager. If there's something truly wrong, they should offer you a new bottle or a new choice.

Sommeliers
of the Year

Whether championing biodynamic producers or letting customers purchase half a bottle of wine for half the price, FOOD & WINE's top sommeliers of the year are inspiring other wine pros around the country. Among the trend-setting obsessions of these seven wine-service stars are a laserlike focus on *terroir* (Clint Sloan); fabulous older wines aged to perfection (Matt Straus); and serious wine lists written in everyday English, not wine-geek gibberish (Steven Grubbs).

MARK EBERWEIN
St. Regis Deer Valley / **Park City, UT** / *starwoodhotels.com*
WHY HE WON Despite the limited catalog of Utah's state-run liquor authority, Eberwein has somehow sourced terrific California Cabernets and great Burgundies for the entire St. Regis Deer Valley resort.
FAVORITE PAIRING 2007 Mas de Gourgonnier les Baux de Provence red with chef de cuisine Matthew Harris's grilled lamb chop with pistachio pesto at J&G Grill.

STEVEN GRUBBS
Empire State South / **Atlanta** / *empirestatesouth.com*
WHY HE WON Grubbs's wine list is smart, quirky and full of great Burgundies and Rieslings, presented in a way that is conversational instead of intimidating.
FAVORITE PAIRING Rare Wine Co. Historic Series Savannah Verdelho Madeira with chef Hugh Acheson's boiled peanuts.

SHEBNEM INCE
Henri / **Chicago** / *henrichicago.com*
WHY SHE WON For this elegant Michigan Avenue restaurant, Ince has scrupulously sourced only wines that are biodynamic, organic and non-interventionist.
FAVORITE PAIRING 2007 Vincent Dancer Meursault with chef Dirk Flanigan's buttery sole meunière.

SOMMELIERS OF THE YEAR

CAT SILIRIE

Menton / Boston / *mentonboston.com*

WHY SHE WON Silirie's beautifully curated wine collection at Menton (chef Barbara Lynch's luxurious new restaurant), combined with tireless staff training and tastings, creates a remarkable wine experience for diners.

FAVORITE PAIRING Pierre Peters Blanc de Blancs Champagne with Lynch's buttery seafood soup.

CLINT SLOAN

Husk / Charleston, SC / *huskrestaurant.com*

WHY HE WON Sloan is bringing attention to the importance of *terroir* by organizing his wines by soil types: alluvial, limestone, gravel and so on.

FAVORITE PAIRING 2001 Chateau Musar from Lebanon with any dish from chef Sean Brock, who changes the menu at Husk twice a day.

JOHN SLOVER

Ciano / New York City / *cianonyc.com*

WHY HE WON Slover has redefined wine service: Guests can try half a bottle for half price, and he will make the rest available to other diners by the glass.

FAVORITE PAIRING 2007 Domaine Chavy Puligny-Montrachet with chef Shea Gallante's scallops with hazelnuts, *mostarda* and brussels sprout leaves.

MATT STRAUS

Heirloom Café / San Francisco / *heirloom-sf.com*

WHY HE WON Straus's obsession with cellaring wines has resulted in a superb library of older vintages from around the world.

FAVORITE PAIRING 1992 Rolet Arbois Vin Jaune, an oxidized white wine from the Jura region of France, with the off-the-menu Epoisses burger (anyone can order it).

OLD WOR

France/
Italy/
Spain/
Portugal/
Germany/
Austria/
Greece

66
ITALY

130
GERMANY

LD

20 FRANCE

102 SPAIN

122 PORTUGAL

140 AUSTRIA

148 GREECE

France

Wine Region

No other country produces more great wine than France. But beyond its world-benchmark bottlings— the great first-growths of Bordeaux, the *grands crus* of Burgundy, the Cristals and Dom Pérignons of Champagne—France offers a varied array of wines from thousands of different vineyards and producers, most of them at surprisingly affordable prices.

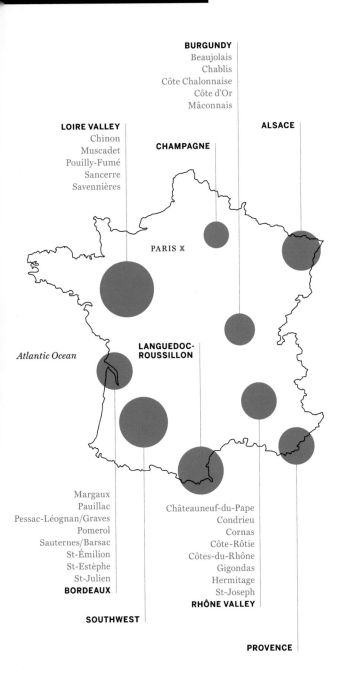

BURGUNDY
Beaujolais
Chablis
Côte Chalonnaise
Côte d'Or
Mâconnais

ALSACE

LOIRE VALLEY
Chinon
Muscadet
Pouilly-Fumé
Sancerre
Savennières

CHAMPAGNE

PARIS X

Atlantic Ocean

**LANGUEDOC-
ROUSSILLON**

Margaux
Pauillac
Pessac-Léognan/Graves
Pomerol
Sauternes/Barsac
St-Émilion
St-Estèphe
St-Julien
BORDEAUX

Châteauneuf-du-Pape
Condrieu
Cornas
Côte-Rôtie
Côtes-du-Rhône
Gigondas
Hermitage
St-Joseph
RHÔNE VALLEY

SOUTHWEST

PROVENCE

21

France

FRANCE PRODUCES A huge quantity of wine: about 1.4 billion gallons a year. More significant, however, is that it produces—in the opinion of most experts and connoisseurs—more *fine* wine than any other nation on earth. France's diverse geography encompasses zones as different as the Atlantic-cooled vineyards of Bordeaux and the Loire Valley, the limestone-studded soils of Burgundy and the sunny regions along the Rhône River and the Mediterranean coast. Centuries of experimentation have honed winemaking into firmly rooted traditions that are admired and emulated around the world.

France has an advantage in quality winemaking in that many of the world's best grape varieties are French, including Chardonnay, Cabernet Sauvignon, Merlot, Pinot Noir, Syrah and Sauvignon Blanc. But while the French care about grapes—and regulate where and how different grapes are grown—what really matters to them is *terroir*. The idea of *terroir*, a term that refers to all the distinguishing elements of a place, such as climate, sun exposure, soil and surrounding flora, is fundamental to French winemaking philosophy. It is the belief that nature and geography make the wine, not man. Perhaps that is why, quite surprisingly, there is no French word for *winemaker*; someone who makes wine is called a *vigneron*—literally, a "vine grower."

Sales of French wine have been declining for several years as competition from New World regions has challenged France's dominance. In response, French winemakers now travel abroad to learn from others; regulation changes have given vintners greater flexibility; and the government has invested in modernizing vineyards and cellars. As a result, established zones such as Bordeaux and the Rhône are turning out some of their greatest wines, while formerly off-the-radar regions, especially in southern France, are making a growing number of fine wines.

FRENCH WINE LABELS

Most French wine labels list appellation (i.e., region or subregion) but not the grape used to make the wine. (Alsace labels are an important exception; see p. 25.) A wine bearing its appellation name must meet regulations designed to guarantee authenticity and quality. The system governing these regulations is known as the Appellation d'Origine Contrôlée (AOC), or "controlled region of origin." In 2008, France added a new category for its lowest priced wines, Vin de France. The following year it introduced new names for some categories to make them consistent with their European Union counterparts, but so far producers have been slow to adopt them. The AOC hierarchy from top to bottom is:

AOC/AOP The AOC category encompasses most French wines exported to the U.S. and ensures that the wines meet regional requirements. Standards vary by region yet typically spell out permitted grapes, winemaking practices, minimum alcohol levels (higher alcohol levels mean the grapes were picked when they were riper, which in theory translates to better wines) and harvest size (overly large grape harvests tend to yield dilute wines). There are AOC regions *within* larger AOC regions as well; generally, the more specific the subregion, the higher the standards. In Burgundy, for example, a wine bearing a district name such as Côte de Nuits–Villages must meet more-stringent requirements than those labeled simply *Bourgogne*. Wines from the Vosne-Romanée, a *village* within the Côte de Nuits, must conform to stricter standards. The standards are even higher for wines from Vosne-Romanée Les Suchot, a *premier cru* denomination of Vosne-Romanée. A new, optional designation for AOC wine is AOP (Appellation d'Origine Protégée), which EU regulators hope all member countries will soon be using.

VIN DÉLIMITÉ DE QUALITÉ SUPÉRIEURE (VDQS) An intermediary step toward AOC status, the VDQS category was eliminated as of the 2011 vintage.

VIN DE PAYS/INDICATION GÉOGRAPHIQUE PROTÉGÉE (IGP) The *vin de pays*/IGP category includes wines from five designated regions (e.g., Vins de Pays du Val de la Loire). These wines are subject to lower standards than AOC wines but are allowed to list their grape varieties. Most *vins de pays* (literally, country wines) are forgettable, but some innovative winemakers who wish to work beyond the constraints of AOC requirements are producing exemplary wines with this designation.

VIN DE TABLE The lowest rung on the quality ladder of wines that fail to meet AOC requirements, *vins de table* (literally, table wines) are being phased out and incorporated into the Vin de France category (see below). *Vins de table* are not permitted to mention vintages or grapes on their labels or give a place of origin more specific than France. Most are dull, but, as with *vins de pays,* certain iconoclasts have chosen to ignore some of the AOC demands and are making great *vins de table.*

VIN DE FRANCE Meant to attract drinkers more interested in grape variety and brand name than origin, this new category allows vintners to blend wines from different regions and still list vintage and variety information on the labels if they choose.

ALSACE

The foothills of Alsace's Vosges mountains, on France's eastern border, yield aromatic white wines from grapes more closely associated with Germany than France. Their mineral flavors, bright acidity and full-bodied style make them great partners for everything from the local choucroute to spicy Asian food.

♣ ALSACE GRAPES & STYLES

Among the Alsace varieties, the four "noble" ones—Riesling, Gewurztraminer, Pinot Gris and Muscat—yield the best wines. Riesling, the region's most widely planted grape, typically makes medium-bodied wines that reflect the mineral, flinty soils. In contrast to German Rieslings, which often have some sweetness,

Alsace versions are usually dry. Pinot Gris is the same grape as Italy's Pinot Grigio, yet the wines are totally different: Alsace Pinot Gris tends to be creamier and fuller-bodied than its light, crisp Italian counterparts. Often made in an off-dry style, Alsace Gewurztraminers display flamboyant lychee and floral aromas and spicy flavors. Pinot Blanc, Muscat and Auxerrois make up the bulk of Alsace's other whites. Pinot Noir, the region's only red grape, makes lighter red and rosé wines. Alsace is also known for glorious dessert wines and for Crémant d'Alsace, a sparkling wine (see p. 266) made with Pinot Blanc.

Alsace white wine blends often include the four noble grapes in combination with Sylvaner, Auxerrois and Chasselas—good if unexceptional varieties that don't generally make great wines on their own. Any of these grapes may be combined in an Edel-zwicker blend, but a Gentil blend must be made up of at least 50 percent noble varieties. Pinot Blanc, the lighter-bodied sibling of Pinot Gris, is also permitted in these blends. However, Alsace wines labeled *Pinot Blanc* are likely to be a blend of Pinot Blanc and Auxerrois, with possible inclusions of Pinot Gris or Pinot Noir that has been vinified as white wine. Chardonnay is approved for AOC Crémant d'Alsace wines but not for still wines.

DEFINING ALSACE

Alsace labels are simple compared with those of most other French regions. Taking a cue from Germany, Alsace labels its wines by grape. Although the European Union requires that the listed grape make up at least 85 percent of a bottle's contents, Alsatian standards insist on 100 percent of the listed grape (wines labeled *Pinot Blanc* are an exception; see above). Blended whites are labeled with the official designation *Edelzwicker* or *Gentil*, or the label may name the vineyard. Most of the wine made in Alsace meets AOC standards. Unlike the complex hierarchy in Burgundy or Bordeaux, Alsace has three AOC designations: Alsace, Alsace Grand Cru (which indicates the grapes were sourced from select vineyards) and Crémant d'Alsace (for sparkling wines). Wines labeled *réserve*, a term used liberally in Alsace to indicate higher-quality wines, may also list a place name. Unfortunately, no uniform system for identifying sweetness levels of Alsace wines exists, though some producers have developed their own scales. Unless you research a wine before you buy it, you won't know from the label if the wine is dry, off-dry or slightly sweet.

Producers/ Alsace

DOMAINE ALBERT MANN

Best known for their luscious Gewurztraminers, Maurice Bar-thelmé and his brother Jacky make wines from 52 acres of biodynamically farmed estate vineyards near the town of Colmar, where warmer temperatures yield riper wines. The Barthelmés come from an old winemaking family; Maurice married Albert Mann's daughter Marie-Claire, and the families gradually combined their vineyards to create a single estate.

○ **Domaine Albert Mann Gewurztraminer / 2009 / $$**
Mann's entry-level Gewurz is silky and lightly sweet, with floral and apricot notes.

○ **Domaine Albert Mann Schlossberg Grand Cru Riesling /** **2009 / $$$** Sourced from a Roman-era vineyard that yields Rieslings with chalky minerality and gorgeous concentration, this stunning wine also shows citrus and apple notes.

○ **Domaine Albert Mann Steingrubler Grand Cru** **Gewurztraminer / 2008 / $$$** This gets its luscious, juicy intensity from grapes grown in an ancient quarry.

DOMAINE MARCEL DEISS

Once dismissed by some as eccentric, owner-winemaker Jean-Michel Deiss is now acknowledged by many as a visionary for his progressive, often unorthodox philosophies on vineyard management. A longtime advocate of biodynamic farming, Deiss makes unusual field blends of different grapes harvested and vinified together. His wines are multilayered and intense.

○ **Domaine Marcel Deiss Pinot Blanc Bergheim / 2009 / $$**
An oak-aged white that's actually a blend of four Pinot varieties: Blanc, Noir, Buerot and plump, satiny Auxerrois.

○ **Domaine Marcel Deiss Grasberg / 2009 / $$$**
This single-vineyard blend of Riesling, Pinot Gris and Gewurztraminer is known for its minerality, which Deiss attributes to the site's limestone soil.

DOMAINES SCHLUMBERGER

This family-owned estate—Alsace's largest—uses horses to plow some of the steep, terraced *grand cru* vineyard slopes. Schlumberger's excellent wines have only improved under Alain Freyburger, who became winemaker in 2000. Major investments in facilities have helped Freyburger bring greater consistency to the wines, made with grapes from some 300 estate-vineyard acres.

○ **Domaines Schlumberger Les Princes Abbés Pinot Blanc** / 2008 / $ Schlumberger's basic wines, including this medium-bodied Pinot Blanc, offer terrific quality.

○ **Domaines Schlumberger Les Princes Abbés Riesling** / 2007 / $$ A few years of bottle aging have brought out a pleasant hint of petrol in this super Riesling.

DOMAINE WEINBACH

Colette Faller runs this top estate with daughters Catherine and Laurence; together they produce some of Alsace's finest benchmark bottlings. Laurence heads up winemaking, each year turning out as many as 20 to 30 different lush, voluptuous wines (entirely sourced from biodynamic vineyards, as of 2010).

○ **Domaine Weinbach Sylvaner Réserve** / 2009 / $ Sylvaners are often bland, yet this slightly sweet apricot-infused example has lots of personality.

○ **Domaine Weinbach Cuvée Théo Riesling** / 2009 / $$ Named for Colette's late husband, Théo Faller, this Riesling layers opulent apple and stone fruit with fresh acidity.

DOMAINE ZIND-HUMBRECHT

In a region where most wineries count their history in centuries, not decades, Zind-Humbrecht is an upstart. Founded in 1959, this biodynamic producer has quickly become one of Alsace's greatest estates. Some of the world's most sumptuous whites are made here, crafted by Olivier Humbrecht, a Master of Wine.

○ **Domaine Zind-Humbrecht Clos Windsbuhl Gewurztraminer** / 2009 / $$$ The 13-acre Clos Windsbuhl vineyard is known for stellar Gewurztraminer, like this spicy, honeyed bottling.

○ **Domaine Zind-Humbrecht Riesling** / 2009 / $$$ Despite a warm vintage, this wine is zesty, citrusy and fresh.

HUGEL ET FILS

Among the best-known vintners in Alsace, the Hugel family has been making wine in the medieval village of Riquewihr since 1639. Their entry-level Classic wines are dry and food-friendly; the Tradition bottlings are made from primarily estate-grown fruit. The finest cuvées, the Jubilee wines, come from the family's 62 vineyard acres, many of which are *grand cru* sites.

○ **Hugel et Fils Gentil / 2009 / $**
A fragrant, floral blend of five grapes, with soft apricot tones.
○ **Hugel et Fils Jubilee Riesling / 2005 / $$$$**
From the *grand cru* Schoenenbourg slope, this mouth-filling Riesling balances mineral citrus flavors with bright acidity.

MAISON PIERRE SPARR SUCCESSEURS

Long a source of affordable wines as well as a few outstanding *grand cru* cuvées, Maison Pierre Sparr was owned for four centuries by Sparr descendants. They sold the winery to a local cooperative in 2009, but judging by the current vintage, the new owners seem intent on upholding the winery's reputation.

○ **Pierre Sparr Réserve Pinot Blanc / 2009 / $**
Fresh apple and pear notes mark this food-friendly wine.
○ **Pierre Sparr Sélection Pinot Gris / 2009 / $$**
A step up from Sparr's basic cuvées, with ripe, bright, lightly sweet apricot tones.

TRIMBACH

Many Alsace producers have switched to making sweeter wines, but Trimbach stays true to the region's dry, mineral-rich, traditional style. Twelfth-generation vintner Pierre Trimbach crafts pure, bracingly dry whites. The most famous is the Clos Ste. Hune Riesling; cuvées such as the Frédéric Emile offer nearly as much complexity and pleasure at more-approachable prices.

○ **Trimbach Pinot Blanc / 2007 / $**
The addition of some Auxerrois contributes a bit of fruitiness to this racy, citrusy Pinot Blanc.
○ **Trimbach Cuvée Frédéric Emile Riesling / 2004 / $$$**
Trimbach ages its wine until it's perfectly ready to drink, like this spicy, beautifully made Riesling.

BORDEAUX

Bordeaux's legendary reputation throughout the world is based on its long-lived, earthy reds and, even more specifically, on a handful of elite and expensive so-called first-growth châteaus with such notable names as Lafite, Latour and Haut-Brion. Beyond this select sampling of renowned wines, Bordeaux turns out a vast amount of affordable reds, whites and even sweet wines.

❧ BORDEAUX GRAPES & STYLES

Nearly 90 percent of Bordeaux wines are red, made from some combination of Cabernet Sauvignon, Merlot, Cabernet Franc, Malbec and Petit Verdot. Which grape grows best in which part of Bordeaux depends on geography. Cabernet Sauvignon excels on the Left (that is, western) Bank of the Gironde River, around the city of Bordeaux, where the Margaux, Pauillac, St-Julien and St-Estèphe subregions produce tannic, cassis- and cedar-inflected reds of impressive structure and longevity. Less famous zones such as Haut-Médoc and Listrac can produce terrific values, as can Graves, which lies upstream from the city. Merlot is at its best on the Right (eastern) Bank; accordingly, wines from this zone are plusher and less tannic than those from the Left Bank. Its Pomerol and St-Émilion subdistricts are the most prestigious.

Although mainly a red wine region, Bordeaux makes many excellent whites, from Sauvignon Blanc, Sémillon and Muscadelle, or some combination thereof. They tend to be crisp and light, offering a refreshing mix of citrus and stone-fruit flavors. The district of Entre-Deux-Mers, literally "between two seas," produces the bulk of Bordeaux white wine, much of which is good and affordable if not terribly complex. The finest white Bordeaux are made in Pessac-Léognan, Graves and Blaye and are worth seeking out for their dry flavors of peach, grass and stone. The most famous Bordeaux *blancs*, however, are the sweet wines from Sauternes and its satellite regions (see p. 280).

DEFINING BORDEAUX

Bordeaux wines are labeled by region; generally, the more specific the regional designation, the better the wine. Wines labeled simply *Bordeaux* can be made anywhere in Bordeaux. The next level up is Bordeaux *supérieur*; these wines are required to be higher in alcohol, which implies that they were made from riper grapes—often a measure of higher quality. Wines from Bordeaux's districts—such as Médoc, Graves and St-Émilion—are required to meet higher standards. Within the districts are communes—Pauillac and Margaux in Médoc, for example—which must meet more-stringent requirements still. Bordeaux's system for ranking wines was established with the famous 1855 classification, which created a hierarchy of wineries (or châteaus) considered superior based on the prices their wines commanded. Known as the *cru classé* system, this ranking grouped 61 superior wineries by *cru* (growth), from first (*premier cru*) on top to fifth. Châteaus that didn't make the cut but were still considered good received the rank *cru bourgeois*. The 1855 system is limited to châteaus in Médoc and Sauternes and a single château in Graves. In 1955 a similar system was set up for the St-Émilion district, but it is subject to revision every 10 years or so. The famed red wines of Pomerol are not ranked. An attempt to revise the *cru bourgeois* ranking in 2003 was overturned by a French court in 2007, and the designation was reestablished as of the 2008 vintage. It is now viewed as a stamp of approval rather than a true classification.

Producers/ Bordeaux

CHÂTEAU BRANE-CANTENAC

This second-growth Margaux estate is owned by Henri Lurton, who inherited it from his father, Lucien, a member of one of Bordeaux's most dynamic wine dynasties. The younger Lurton is also the winemaker, and although he's a trained enologist, it's his focus on the vineyards that has most rejuvenated quality. The winery's second wine, Baron de Brane, is a great value.

- Baron de Brane / 2008 / Margaux / $$
  With less Cabernet Sauvignon and less concentration than the winery's top wine, this offers approachable flavors of juicy black cherries and smoky incense.
- Château Brane-Cantenac / 2008 / Margaux / $$$
  An old-school Margaux with layers of smoky cherry and spice woven through its pretty herb notes.

CHÂTEAU CANTENAC BROWN

Château Cantenac Brown burst out of the middle ranks of Margaux estates with its latest vintages, made under Simon Halabi, a former billionaire who bought the property in 2006 and has spent lavishly to update it. Halabi's finances have not fared well—a London court declared him bankrupt in 2010—so whether the estate can continue to invest in such quality remains to be seen.

● **Château Cantenac Brown Grand Cru Classé / 2008 / Margaux / $$$** Smooth and rich, with loads of vibrant fruit, this supple Cabernet-dominated red is unusually brawny.

CHÂTEAU CARBONNIEUX

This Graves estate spreads across a hilly outcrop of especially deep gravel in Pessac-Léognan. The soil is one reason Carbonnieux's white is among the finest in Bordeaux. Another factor keeping quality high is Denis Dubourdieu, the superstar winemaking consultant who has lent his talents here since the 1980s.

○ **Château Carbonnieux Grand Cru Classé de Graves / 2007 / Pessac-Léognan / $$$** Fleshy, dense and infused with notes of candied lemon rind, this blend of 65 percent Sauvignon Blanc and 35 percent Sémillon drinks beautifully now.

● **Château Carbonnieux Grand Cru Classé de Graves / 2008 / Pessac-Léognan / $$$** A structured yet generous Graves red composed of mostly Cabernet and Merlot.

CHÂTEAU DE FIEUZAL

This historic Pessac-Léognan estate produces more red wine than white, but lately Fieuzal's stylish white—a flavorful blend of Sauvignon Blanc and Sémillon—has generated more excitement. Irish banker Lochlan Quinn purchased the estate over a decade ago and immediately improved it; one of his wisest moves was hiring talented winemaker Stéphen Carrier in 2007.

○ **Château de Fieuzal / 2008 / Pessac-Léognan / $$$** Recent vintages have been climbing in price, but quality also has gone up—meaning this white is still worth seeking out.

● **Château de Fieuzal / 2008 / Pessac-Léognan / $$$$** Carrier's influence is already apparent in the 2008 red, which offers compelling plush cherry flavors and a reasonable price.

CHÂTEAU DE PEZ

The claim to fame of Château de Pez, founded in 1452, used to be that it was one of the oldest estates in St-Estèphe. But since being acquired by the Rouzaud family (who own several top wine houses, including Louis Roederer and Château Pichon Longueville Comtesse de Lalande) in 1995, it has been attracting equal fame for the pristine quality of its wine.

● Château de Pez / 2008 / St-Estèphe / $$$
While most St-Estèphe estates rely primarily on Cabernet Sauvignon, this bottling is nearly half Merlot, which gives its fresh black cherry layers a silky roundness.

CHÂTEAU D'ISSAN

Not long after taking over his family's Margaux estate in 1995, Emmanuel Cruse began a massive renovation: regrafting vines, building a new cellar and bringing in winemaking star Jacques Boissenot to consult. These days Château d'Issan is making wines worthy of its illustrious heritage (Issan wine, it is said, was served at Eleanor of Aquitaine's wedding in 1152).

● Blason d'Issan / 2007 / Margaux / $$
A boost of old-vine grapes lends this velvety, black-fruited blend a touch of richness.
● Château d'Issan / 2007 / Margaux / $$$
Tobacco and smoke notes—the result of 18 months of aging in oak barrels—underscore plump, dense black-fruit flavors.

CHÂTEAU FOMBRAUGE

Wine magnate Bernard Magrez bought this sizable St-Émilion *grand cru* estate in 1999 and diligently improved the vineyards and the winery—something he has done many times before with other châteaus in his portfolio, including Pape Clément and La Tour Carnet. Made in a minimalist winemaking fashion under the direction of famed consultant Michel Rolland, the wine has become one of the best values in St-Émilion.

● Château Fombrauge / 2008 / St-Émilion Grand Cru / $$$
A Merlot-dominated red that displays the classic flavors imparted by St-Émilion's clay and limestone soils: refined, bright fruit underpinned by firm minerality.

CHÂTEAU GREYSAC

Château Greysac is a standard-bearer for well-made, widely available and accessibly priced Bordeaux red wines. The estate, which offers just two bottlings each year (the second is called Château de By), is located north of St-Estèphe in Bégadan, a small town. The top wine gets its supple tannins from a relatively high percentage of Merlot in the blend—a full 50 percent in the 2008 vintage, for example.

● **Château Greysac / 2008 / Médoc / \$\$**
Despite a challenging growing season, Château Greysac delivers another reliable plum-infused red, this one accented with hints of herb and toast.

CHÂTEAU LA TOUR CARNET

Bernard Magrez owns some 35 luxury wine estates in France and abroad (see Château Fombrauge, opposite), and he seems to have a knack for bringing out the best in them, often enlisting the help of winemaking talent Michel Rolland. He has succeeded again with La Tour Carnet, an overachieving fourth-growth Haut-Médoc estate that produces exceptionally classy wines at very fair prices.

● **Château La Tour Carnet Grand Cru Classé / 2008 / Haut-Médoc / \$\$\$** Hand-sorting, manual destemming and small-batch fermentation result in La Tour's New World–styled red, uncommonly fruit-driven for Bordeaux. Its lush black fruit is augmented by vanilla-tinged oak.

CHÂTEAU LYNCH-BAGES

Though classified as a less prestigious fifth-growth producer, Château Lynch-Bages has long aimed far above its rank and is responsible today for some of Pauillac's top wines. Made in a powerful, firmly structured style, the wines are also more reasonably priced than bottlings of similar quality (thanks to the estate's unfairly low status). Also a smart buy is the estate's second wine, Echo de Lynch-Bages.

● **Château Lynch-Bages Grand Cru Classé / 2007 / Pauillac / \$\$\$\$** A stunner even in the modest 2007 vintage, this red displays dark currant and graphite notes.

CHÂTEAU PALMER

Named for a British major general who acquired the estate in 1814, spent a fortune and ran it into the ground, Château Palmer is today among the stars of Margaux. It's now owned by the Sichel and Mähler-Besse families, who have kept the long-lived *grand vin* on a steady course while introducing a second wine, Alter Ego, which delivers plenty of class at a more modest price.

● **Alter Ego / 2006 / Margaux / $$$$**
Unlike most second wines, which simply use up grapes that do not make the cut for the top bottling, this supple red is sourced exclusively from a single designated plot on Palmer's estate.

● **Château Palmer / 2008 / Margaux / $$$$**
Polished and intense, not to mention underpriced when compared with the much-hyped 2009 bottlings.

CHÂTEAU PAPE CLÉMENT

This Pessac-Léognan estate was turning out fine wine as early as 1305, when its owner was Pope Clement V (hence its name). Pape Clément's modern reputation can be traced to the 1950s and the involvement of Émile Peynaud (one of France's best winemakers). Today, part-owner Bernard Magrez and consultant Michel Rolland are the stewards of its benchmark wines.

○ **Château Pape Clément Grand Cru de Graves / 2008 / Pessac-Léognan / $$$$** Lovely peach-and-melon fruit reveals the strength of the 2008 vintage for Bordeaux whites.

● **Château Pape Clément Grand Cru Classé de Graves / 2007 / Pessac-Léognan / $$$$** Smoky stone, leather, dark fruit: all the elements of classic Pessac-Léognan.

CHÂTEAU TROTANOY

Pomerol does not officially rank its chateaus, but if it did, Trotanoy no doubt would place at the top. Owned by the Moueix family, Trotanoy is small and (like all Pomerol estates) focused on Merlot. Its 18 acres turn out just 2,000 or so cases of the *grand vin* each year, and the wine's price reflects its rarity.

● **Château Trotanoy / 2008 / Pomerol / $$$$**
Christian Moueix claims that of all the wines he has produced, this vintage is the most enjoyable in its youth.

CHRISTIAN MOUEIX

The Moueix family owns several of the most prestigious châteaus of Bordeaux, including Pétrus and Trotanoy in Pomerol. Winemaker and president of the family company, Christian Moueix also makes lovely, affordable *négociant* wines from grapes both purchased from select growers and declassified from estate properties. Not surprisingly, the Pomerol stands out.

> **WINE INTEL**
> Recent legal changes now allow the spicy, Left Bank variety Petit Verdot to be planted in Pomerol. Christian Moueix is likely to be among the first to take advantage of the new rules.

● **Christian Moueix** / 2006 / **Pomerol** / $$
This wine shows off the rich, plump side of Merlot, with velvety black-fruit flavors and a pretty floral note.

● **Christian Moueix** / 2006 / **St-Estèphe** / $$
A few years of bottle aging have helped integrate this Cabernet-based blend's expansive layers of cherry, mocha and smoke.

L'AURA DE CAMBON

New vineyards are rare in Margaux. When the town butcher was willing to sell a 1.2-acre plot next to Château Margaux in 2002, vintner Jean-Pierre Marie, owner of Château Cambon La Pelouse, bought it and planted vines. The resulting wine is a stunner.

● **L'Aura Cambon La Pelouse** / 2007 / **Margaux** / $$$
A terrific value, with fine tannins and distinctive floral tones.

BURGUNDY

Burgundy's ethereal, smoky wines are among the most prized in the world. Yet as one of France's northernmost and coolest wine regions, it can produce disappointing vintages. In contrast to Bordeaux, Burgundy's wines are classified by the vineyard from which they originate, rather than by the producer.

❧ BURGUNDY GRAPES & STYLES

Most Burgundy whites are made from Chardonnay, except for a bit of Sauvignon Blanc (grown in and around St-Bris) and Aligoté (mostly from the Côte Chalonnaise) and tiny amounts of Pinot Blanc and Pinot Gris. Pinot Noir is responsible for nearly all Burgundy reds, with the exception of Beaujolais reds, which are made with Gamay. Though considered part of Burgundy, Beaujolais has a different *terroir* and style of wine.

Basic white Burgundy takes two forms: Bourgogne Blanc, made from Chardonnay, and the much scarcer Bourgogne Aligoté. For affordable Chardonnay, look to Côte Chalonnaise and the Mâconnais. The simplest Mâconnais wines are labeled *Mâcon*; more-complex wines usually have a village name as well, Mâcon Lugny, for instance. Rich and oaky Pouilly-Fuissé is regarded as the apex of the Mâconnais region's wines.

The Côte d'Or, Burgundy's premier region for reds and whites, is split in two: northern Côte de Nuits and southern Côte de Beaune. The latter produces some of the world's best Chardonnays, from villages such as Puligny-Montrachet and Meursault.

Far to the north is the cool region of Chablis, known for high-acid, minerally Chardonnays. Unlike most other white Burgundies, they spend very little if any time in oak barrels, which leaves them fresh and pure. The region's best wines are labeled with their *grand* or *premier cru* vineyard names, followed by the *Chablis* appellation; lesser wines are labeled simply *Chablis*. Petit Chablis wines are from the least prestigious subregions.

Burgundy's finest red wines hail from the Côte d'Or. The more renowned villages and *grands crus* are in the Côte de Nuits, including Chambolle-Musigny, Gevrey-Chambertin and Nuits-St-Georges. Corton is the only red *grand cru* in the Côte de Beaune, where reds tend to be on the lighter side. Wines labeled *Côte de Nuits–Villages* may be red or white; those labeled *Côte de Beaune–Villages* are always red. Such wines don't qualify for a village designation or are blends of wines from several villages. The Côte Chalonnaise is better known for whites, although the villages of Mercurey and Givry make good-value reds.

DEFINING BURGUNDY

Burgundy labels list the region; some also list the subregion, and the most prestigious include a vineyard name. Generally, the more specific the locality on a label, the finer the wine, but vintage is also very important when assessing quality in this region. Many of the familiar producers of Burgundy are *négociants*, merchants who buy wine or grapes from small grower-producers.

REGION The most basic wines of Burgundy are labeled with just the name of the region, Bourgogne, and occasionally with the grape. Though these wines are often unassuming, some of them nonetheless offer good quality at a reasonable price.

DISTRICT A district appellation (such as Chablis or Mâconnais) is the next step up in terms of quality in Burgundy. The grapes must be grown exclusively in the named district. Wines labeled with *Villages* after the district name are theoretically superior.

VILLAGE A wine is permitted to take the name of a specific village if all of its grapes have been grown within that village's boundaries. This is often a good sign, as grapes from the same *terroir* typically display similar characteristics and flavors.

PREMIER CRU Certain vineyards with a lengthy history of producing superior wines have earned the *premier cru* distinction. These special wines must be made only with grapes grown in the designated vineyards, which are often included in the wine's name (e.g., Meursault Premier Cru Genevrières). In Burgundy *premier cru* is the second-highest distinction, after *grand cru*.

GRAND CRU The exceptional *grand cru* vineyards of Burgundy are so elite that some, like Montrachet, don't include the *grand cru* title on their labels. Such is their prestige that some villages added the name of the local *grand cru* vineyard to their own names. Wines from Chassagne became Chassagne-Montrachet, but while many are superb, they're not true Montrachet.

Producers/ Burgundy

BOUCHARD PÈRE & FILS

Bouchard has been on a roll lately. A relatively new winery near Savigny (courtesy of the Henriot family, who bought Bouchard in 1995) contains all the high-tech tools that winemakers covet, while land purchases have made it the largest vineyard owner in the Côte d'Or. Bouchard pays for purchased grapes based on ripeness, not weight, helping to keep quality uniformly high.

● **Domaine Bouchard Père & Fils Beaune du Château / 2009 / Beaune Premier Cru / $$$** Made since 1907, this earthy, fruity cuvée blends fruit from a handful of *premier cru* vineyards.

CHÂTEAU-FUISSÉ

Antoine Vincent turns out serious Mâconnais whites at this underrated estate owned by the Vincent family since the 1860s (the domaine itself dates back to the 1600s); most of its vineyards are in Pouilly-Fuissé. Château-Fuissé's most interesting wines may be its outstanding single-vineyard cuvées, Le Clos, Les Brûlés and Les Combettes. Each wine brilliantly highlights vineyard-driven differences in flavors.

○ **Château-Fuissé Le Clos** / 2009 / Pouilly-Fuissé / $$$
Most of this single-vineyard cuvée spent time in new oak, which added creamy, smoky notes to its ripe-apple profile.

○ **Château-Fuissé Les Combettes** / 2009 / Pouilly-Fuissé / $$$
Aged in 3-to-5-year-old oak, this is brighter and more citrusy than the estate's other offerings, with terrific minerality.

DOMAINE BILLAUD-SIMON

Though this estate produces acclaimed *grand cru* Chablis, owner Bernard Billaud believes humble wines best show a winemaker's expertise; hence the care lavished even on Billaud's Petit Chablis vineyards. Using grapes from 50 acres of vineyards and a boutique, state-of-the-art winery, Billaud crafts unoaked, elegant Chablis that's very well priced.

○ **Domaine Billaud-Simon** / 2009 / Petit Chablis / $$
Chablis's less prestigious zone is a source of delicious, affordable whites, including this ripe, lime-inflected bottling.

○ **Domaine Billaud-Simon Les Vaillons** / 2009 / Chablis Premier Cru** / $$$ Dense and citrusy, this complex Chablis is filled out with sweet vanilla and mineral notes.

○ **Domaine Billaud-Simon Les Blanchots Vieille Vigne** / 2008 / Chablis Grand Cru** / $$$$ This shows a seductive intensity and layers of satiny apple, mineral and smoke flavors.

DOMAINE CHRISTIAN MOREAU PÈRE & FILS

This is a newish domaine from an old Chablis family: The Moreaus sold their J. Moreau et Fils wine-merchant business in 1985 but held on to a few stellar vineyards. Today Christian Moreau, along with his son Fabien (back from a winemaking stint in New Zealand) and his Canadian wife, Christine, turns out impressive offerings from these prime sites.

○ **Domaine Christian Moreau Père & Fils** / 2009 / Chablis / $$
Moreau's basic Chablis is a knockout, defined by a silky texture and vivid green apple flavors

○ **Domaine Christian Moreau Père & Fils Vaillon** / 2009 / Chablis Premier Cru / $$$ Old vines, limestone soils and a sunny vintage make for a vibrant, powerful white.

○ **Domaine Christian Moreau Père & Fils Les Clos** / 2009 / Chablis Grand Cru / $$$$ A creamy, crisp, lemon- and apple-driven Chardonnay from the largest of Chablis's *grands crus*.

DOMAINE DUJAC

Proprietor Jacques Seysses christened his estate with his first name instead of his family name, which even the French find hard to pronounce (for the record, it's *sayss*). His father bought the property for him in 1967, and Dujac's wines earned nearly instant acclaim. Today Jacques leaves day-to-day decisions to sons Jeremy and Alec and Jeremy's American wife, Diana. The team crafts impeccably refined reds and whites.

● **Domaine Dujac** / 2008 / Morey-Saint-Denis / $$$$
More affordable than most of Dujac's estate-grown reds, this sleek, outstanding wine melds sweet red cherry with fragrant violet and spice notes.

● **Domaine Dujac Aux Combottes** / 2009 / Gevrey-Chambertin Premier Cru / $$$$ Seysses picked grapes early to keep this delicious, cherry-scented red fresh and elegant.

DOMAINE FAIVELEY

Following in the footsteps of six generations might intimidate even the most self-assured 25-year-old, but Erwan Faiveley wasn't afraid to make big changes when he took over his family's domaine in 2007. Recent vintages have been the best in years. Known for its elegant, ageworthy reds, the winery owns one of the Côte d'Or's largest portfolios of top vineyards.

● **Domaine Faiveley La Framboisière** / 2009 / Mercurey / $$$
A straightforward, affordable taste of textbook Burgundy, with graceful red fruit and spice.

● **Domaine Faiveley** / 2009 / Nuits-St-Georges / $$$$
Faiveley's reds are typically muscular and rich, as in this earthy, cherry-scented offering.

DOMAINE GUFFENS-HEYNEN/VERGET

Jean-Marie Guffens and Maine Heynen buy grapes all over Burgundy and the Luberon for their Maison Verget label, but it's their Mâconnais estate wines that define their style. They keep yields radically low, pick late and add no acidity, sugar or yeasts. The result: penetrating whites unlike any others in the Mâconnais.

○ **Verget Cuvée des 20 Ans / 2009 / Chablis / $$**
Savory mineral, smoke and apple notes inflect this rich cuvée, created to commemorate the winery's 20th anniversary.

○ **Domaine Guffens-Heynen Tri de Chavigne / 2009 / Mâcon-Pierreclos / $$$$** Selecting only perfectly ripe grapes resulted in this intensely mineral, creamy white.

DOMAINE JACQUES PRIEUR

Just a few women winemakers run prestigious Burgundy estates; the talented Nadine Gublin is one of them. It was big news when Jean Prieur named her winemaker of his family's famed domaine in the late '80s. She draws chiefly on grapes from *grand* and *premier cru* vineyards throughout the Côte d'Or's top *terroirs*.

○ **Domaine Jacques Prieur Clos de Mazeray / 2009 / Meursault / $$$$** This smoky, opulent white is made with grapes from a walled vineyard owned entirely by Prieur.

● **Domaine Jacques Prieur / 2008 / Corton-Bressandes Grand Cru / $$$$** Powerful and poised, with fresh, minerally red fruit.

● **Domaine Jacques Prieur / 2008 / Gevrey-Chambertin Premier Cru / $$$$** Satiny cherry and earth flavors are pure and long.

DOMAINE LAROCHE

Fifth-generation vintner Michel Laroche took his family's unremarkable 15-acre winery and turned it into one of the top large estates in Chablis. Laroche challenges convention, advocating screw-caps—even for *grand cru* wines—and aging some wines in new oak. In 2010 he sold control of the domaine, but he and winemaker Denis de la Bourdonnaye remain on board.

○ **Laroche / 2009 / Petit Chablis / $$**
A stellar, affordable Chablis: bright, zesty and mineral-rich.

○ **Domaine Laroche Les Clos / 2007 / Chablis Grand Cru / $$$**
A superb Chablis, displaying lushness, verve and balance.

DOMAINE LEFLAIVE

This is one of the finest domaines in Puligny-Montrachet, one of the great sources of white Burgundy. Winemaker Anne-Claude Leflaive (whose grandfather Joseph Leflaive began the winery in 1920) and cellarmaster Eric Rémy craft brilliant whites in tiny quantities from some of the world's most famous vineyards. Look for its more-accessibly priced cuvées from the Mâcon district.

○ **Domaine Leflaive** / 2008 / **Bourgogne** / **$$$**
Fruit from two biodynamically farmed vineyards yielded this rich wine full of pear and peach flavors that finish clean.

○ **Domaines Leflaive** / 2009 / **Mâcon-Verzé** / **$$$**
Leflaive's most affordable bottling, this offers a lush, seductive taste of the winery's classic style.

JEAN-MARC BROCARD

Jean-Marc Brocard began with a few acres of vines in the 1970s. Today he makes a range of terrific, unoaked wines from nearly 450 acres of vineyards throughout Chablis and beyond. His son Julien is converting the estate to biodynamic farming; look for ladybugs or moons on the labels of wines from "green" sites.

○ **Jean-Marc Brocard En Sol Kimméridgien Chardonnay** / 2008 / **Bourgogne** / **$$** A bright, citrusy white with the hallmark minerality imparted by Burgundy's chalky clay soils.

○ **Jean-Marc Brocard Sauvignon** / 2009 / **St-Bris** / **$$**
From the only zone in Burgundy that allows Sauvignon Blanc, this is juicy, zippy and floral-scented.

LOUIS LATOUR

One of Burgundy's largest producers, Louis Latour offers wine from nearly every major appellation in Burgundy. (It also produces *vins de pays* from vineyards farther south.) Latour's portfolio gets its sheen from a handful of flagship whites hailing from *grand cru* Côte d'Or vineyards such as Corton-Charlemagne.

○ **Louis Latour** / 2009 / **Pouilly-Fuissé** / **$$**
Zero oak aging keeps this wine's apple flavors fresh and pure.

● **Louis Latour Château Corton Grancey** / 2009 / **Corton Grand Cru** / **$$$$** Made only in the best vintages, this features the ideal Burgundy combination of structure and seductive grace.

LUCIEN LE MOINE

This boutique winery is the creation of Lebanon native Mounir Saouma and his wife, Rotem Brakin. Saouma worked at a wine-making monastery in the Middle East in the late 1980s and studied wine in France before starting this small *négociant* business in Beaune, known for its lush, ageworthy whites and reds.

- **Lucien Le Moine / 2009 / Bourgogne / $$$**
  In a solid vintage like 2009, mid-priced regional blends from top names such as Le Moine make great value bets.
- **Lucien Le Moine / 2009 / Bonnes Mares / $$$$**
  Made in tiny quantities from revered sites—like this Côte de Nuits *grand cru*—Le Moine's top wines are splurge-worthy.

MAISON JEAN-CLAUDE BOISSET

This Burgundy *négociant* was once known for making large amounts of dull wine. But under current head Jean-Charles Boisset, it is now a go-to label for expressive, well-made wines. Since joining in 2002, star winemaker Grégory Patriat has switched to traditional, small-winery techniques that have paid off.

- **Jean-Claude Boisset Grand Clos Rousseau / 2006 / Santenay Premier Cru / $$$** Vines around Santenay generally yield intense, rustic wines, yet this example is slightly more refined.
- **Jean-Claude Boisset Les Grèves / 2006 / Beaune Premier Cru / $$$** Medium-bodied and fragrant, with red-fruit notes.

MAISON JOSEPH DROUHIN

Since 1880, the Drouhin family has steadily added to its collection of Côte d'Or vineyards, which include parts of such legendary plots as Musigny and Vosne-Romanée. Today more than half of Drouhin's Burgundy offerings are made with estate grapes, all organically farmed. That control, plus the family's focus on quality, keeps Drouhin among Burgundy's finest producers.

- ○ **Joseph Drouhin / 2009 / Saint-Véran / $$**
  A good example of the values that can be found in lesser zones, this shows graceful layers of apple and mineral.
- **Joseph Drouhin Clos des Mouches / 2009 / Beaune Premier Cru / $$$$** Gorgeously perfumed and seductively supple, this is a great mix of cherries, herbs and earth.

MAISON LOUIS JADOT

Few producers anywhere match this *négociant*'s ability to turn out both juicy, value-packed everyday wines and world-class cuvées. This is due partly to the skill of Jacques Lardière, Louis Jadot's technical director for 30-plus years, and to the inarguable quality of the company's fruit—even in basic bottlings.

● **Louis Jadot / 2009 / Beaujolais-Villages / $**
An excellent vintage gave this basic wine depth and richness.
● **Louis Jadot Pinot Noir / 2008 / Bourgogne / $$**
With supple earth and cherry notes, this is a straightforward, well-made Pinot at a reasonable price.

OLIVIER LEFLAIVE

Born into a prominent wine family, Olivier Leflaive began his own label in 1984 as a side business, using purchased grapes. He later left his family's legendary domaine (see p. 41) to concentrate on his eponymous wine venture (plus a new hotel and restaurant). Gifted winemaker Franck Grux crafts Leflaive's vibrant, beautifully layered wines, most of which are white.

○ **Olivier Leflaive / 2009 / Puligny-Montrachet / $$$**
Leflaive combines wine made from dozens of tiny plots around Puligny to create this creamy, harmonious blend.
○ **Olivier Leflaive Les Folatières / 2009 / Puligny-Montrachet Premier Cru / $$$$** A gorgeous, peach- and mineral-inflected offering from one of the best-known vineyards in Puligny.

VINCENT GIRARDIN

Though his wines can be quite traditional, Vincent Girardin is a thoroughly modern winemaker. Made in a state-of-the-art facility in Meursault, Girardin's seductive, fruit-driven Côte d'Or reds and whites—mostly *grands* and *premiers crus*—have made his reputation (though his Mâconnais wines offer great value).

○ **Vincent Girardin Les Vieilles Vignes / 2009 / Pouilly-Fuissé / $$** Old vines (*vieilles vignes*) give the vibrant, silky citrus flavors in this wine a lovely intensity.
○ **Vincent Girardin Rully Vieilles Vignes / 2009 / Rully / $$**
Rully is a good source of affordable offerings, such as this juicy, green apple–driven white.

WILLIAM FÈVRE

Sometimes selling out to a larger company improves a winery. William Fèvre sold this terrific estate over a decade ago to the Henriot Champagne company. Henriot sent in winemaker Didier Séguier, who increased grape quality by reducing vineyard yields and decreased the amount of new oak used for aging. The result has been more-complex wines with purer, fresher flavors.

○ **Domaine William Fèvre / 2009 / Chablis / $$**
A bright, approachably styled Chablis that shows the ripeness of the vintage but stays fresh.

○ **Domaine William Fèvre Vaillons / 2009 / Chablis Premier Cru / $$$** A seven-acre estate-owned plot in the Vaillons vineyard produced the grapes for this focused, citrusy cuvée.

BURGUNDY

BEAUJOLAIS

As Burgundy's southernmost region, Beaujolais is distinctly different from its neighbors to the north. Red wines here are made exclusively with the Gamay grape (not Pinot Noir), and the region has its own ranking system for quality. Beaujolais produces an abundance of inexpensive, tasty red wines, as well as a number of high-quality bottles that can satisfy a Burgundy lover's palate at a fraction of the cost. A very small amount of Chardonnay-based white wine is also made here.

BEAUJOLAIS NOUVEAU Designed to be consumed within weeks of harvest, Beaujolais Nouveau is as light and simple as reds get. By law, it is released the third Thursday of every November, conveniently coinciding with the start of the U.S. holiday season.

BEAUJOLAIS Wines made from grapes grown anywhere within the designated region earn the moniker *Beaujolais*. These reds are marked by distinctive light, fruity flavors and are a bit more substantial than Beaujolais Nouveau.

BEAUJOLAIS-VILLAGES The title *Beaujolais-Villages* is given to any wine made from grapes grown within the 39 villages occupying the gentle hills at the center of the region. These wines are typically made with more care and precision, producing bright fruit flavors as well as an added depth of mineral and spice.

CRU BEAUJOLAIS The region's greatest wines come from 10 hillside villages in the northern part of Beaujolais. Often, these *cru* Beaujolais wines deliver real complexity at approachable prices. They show greater flavor concentration than Beaujolais-Villages, plus ample tannins, which allow them to age, unlike other Beaujolais. *Cru* Beaujolais labels often list only the village name: Brouilly, Chénas, Chiroubles, Côte de Brouilly, Fleurie, Juliénas, Morgon, Moulin-à-Vent, Régnié or St-Amour.

Producers/ Beaujolais

GEORGES DUBOEUF

Even more remarkable than this *négociant*'s huge output (some 2.5 million cases of Beaujolais wine yearly) is that so much of it is so delicious. Duboeuf helped to create the Beaujolais Nouveau craze in the 1970s; today its lineup also includes many Beaujolais-Villages bottlings (with the well-known "Flower Label"), plus *cru* wines offering more-serious drinking pleasure.

● **Georges Duboeuf "Flower Label"** / 2009 / Morgon / $
Juicy, fruit-forward and affordable, this *cru* Beaujolais from the superb 2009 vintage is a true bargain.

● **Georges Duboeuf "Flower Label"** / 2009 / Fleurie / $$
Delivers loads of ripe black-fruit flavors and notable tannins.

MARCEL LAPIERRE

Iconoclast vintner Marcel Lapierre, who died in 2010, believed in hands-off winemaking: no chemicals, no added yeast and minimal sulfur. His son Mathieu continues this approach with expert results. The winery's alluring, deeply fruity cuvées serve as Beaujolais benchmarks.

● **Marcel Lapierre Raisins Gaulois** / 2010 / Vin de France / $
A light, easy-drinking, berry-driven red that's great with food.

● **Marcel Lapierre** / 2009 / Morgon / $$
This gorgeous, mineral-edged wine demonstrates just how complex and elegant the best Beaujolais can be.

POTEL-AVIRON

Nicolas Potel made his name as a micro-*négociant*, selecting tiny lots of grapes from choice vineyards to make top-notch wines. While Potel now owns an estate in Beaune, his Beaujolais *négociant* partnership with Stéphane Aviron is wildly successful. Their secret is treating Gamay like serious Pinot Noir, including aging it in small oak barrels. Smoky, dark and tannic, the wines are arguably the most exciting Beaujolais made today.

- **Potel-Aviron Vieilles Vignes / 2009 / Fleurie / $$**
  Grapes from two vineyards more than half a century old create a velvety, black currant–infused blend.
- **Potel-Aviron Vieilles Vignes / 2009 / Moulin-à-Vent / $$**
  Made only in the best vintages from very old vines, this is structured and serious, with lush, spicy fruit.

LOIRE VALLEY

Stretching some 300 miles along the Loire River, the fertile Loire Valley is one of France's largest and most diverse wine regions—and one of its most underappreciated. Loire wines range from dry still reds, whites and rosés to sparklers and dessert bottles; almost all are marked by relatively high acidity.

❦ LOIRE VALLEY GRAPES & STYLES

The Loire Valley's vast range of white wines, from simple aperitifs to profound, complex cuvées designed for aging, are made from three primary grapes: Melon de Bourgogne, Sauvignon Blanc and Chenin Blanc. Melon de Bourgogne is the only grape used for Muscadet, a typically light-bodied white that's one of the world's great shellfish wines. The best Muscadet comes from the subappellation Muscadet Sèvre et Maine, where many wines develop richer flavors from aging *sur lie* (on lees). Sauvignon Blanc wines from the Loire Valley are defined by refreshing acidity, flinty aromatics and ripe grapefruit and grass flavors. Benchmark examples hail from Sancerre and Pouilly-Fumé, with the former fuller-bodied and the latter lighter and more perfumed. Nearby Menetou-Salon, Quincy and Reuilly offer more-affordable alternatives.

Chenin Blanc is the Loire's most versatile and ageworthy grape, capable of creating wines that range from light and tart to sweet and rich, as well as sparkling wines, all featuring bright acidity. The Vouvray subregion offers off-dry and dry versions of Chenin Blanc; Montlouis-sur-Loire is a tiny up-and-comer. Many Chenin Blancs from Savennières, Saumur and Anjou can age for decades, developing honey, truffle and smoke flavors.

Made chiefly from Cabernet Franc, Loire Valley reds show the crisp red-fruit flavors and herbal and pepper notes typical of cool-climate reds; top examples from Chinon, Bourgueil and Saumur-Champigny are full-bodied, smoky and tannic. In Sancerre and Menetou-Salon, small amounts of red and rosé are made from Pinot Noir, while Gamay reigns in Touraine.

DEFINING THE LOIRE VALLEY

Because there is no broad AOC Loire appellation for still wines, only the pink Rosé de Loire and the sparkling Crémant de Loire actually bear *Loire* on their labels. (There is a *vin de pays* designation for the region, Vin de Pays du Val de la Loire.) Most Loire wines are identified by more precise appellations, and since blending of grapes is rare, the appellation name is usually enough to determine the variety. Wines made from grapes not tied to a region will list both the grape and the region.

Producers/ Loire Valley

ALPHONSE MELLOT DOMAINE LA MOUSSIÈRE

Founded in 1513 and handed down from one Alphonse Mellot to another ever since, this Sancerre estate is now run by Alphonse No. 19. He has converted the vineyards to biodynamic farming, created two of the Loire's most expensive red wines (both Pinot Noirs) and introduced two *vins de pays*. The prices of its top wines reflect the estate's prestige.

○ **Alphonse Mellot La Moussière** / 2010 / Sancerre / $$$
Limestone soils impart a flinty minerality to this elegant, lemon-inflected white.

○ **Alphonse Mellot Génération XIX** / 2009 / Sancerre / $$$$
Broad, honey-tinged citrus and floral flavors make this weighty cuvée utterly distinctive.

CHÂTEAU DE SANCERRE

Sancerre's vineyards are a kaleidoscopic mix of soils, each type yielding dramatically different wines. Château de Sancerre owns vineyards that span all of the region's major soil types. Using only estate-grown fruit, winemaker Gerard Cherrier blends lots to achieve balanced, layered wines—from the flagship, steely Sancerre Blanc to the small-lot Cuvée du Connetable.

○ **Château de Sancerre / 2010 / Sancerre / $$**
Cherrier makes the winery's flagship bottling in a consistently flinty, zesty style that's textbook Sancerre.

○ **Château de Sancerre Cuvée du Connetable / 2010 / Sancerre / $$$** The best grapes go into this cuvée, which is partially fermented in oak to add a hint of creaminess.

DOMAINE BERNARD BAUDRY

Bernard Baudry and his son Matthieu turn out some of the Loire's best Cabernet Francs from this 75-acre estate in Chinon. Their five different cuvées are distinguished by the diverse terrain of the vineyards. All of the domaine's wines, though, reflect the Baudrys' preference for supple, classically elegant Chinon.

● **Bernard Baudry Le Clos Guillot / 2008 / Chinon / $$**
Ripe red currant flavors are offset by minerals and herbs.

● **Bernard Baudry La Croix Boissée / 2008 / Chinon / $$$**
Uncommonly lush and silky, with raspberry and cherry notes.

DOMAINE DES BAUMARD

Depth and concentration are not qualities often associated with Loire Valley Cabernet Franc, but Anjou vintner Florent Baumard seems able to turn his hand to any grape or style and craft wines of rare complexity. From mineral and tart Chenin Blancs to lush Cabernet Francs and long-lived dessert wines, Baumard's portfolio is a tour de force of Loire Valley winemaking.

○ **Domaine des Baumard / 2007 / Savennières / $$**
Aged in stainless steel, this is full of ripe peach and minerals.

○ **Domaine des Baumard Clos du Papillon / 2006 / Savennières / $$$** One of the Loire's most famous wines, this is still remarkably affordable; glossy-textured, with chalky minerality, it's brimming with ripe peach notes.

DOMAINE FRANÇOIS CHIDAINE

The Chidaine family comes from Montlouis, which in Vouvray is seen as the wrong side of the tracks—or in this case, of the Loire River. Yet since acquiring one of Vouvray's most famous vineyards, Clos Baudoin, François Chidaine has been making some of the region's most compelling whites, marked by freshness and minerality evident even in his two basic Touraine wines and in those he makes from family vineyards in Montlouis.

○ **François Chidaine Sauvignon** / 2009 / **Touraine** / $
Biodynamically farmed vines yielded this tangy, citrusy Sauvignon Blanc with a smooth texture and notes of herb.

DOMAINE HUET

Huet's definitive white wines are some of the most highly regarded in Vouvray—and the Loire Valley. The relative obscurity of Loire wines means this greatness still comes at amazingly reasonable prices. Noël Pinguet, who learned winemaking from his father-in-law, Gaston Huet, farms biodynamically and handpicks his vineyard. He also crafts dry and semisweet sparkling and dessert wines remarkable for their purity and balance.

○ **Domaine Huet Le Haut-Lieu Sec** / 2009 / **Vouvray** / $$
Pinguet fermented this cuvée until dry (*sec*), achieving a full-bodied white with succulent citrus and apple tones.

○ **Domaine Huet Le Haut-Lieu Demi-Sec** / 2009 / **Vouvray** / $$$
From the same vineyard as Le Haut-Lieu Sec, this lightly sweet bottling offers honey-tinged pear flavors.

DOMAINE LUCIEN CROCHET

"Soil" is a misnomer for the carpet of whitish rocks that crunches underfoot in the Crochet family's Le Chêne vineyard. The estate's 94 vineyard acres in Sancerre include prized limestone-studded holdings such as Le Chêne and Clos du Roy plus a clutch of top sites on south-facing hillsides. The extra sun exposure translates to especially ripe grapes, which means that even the reds crafted by winemaker Gilles Crochet are unusually lush.

○ **Lucien Crochet La Croix du Roy** / 2008 / **Sancerre** / $$
Abundant minerals and ripe apple tones define this classically styled bottling from the famous Clos du Roy vineyard.

DOMAINE LUNEAU-PAPIN

Easy-drinking Muscadet gains complexity and character at this terrific estate that has been in the Luneau-Papin family for eight generations. Old vines, hand-harvested grapes (rare in Touraine) and a laserlike focus on *terroir* help Pierre and Monique Luneau-Papin turn out outstanding wines such as their L d'Or—possibly the best Muscadet made today—as well as four small-lot cuvées that showcase a quartet of distinct soil types.

○ **Luneau-Papin Pierre de la Grange Vieilles Vignes** / 2009 / **Muscadet de Sèvre et Maine Sur Lie** / $ A fabulous bargain, this fresh, captivating wine is made with grapes from old vines.

○ **Luneau-Papin L d'Or** / 2007 / **Muscadet de Sèvre et Maine Sur Lie** / $$ With penetrating citrus notes and slatelike minerality, this wine illustrates just how complex Muscadet can be.

DOMAINE PASCAL JOLIVET

Pascal Jolivet comes from a winemaking family, but he started his own wine business from scratch in the 1980s, buying grapes from all over Sancerre and Pouilly-Fumé. These regions are still the focus of his portfolio, but Jolivet now owns substantial vineyard acreage as well. A commitment to quality makes his a go-to name for traditionally made, reliably delicious reds and whites.

○ **Pascal Jolivet** / 2010 / **Pouilly-Fumé** / $$
Mouthwatering Sauvignon with minerally grapefruit tones.

○ **Pascal Jolivet Clos du Roy** / 2009 / **Sancerre** / $$$
This steel-fermented white features the chalky, zesty intensity typical of wines from the famous Clos du Roy site.

○ **Pascal Jolivet Exception** / 2008 / **Sancerre** / $$$$
Produced from the best lots from three famous vineyards, this offers remarkable concentration and crushed-stone notes.

DOMAINE VACHERON

Since taking over this Sancerre estate from their fathers, Vacheron cousins Jean-Laurent and Jean-Dominique have made this already respected domaine one to watch. Extremely low yields, handpicked and hand-sorted fruit and biodynamic farming are among the rigorous practices that keep the quality ratcheting up. Another factor: about 100 acres of prime vineyards, mainly old vines and mostly located on flint-rich rock.

○ **Domaine Vacheron** / 2010 / Sancerre / $$$
Elegant and beautifully structured, with a hint of saline
freshness to its rich white peach and citrus flavors.

● **Domaine Vacheron Rosé** / 2010 / Sancerre / $$
A silky, salmon-colored rosé made from Pinot Noir, with juicy
blood orange and peach tones.

NICOLAS JOLY

Nicolas Joly's business card reads *Nature Assistant,* which is
how this Savennières winemaker prefers to describe his role.
Joly is France's most visible evangelist for biodynamics, a radically holistic, organic farming philosophy. The legendary Coulée
de Serrant, one of three impressive Joly cuvées, hails from a
world-renowned Chenin Blanc vineyard.

○ **Nicolas Joly Clos de la Bergerie** / 2008 / Savennières
Roche-aux-Moines / $$$ Despite its high 15.5 percent alcohol
content, this white is remarkably balanced and full of fresh
pineapple, flowers and smoky minerals.

○ **Nicolas Joly** / 2008 / Clos de la Coulée de Serrant / $$$$
Joly's wines are famous for showing intriguing hints of
oxidation; this one is rich, nutty and lightly honeyed.

RHÔNE VALLEY

France's Rhône Valley has risen to viticultural greatness only
relatively recently. Its wines, once dismissed as sturdy, coarse
and second-class, have the potential to express unbridled power,
intense spiciness and an appealing earthy character. While Côtes-
du-Rhônes are simple, easy-drinking reds, many single-vineyard
Rhône Valley reds are world-class wines, as profound as the best
Burgundies or Bordeaux, with prices that reflect their rarity.

RHÔNE VALLEY: AN OVERVIEW

The Rhône River flows from the Swiss Alps down into France's
Jura mountains and on to the Mediterranean. The Rhône Valley
wine region is divided into northern and southern parts, which
differ greatly in terms of grapes, wine philosophies, soils and
microclimates. The Rhône Valley ranks second in total wine
production among major French regions, and while every style
of wine is made here, red wines represent approximately 90
percent of the region's AOC production.

NORTHERN RHÔNE

The northern Rhône is a narrow 50-mile-or-so stretch of steep, terraced hills bookended by the appellations of Côte-Rôtie in the north and Cornas and St-Péray in the south. The region's output is small, accounting for less than 5 percent of all Rhône Valley wine production. Some of the area's most coveted wines hail from its steepest vineyard sites. The northern Rhône lies between cooler-climate Burgundy to the north and the warm, sunny Mediterranean-influenced southern Rhône region, and its wines, both reds and whites, reflect this geographical and climatic diversity in their alluring combination of elegance and robust flavors.

❦ NORTHERN RHÔNE GRAPES & STYLES

Though Viognier produces the Rhône Valley's most celebrated whites in the Condrieu appellation, two other white grapes play significant roles in the north: Marsanne and Roussanne, which often are blended together to create the full-bodied, nutty, pear-scented whites of Hermitage, Crozes-Hermitage, St-Péray and St-Joseph. These wines are not high in acidity, yet many have the ability to age for a decade or more. The only red grape permitted in the production of northern Rhône red wines is Syrah, which can achieve great power and complexity, often displaying black pepper, meat and game flavors. Most northern Rhône red wines are allowed to include regional white grapes, except in Cornas, where Syrah must stand alone. Crozes-Hermitage is responsible for about half of the region's wine, mostly everyday reds and whites, while the smaller Hermitage appellation produces more-powerful renditions.

DEFINING THE NORTHERN RHÔNE

Very little basic Côtes-du-Rhône comes from the northern Rhône; most northern Rhône wines meet higher standards and are entitled to label their wines with one of the region's eight *crus*. Labels generally include the *cru* and a producer or *négociant*. In the *crus* that produce red and white wines, such as Crozes-Hermitage, the label might say *rouge* or *blanc*, as grape varieties are not given. The top wines from important Rhône producers, such as M. Chapoutier and E. Guigal, often bear a specific vineyard name in addition to the *cru*.

Producers/ Northern Rhône

ALAIN GRAILLOT

Alain Graillot's ability to produce knockout wines from less-prestigious northern Rhône regions has earned new respect for Crozes-Hermitage and St-Joseph. Since his debut vintage in 1985, Graillot's success at crafting sumptuous reds that taste as good as wines twice their price has energized a generation of local winemakers. Though Graillot once worked in the agrochemicals industry, he is a firm believer in organic methods and farms his 54-acre estate without pesticides or chemical fertilizers.

- **Alain Graillot Crozes-Hermitage / 2009 / Crozes-Hermitage / $$$** Pristine, handpicked grapes from estate vines give this cherry-driven red outstanding complexity.

DELAS FRÈRES

In the past 15 years, Delas Frères has undergone a transformation. What was once a lackluster portfolio has become a treasure trove of stunning wines. Thanks to an all-star team, including managing director Fabrice Rosset, enologist Jacques Grange and winemaker Jean-François Farinet, plus an infusion of cash from corporate parent Louis Roederer, this *négociant* is at last living up to the potential of its vineyards (which include parcels in Hermitage and Côte-Rôtie) and turning out great wines from both northern and southern Rhône regions.

- **Delas / 2009 / Côtes du Ventoux / $** Aging in stainless steel keeps this southern Rhône red's focus on juicy, ripe plum flavors.
- **Delas Saint-Esprit / 2009 / Côtes-du-Rhône / $** The rugged southern Rhône region of the Ardèche—famous for its spectacular river gorge—yielded this red loaded with notes of luscious raspberry.
- **Delas Chante-Perdrix / 2009 / Cornas / $$$** Wines from the terrific 2009 vintage, such as this red from one of the northern Rhône's smallest regions, are worth seeking out.

E. GUIGAL

A Côte-Rôtie specialist, Guigal makes more wine from the northern Rhône than any other producer—and some of the region's finest wines. Crowned by three pricey Côte-Rôtie wines from the La Turque, La Mouline and La Landonne vineyards, Guigal's portfolio offers a tour of every key Rhône appellation.

○ **E. Guigal / 2007 / Hermitage / $$$$**
Though not inexpensive, Guigal's consistently stunning Hermitage is a bargain when compared with similar wines.

● **E. Guigal / 2007 / Côtes-du-Rhône / $$**
Philippe Guigal experiments with hundreds of blends to create this harmonious, earth- and cassis-inflected red.

JEAN-LUC COLOMBO

Jean-Luc Colombo owns a 49-acre estate in Cornas and a thriving *négociant* business, but his real influence is as a consultant, passing on his secrets for making the kind of flashy, concentrated wines he's known for. His Cornas bottlings include four estate cuvées; a great array of *négociant* wines deliver value.

● **Jean-Luc Colombo Cape Bleue Rosé / 2010 / Coteaux d'Aix-en-Provence / $** Crisp and refreshing, with mouthwatering peach and strawberry tones.

● **Jean-Luc Colombo Terres Brûlées / 2009 / Cornas / $$$**
Cornas reds, made only from Syrah, are known for being rustic, but this one is refined, with spice, mineral and cherry notes.

M. CHAPOUTIER

Michel Chapoutier's spectacular estate wines from Hermitage and Châteauneuf-du-Pape are so celebrated, they divert attention from his great lineup of affordable reds and whites. These come from vineyards elsewhere in the Rhône Valley and southern France. An ardent proponent of biodynamic farming, the prolific Chapoutier also makes wine in Portugal and Australia.

○ **M. Chapoutier Petite Ruche / 2009 / Crozes-Hermitage / $$**
This Marsanne is fresh, broad and peach- and pear-driven.

● **M. Chapoutier La Bernardine / 2008 / Châteauneuf-du-Pape / $$$** Grenache gives this single-vineyard blend its deep raspberry flavors and plump, silky texture.

PAUL JABOULET AÎNÉ

Jaboulet is arguably the most important Rhône wine house of the past century. Its Hermitage La Chapelle set a world-class standard, and basic cuvées such as Parallèle 45 are seemingly ubiquitous. After an unstable period in the early 2000s, Jaboulet has rebounded under Denis Dubourdieu's direction and the ownership of the Frey family, who bought the winery in 2006.

○ Paul Jaboulet Aîné Domaine Mule Blanche / 2009 / Crozes-Hermitage / $$$ Citrusy acidity cuts the melon and peach flavors of this fabulous, 50-50 Roussanne-and-Marsanne blend.

● Paul Jaboulet Aîné La Chapelle / 2007 / Hermitage / $$$$ This lives up to its iconic reputation, with immense power, voluptuous grace and mineral-laden cherry and licorice notes.

RHÔNE VALLEY

SOUTHERN RHÔNE

Some 30 miles south of the northern Rhône, the sunnier southern Rhône begins. Its gentle hills are home to vineyards that yield about 95 percent of the Rhône Valley's production.

❧ SOUTHERN RHÔNE GRAPES & STYLES

Many grapes are permitted in various appellations across the southern Rhône, most selected for their ability to withstand the hotter Mediterranean climate—in Châteauneuf-du-Pape, 13 varieties are allowed. The most important whites include Grenache Blanc, Clairette and Bourboulenc, plus the northern Rhône varieties Marsanne, Roussanne and Viognier. They are typically blended to yield medium-bodied wines with peach, citrus and/or nut flavors. The southern Rhône's dark, fruity, earth-driven red wines are made primarily with Grenache, which usually is blended with Cinsaut, Syrah, Mourvèdre and/or Carignane. Rosés and good sweet wines are also made here.

DEFINING THE SOUTHERN RHÔNE

Côtes-du-Rhône is the southern Rhône's most basic category, and represents the vast majority of wines made here. Most Côtes-du-Rhône wines come from the south, although the entire Rhône Valley is permitted to use the designation. Wines made in the dozens of villages that satisfy stricter requirements are labeled *Côtes-du-Rhône Villages*. Eighteen high-quality villages have earned the right to add their name to the wine label, such as Côtes-du-Rhône Villages Cairanne. The best—including Gigondas, Vacqueyras and Châteauneuf-du-Pape—have their own appellations. Satellite regions such as Luberon, Ventoux and Costières de Nîmes make wines that are similar to the basic Côtes-du-Rhône, while Lirac and Tavel are best known for their rosés.

Producers/ Southern Rhône

CHÂTEAU DE BEAUCASTEL/PERRIN & FILS

One of most revered names in Châteauneuf-du-Pape, Château de Beaucastel is the southern Rhône's flagship producer. The Perrin family owns over a thousand acres and produces a huge variety of wine, including the Vieille Ferme label as well as such cult classics as Mourvèdre-based Hommage à Jacques Perrin.

○ **La Vieille Ferme** / 2010 / Côtes du Luberon / $
From Rhône's southernmost zone, this is fresh and peachy.

● **Perrin & Fils** / 2009 / Côtes-du-Rhône Villages / $
Exuberantly fruity, with raspberry and sweet cherry tones.

● **Château de Beaucastel** / 2008 / Châteauneuf-du-Pape / $$$$
This powerful, deeply layered red proves that even in so-so vintages, great producers make great wines.

CHÂTEAU DE SAINT COSME

Winemaker Louis Barruol's family acquired this ancient Gigondas estate in 1490. Saint Cosme is known for a supremely well-crafted lineup of wines from estate and purchased grapes (the latter under the Saint Cosme and Little James' Basket Press labels). Barruol has farmed organically since the 1970s.

○ **Little James' Basket Press** / 2010 / Vin de Pays d'Oc / $
This unusual, crisply delicious blend of lush, tropical Viognier and zesty Sauvignon Blanc comes at a compellingly low price.

● **Château de Saint Cosme** / 2009 / Gigondas / $$$
A freak spring hailstorm in 2009 reduced yields in Gigondas, making for a dense, full-bodied—yet gracefully polished—red.

CHÂTEAU GUIOT

Château Guiot is the leading winery in the Costières de Nîmes region. This slice of Provence used to be considered part of the Languedoc but was elevated in 2004 to the more esteemed Rhône Valley appellation. Sylvie Cornut makes the wines, while husband François tends their 216 vineyard acres. Their top red cuvées are dense blends; their two Vins de Pays du Gard are great values.

● **Château Guiot** / 2010 / **Costières de Nîmes** / $
This zesty rosé, redolent of raspberries and flowers, is a steal.

● **Mas de Guiot 40% Grenache–Syrah 60%** / 2010 / **Vin de Pays du Gard** / $ Plush Grenache and spicy, plummy Syrah come together nicely in this terrific value wine.

CHÂTEAU LA NERTHE

Alain Dugas found an ideal partner in the Richard family, who had the cash to buy this Châteauneuf estate in 1985 and the wisdom to let him run it. Along with his protégé, Christian Voeux, and winemaker Philippe Capelier, Dugas turned Château la Nerthe into one of the region's stars. Since Dugas's retirement in 2008, Voeux has been at the helm, keeping quality high.

● **Château La Nerthe** / 2007 / **Châteauneuf-du-Pape** / $$$
La Nerthe finished harvesting right before rain arrived in September, so this red's spicy cherry flavors are undiluted.

● **Château La Nerthe Cuvée des Cadettes** / 2005 / **Châteauneuf-du-Pape** / $$$$ The estate's most famous cuvée achieves brilliance in the stellar 2005 vintage.

DOMAINE DE FONDRÈCHE

This dynamite estate winery is drawing new attention to the Ventoux region. Radically low yields and organic farming give an inkling of vintner Sébastien Vincenti's commitment to quality. His powerful wines offer the complexity of bottlings from the Rhône's better-known regions at a fraction of the price.

● **Domaine de Fondrèche Nadal** / 2009 / **Côtes du Ventoux** / $$
A meaty blend of Syrah and Grenache with a little Mourvèdre.

● **Domaine de Fondrèche Cuvée Persia** / 2008 / **Côtes du Ventoux** / $$$ Just a few more dollars than the Nadal, this opulent Syrah-dominated red delivers serious structure.

DOMAINE DE LA JANASSE

In 1990, Aimé Sabon let his son Christophe, then only 19 years old, take charge of winemaking at this Châteauneuf estate. Under Christophe's precocious direction, quality soared. Today the domaine makes some of region's most sought-after reds. Chief among these is the extremely rich cuvée Chaupin, but even Sabon's "basic" wines are anything but.

- **Domaine de la Janasse Terre d'Argile** / 2008 / Côtes-du-Rhône Villages / $$ A lively, licorice-inflected red of equal parts Syrah, Grenache and Mourvèdre.
- **Domaine de la Janasse** / 2008 / Châteauneuf-du-Pape / $$$ Only a small portion of this smooth, elegant blend was aged in oak, allowing the wine's minerality to come through.

DOMAINE DE LA MORDORÉE

Winemaker Christophe Delorme is celebrated for his extraordinary Châteauneuf-du-Pape; not surprisingly, it's superexpensive. Look instead for Delorme's excellent rosés and reds from his organic vineyards in the humbler Tavel district. Delorme's style is consistent across his portfolio, with hedonistic fruit flavors checked by natural acidity and the modest use of oak.

- **Domaine de la Mordorée La Dame Rousse** / 2010 / Tavel / $$ Minerally red berry flavors mark this relatively hearty rosé.
- **Domaine de la Mordorée La Reine des Bois** / 2009 / Châteauneuf-du-Pape / $$$$ Mostly Grenache, this powerhouse bottling shows dense fruit flavors and supple tannins.

DOMAINE DE LA SOLITUDE

Florent Lançon's father and uncle, Michel and Jean Lançon, brought this historic Châteauneuf estate to the region's front ranks by making riper, modern-style wines. But Florent recently returned to a more traditional style with Cornelia Constanza, a powerful, spicy cuvée that dials back on new oak and extraction.

- **Domaine de la Solitude** / 2009 / Châteauneuf-du-Pape / $$$ A creamy wine layered with stone-fruit and mineral flavors.
- **Domaine de la Solitude Cornelia Constanza** / 2007 / Châteauneuf-du-Pape / $$$$ Sourced from century-old Grenache vines, this is gorgeously rich, smooth and complex.

DOMAINE DU CAILLOU

Caillou means "stone" in French—an apt moniker for this rock-strewn estate in Châteauneuf-du-Pape and Côtes-du-Rhône. Sylvie Pouizin inherited the property in 1996 and, together with her late husband, winemaker Jean-Denis Vacheron, started turning out stellar estate wines. Today winemaker Bruno Gaspard and consultant Philippe Cambie craft the wines, which are some of the region's most compelling.

● **Le Clos du Caillou** / 2010 / **Côtes-du-Rhône** / **$$**
Exactly what a summer rosé should be: fresh, fragrant and berry-flavored, with ample mouthwatering acidity.

● **Le Clos du Caillou Vieilles Vignes** / 2009 / **Côtes-du-Rhône** / **$$** A seductive bottling that aims for finesse over sheer power, with firm red-fruit flavors and a creamy texture.

DOMAINE DU PÉGAU

Domaine du Pégau makes its modern-style Châteauneuf wines the old-fashioned way: Winemaker Laurence Féraud does little more than bring in grapes, crush them and let them ferment. She attributes the fabulous concentration of Pégau's top-tier wines to extremely low yields and old vines.

● **Plan Pégau Lot 2009** / **NV** / **$$**
Although this blend lacks an appellation and can't legally list a vintage (it's a 2009), it delivers plenty of rich cherry flavors.

● **Domaine du Pégau Cuvée Reservée** / 2008 / **Châteauneuf-du-Pape** / **$$$$** A cooler vintage gave this top cuvée's sweet, smoky blackberry tones a savory edge.

DOMAINE LA RÉMÉJEANNE

Vintner Rémy Klein is bringing new attention to Sabran, a village in an unheralded corner of the Rhône. The site's superb *terroir* (lean soils, higher elevation and cooler temperatures) and Klein's craftsmanship yield wines of remarkable depth and finesse. But the district's obscurity and affordable real estate mean Klein can sell his Côtes-du-Rhônes at reasonable prices.

● **Domaine La Réméjeanne Les Arbousiers** / 2009 / **Côtes-du-Rhône** / **$$** Grown in rocky hillside soils, this plush Grenache-Syrah blend is ripe and dark fruit–flavored.

59

DOMAINE SANTA DUC

Until Yves Gras took over his family's Gigondas estate in 1995, Domaine Santa Duc sold its fermented juice in bulk. Gras took a bet on estate-bottled wines that has paid off handily. Top cuvées like the Prestige des Hautes Garrigues rank among the region's best; look for affordable bottlings made from purchased grapes, such as Les Vieilles Vignes Côtes-du-Rhône.

- **Domaine Santa Duc Les Vieilles Vignes** / 2007 / Côtes-du-Rhône / $$ An overachieving Grenache-based blend that coats the palate with plush blackberry flavors.
- **Domaine Santa Duc** / 2008 / Gigondas / $$$ Sleeker than Gras's usual lush style, thanks to a cool vintage.
- **Domaine Santa Duc Les Garancières** / 2007 / Gigondas / $$$ Gras's expertise is on display in this opulent, smoke-inflected red created from parcels scattered across the appellation.

LES CAILLOUX/FÉRAUD-BRUNEL

It's harder to make large amounts of fantastic everyday wine than it is to make a few hundred cases of a cult bottling, but André Brunel makes both look easy. The proprietor of Châteauneuf's Les Cailloux is best known for his estate cuvées, but a joint *négociant* venture with the famed Domaine du Pégau's Laurence Féraud (the Féraud-Brunel label) and forays into Côtes-du-Rhône vineyards have expanded his range.

- **Féraud-Brunel Rasteau** / 2009 / Rasteau / $$ Unlike most rustic wines from Rasteau, this bottling shows polished cherry, herb and earth layers and firm tannins.
- **Les Cailloux** / 2008 / Châteauneuf-du-Pape / $$$ Brunel's estate provided grapes for this flashy, dense Grenache-based red blend.

MAS CARLOT

This winery helped draw deserved attention to the Costières de Nîmes area (actually part of southern Rhône but often associated with Languedoc). Nathalie Blanc-Marès (whose husband owns Mas des Bressades, another local star) owns this property and crafts decadent, velvety reds made mostly from Syrah, Grenache and Mourvèdre and whites featuring local grape varieties such as the fresh, minerally Clairette.

○ **Mas Carlot Clairette de Bellegarde** / 2010 / *Clairette de Bellegarde* / $ Thanks to very old vines, the humble Clairette grape yields this pleasant white with silky stone-fruit flavors.

● **Mas Carlot Costières de Nîmes Tradition** / 2010 / *Costières de Nîmes* / $ An easy-drinking blend of Grenache and Syrah with a mix of vibrant red-fruit flavors.

TARDIEU-LAURENT

This small-scale *négociant* owes its success to two individuals: manager Michel Tardieu, who has a knack for sniffing out prime vineyards, and the brilliant winemaking consultant Philippe Cambie. Tardieu zeroes in on ancient, well-situated plots up and down the Rhône—which is partly how his boldly styled wines get their signature intensity. The array of bottlings includes accessibly priced appellation-wide blends plus small lots from prestigious subzones such as Hermitage.

○ **Tardieu-Laurent Guy Louis** / 2009 / *Côtes-du-Rhône* / $$ Grapes from Marsanne vines more than half a century old impart minerals and deep flavor to this terrific, peachy blend.

● **Tardieu-Laurent Les Becs Fins** / 2009 / *Côtes-du-Rhône Villages* / $$ Unoaked aging and a ripe vintage made this red very fruity and fresh, with sweet raspberry tones.

SOUTHERN FRANCE

The appellations of France's Mediterranean coast (Provence, Languedoc and Roussillon) and of the Southwest region were long known primarily for the quantity, not quality, of their wine production. But ongoing global demand for more affordable wines has brought the area renewed attention, and the wines have been improving dramatically.

SOUTHERN FRANCE: AN OVERVIEW

Le Midi, the storied south of France, includes the Languedoc, Roussillon and Provence regions (the first two are often referred to as a single hyphenated entity, Languedoc-Roussillon, or as just Languedoc). This area is blessed with so much Mediterranean sunlight that it is possible to make wines of every imaginable style here. The lands of the French Southwest (*le Sud-Ouest*) are under the combined influences of the Pyrenees mountains and the Atlantic Ocean.

❧ SOUTHERN FRANCE GRAPES & STYLES

The prolific Languedoc has become the source of many of the best values in French wine today, with its top subregions turning out increasingly serious and complex wines at prices that don't carry the prestige tax of its northern neighbors. Unlike most parts of France, the Languedoc grows a range of grapes—some native to the region, others from different French regions. Red grapes dominate, especially Carignane, which is capable of delicious spicy wines; excellent examples are made in Corbières. Syrah, Grenache and Mourvèdre are typically blended to create the hearty wines of Minervois and Fitou, as well as those of the Roussillon appellations. Cabernet and Merlot are used mostly for inexpensive wines destined for export. White grapes Grenache Blanc, Maccabéo, Muscat, Picpoul Blanc and Rolle create fresh, interesting wines; Viognier yields richer, more complex whites. Chardonnays from Limoux are worth exploring too.

Provence is known for its delicious, dry rosés. Typically made from a blend of Cinsaut, Grenache and Mourvèdre, they're meant to be consumed young. Those from Bandol are considered the finest, but rosés from Côtes de Provence and Coteaux d'Aix-en-Provence are also well made. Provence's citrusy whites are usually blends of local grapes Bourboulenc, Rolle, Clairette, Grenache Blanc and/or Ugni Blanc; the best come from Cassis. Bandol's minerally whites are full-bodied, as are its reds, made mostly with Mourvèdre. Grenache, Carignane, Cabernet, Cinsaut and Syrah are also grown in Provence. The best Provençal reds are from Les Baux de Provence and Coteaux d'Aix-en-Provence.

The wines of the Southwest, outshone by those of neighboring Bordeaux, are little known in the U.S., but that is changing. Bergerac reds are made with the same grapes as Bordeaux— Cabernet, Merlot, Malbec and Cabernet Franc—and often exhibit a similar finesse. Vintners in Cahors use the grape Auxerrois (known elsewhere as Malbec or Côt) to craft reds of massive power. The Sauternes-like sweet wines from Monbazillac cost far less than Bordeaux's famed sweet wines. In Madiran, winemakers produce dark, full-bodied and tannic wines from the Tannat grape. The Basque Country's hearty wines are made from a blend of local grapes. Jurançon, for example, is a full-bodied white wine produced from Petit and Gros Manseng grapes in dry and sweet styles. Vins de Pays des Côtes de Gascogne are light- to medium-bodied and made from local and international grapes.

Producers/ Southern France

BIELER PÈRE ET FILS

Charles Bieler is a champion of great wines in lowbrow packaging: His Three Thieves brand has put wine in jugs and Tetra Pak boxes, and his Gotham Project wines come in kegs. But pink wines are a family specialty. Bieler's family founded Château Routas, and his Bieler Père et Fils label consists of a single rosé.

● **Bieler Père et Fils Rosé** / 2010 / Coteaux d'Aix-en-Provence / $
A blend of Syrah, Grenache, Cinsaut and Cabernet, this elegant rosé is marked by strawberry and watermelon flavors.

CHÂTEAU DE JAU

This Roussillon winery makes robust, spicy reds that deliver loads of southern French character at reasonable prices. Château de Jau was bought and rehabilitated by the Dauré family in the 1970s. Its distinguishing asset is a huge limestone plateau, where the Daurés planted their Grenache and Carignane vines.

○ **Le Jaja de Jau Sauvignon Blanc** / 2010 / Vin de Pays d'Oc / $
Tart and refreshing, with lime and grapefruit flavors.
● **Château de Jau** / 2008 / Côtes du Roussillon Villages / $
A sleek blend of Syrah, Mourvèdre, Carignane and Grenache.

CHÂTEAU LAGRÉZETTE

Alain Dominique Perrin acquired this Cahors estate in 1980 and hired star consultant Michel Rolland to mastermind the wines. His Malbec-based reds have turned Lagrézette into Cahors's leading winery. The top cuvée is Le Pigeonnier; a range of wines made from bought grapes offers a more affordable taste of Lagrézette's style.

● **Château Lagrézette Cuvée Dame Honneur Malbec** / 2003 / Cahors / $$$$ Voluptuous blackberry, spice and mineral tones are up front in this reserve cuvée made from older vines.
● **Château Lagrézette Le Pigeonnier** / 2003 / Cahors / $$$$
A massive, single-vineyard Malbec with smoky black fruit.

CHÂTEAU ROUTAS

Château Routas is a go-to producer in the little-known Provençal appellation of Coteaux Varois. Founded by entrepreneur Philippe Bieler in 1993, Routas is now owned by Scottish billionaire Sir David Murray. Of the winery's six bottlings—all made with estate-grown grapes, most of them Rhône varieties—the rosé gets the most attention, but the whites and reds are equally well made.

○ **Château Routas Coquelicot Estate Vines / 2009 / Vin de Pays du Var / $$** A creamy blend of Viognier and Chardonnay.

● **Château Routas Rouvière / 2010 / Côteaux Varois en Provence / $** This vivid rosé's strawberry, tangerine and mineral notes are pure and refreshing.

CHÂTEAU ST-MARTIN DE LA GARRIGUE

This Languedoc winery made a name for itself by turning out excellent Picpoul, a tangy native white. But thanks to the area's sunny climate, red varieties such as Syrah, Mourvèdre, Grenache and Carignane thrive in St-Martin de la Garrigue's vineyards too. Winemaker Jean-Claude Zabalia ferments some of his red grapes as whole clusters, which softens their tannins and yields supple wines with great character (and friendly prices).

○ **Château St-Martin de la Garrigue Picpoul de Pinet / 2010 / Coteaux du Languedoc / $$** The Picpoul (pronounced "peek pool") grape makes zingy, super-refreshing whites such as this citrusy, mineral-rich version.

COMMANDERIE DE LA BARGEMONE

Fabulous dry rosé wines are the hallmark of this Provençal winery. Founded by Knights Templar in the 1200s, the estate is now owned by the Garin family. Key to Bargemone's success has been a focus on estate-grown fruit: All its wines, including newer blends such as Cuvée Marina, come from Garin vineyards.

● **Commanderie de la Bargemone / 2010 / Coteaux d'Aix-en-Provence / $$** A great candidate for a house rosé, bursting with juicy melon, berry and orange-zest notes.

● **Commanderie de la Bargemone Cuvée Marina / 2010 / Coteaux d'Aix-en-Provence / $$** Still juicy and fresh, this rosé gets its weightier flavors from a blend of Cabernet and Syrah.

DOMAINE TEMPIER

The leading estate in Bandol, Domaine Tempier makes some of the world's finest Mourvèdre-based reds. But its best-known wine is its dry rosé, a delicious wine that proves pink wines can be complex. Owned for generations by the Péyraud family, the estate has gained momentum in recent years under winemaker Daniel Ravier, who has improved the single-vineyard cuvées.

- **Domaine Tempier / 2010 / Bandol / $$$**
  Smooth, silky and lush, this is one of the few rosés that invites contemplation as much as sipping.
- **Domaine Tempier La Tourtine / 2008 / Bandol / $$$**
  This lush, spicy red uses fruit from a single 12-acre vineyard known for producing grapes with powerful tannins.

MAS AMIEL

Olivier Decelle is putting the under-the-radar Maury district on the map with Mas Amiel, an old domaine he bought in 1999. Decelle converted the estate's 420 acres of prized old vines to biodynamic farming and hired well-known consultants Stéphane Derenoncourt and Claude Bourgignon. The team's plush reds have quickly become benchmarks for the region.

- **Mas Amiel Notre Terre / 2006 / Côtes du Roussillon Villages / $**
  A soft blend of Grenache, Carignane, Syrah and a bit of Mourvèdre, with cherry and raisin notes and firm tannins.

MAS DE GOURGONNIER

Rocky Les Baux de Provence, a small corner of southern France that's home to Mas de Gourgonnier, will look familiar to fans of Van Gogh, who lived and painted for a time near the winery's current location. This dynamite winery—organic since the 1950s—is run by the Cartier family and turns out powerful, reasonably priced red blends as well as crisp whites and rosés.

- **Mas de Gourgonnier / 2010 / Les Baux de Provence / $$**
  Redolent of sweet herbs, flowers and ripe raspberries, this is a quintessential Provençal rosé.
- **Mas de Gourgonnier Réserve du Mas / 2009 / Les Baux de Provence / $$$** A full-bodied blend of equal parts Cabernet, Grenache and Syrah, with blackberry and dried-herb notes.

Italy

Wine Region

It's a testimony to the variety
offered by Italian wine that even
experts have trouble keeping track
of how many official wine regions
exist in the country. From the
foothills of the Alps in the north
to the island of Sicily in the south,
Italy's wealth of great reds and
whites seems only to increase each
year, especially as top winemakers
experiment more and more
with the country's vast number
of indigenous grape varieties.

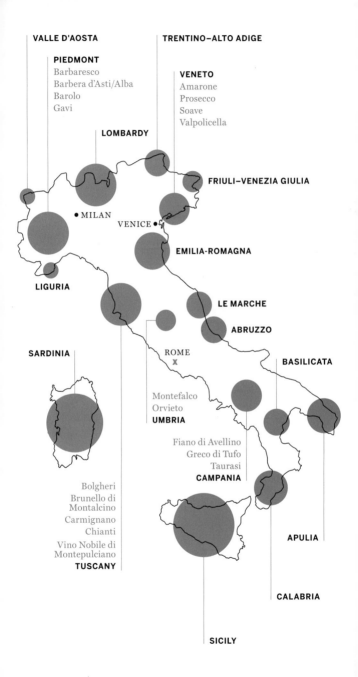

VALLE D'AOSTA

TRENTINO–ALTO ADIGE

PIEDMONT
Barbaresco
Barbera d'Asti/Alba
Barolo
Gavi

VENETO
Amarone
Prosecco
Soave
Valpolicella

LOMBARDY

FRIULI–VENEZIA GIULIA

• MILAN

VENICE •

EMILIA-ROMAGNA

LIGURIA

LE MARCHE

ABRUZZO

SARDINIA

ROME
✕

BASILICATA

Montefalco
Orvieto
UMBRIA

Fiano di Avellino
Greco di Tufo
Taurasi
CAMPANIA

Bolgheri
Brunello di
Montalcino
Carmignano
Chianti
Vino Nobile di
Montepulciano
TUSCANY

APULIA

CALABRIA

SICILY

Italy

WITH ITS QUALITY at an all-time high, the vast and varied world of Italian wine is more exciting to explore than ever. Piedmont and Tuscany lead in prestige, but up-and-coming regions are crafting delicious wines, mostly with native grapes. Italy has more than 300 DOC and DOCG zones (see Italian Wine Labels, below), but two regions stand out: Piedmont, in the northwest, where the Nebbiolo grape yields powerful, long-lived Barolo and Barbaresco; and Tuscany, home of the Sangiovese grape, responsible for two of Italy's most acclaimed wines—Chianti and Brunello di Montalcino. Southern Italy has reestablished its fine-wine tradition, while in the north the crisp whites of Friuli and Trentino–Alto Adige are gaining new respect. Central Italy too offers a wealth of wine, including Umbria's dark Sagrantino di Montefalco and Lazio's lighter wines.

ITALIAN WINE LABELS

Most Italian wines are labeled by region; some list the grape if it defines a region, such as Montepulciano d'Abruzzo, made from the Montepulciano grape in Abruzzo. Grape names commonly appear on wines from Alto Adige and Friuli–Venezia Giulia and from the south. Italy's regulatory system is the Denominazione di Origine Controllata (DOC), which sets basic standards. Stricter standards apply to wines labeled *DOCG* (Denominazione di Origine Controllata e Garantita). The term *classico* indicates a prestigious subregion. For much of the system's history, wines not adhering to DOC or DOCG standards were given the humble title *vino da tavola* (table wine). Since the 1994 vintage, the Indicazione Geografica Tipica (IGT) classification has been used for many regional table wines. It's also used for better wines that don't qualify for higher designations because of the use of unorthodox grape varieties or production methods.

PIEDMONT

Northwestern Italy's Piedmont region is a gastronome's paradise. Its aristocratic, truffle-infused cuisine is matched by its equally noble red wines, Barolo and Barbaresco, as well as by many other less famous but still impressive wines.

PIEDMONT: AN OVERVIEW

Made from the Nebbiolo grape, Barolo and Barbaresco wines come from a small number of vineyards surrounding the town of Alba, and their steep prices reflect their scarcity. Nebbiolo-based wines from zones outside Barolo and Barbaresco can offer great quality for the price. For everyday values, look to the supple, juicy, food-friendly reds made from the Barbera and Dolcetto grapes.

PIEDMONT GRAPES & STYLES

Nebbiolo's powerful tannins and firm acidity are behind the longevity of Barolo and Barbaresco; they also make these wines difficult to drink when young. For this reason, Barolo—more substantial than Barbaresco—must be aged three years, two in barrel, before release; Barbaresco must be aged two years, one in barrel. Many of these reds are best after a decade or more of age.

Traditional vintners craft these wines in an austere, earthy style, while modern-minded producers opt for fruit-forward, oak-influenced wines. Either way, Nebbiolo displays a signature mix of savory and floral scents reminiscent of tar and roses. Nebbiolo-based reds from Gattinara, Ghemme, Alba and especially Langhe offer a taste of the grape at a fraction of the cost.

Barbera and Dolcetto are Piedmont's more accessible offerings. Both display supple tannins, berry flavors and juicy acidity, though Barbera is capable of greater complexity.

While its renown is based on reds, Piedmont offers fine whites too. Gavi, from the Cortese grape, was upgraded to DOCG status in 1998; although many bottlings are excellent, lots of mediocre versions are still being made. Another local grape, the bright, almond-flavored Arneis, has come back from near extinction; the best examples of its wines are from the Roero subregion. Piedmont's Chardonnays are sometimes overlooked, but many prominent vintners are producing worthwhile versions.

Producers/ Piedmont

BRUNO GIACOSA

Modern wine orthodoxy glamorizes estate-grown fruit, yet Bruno Giacosa proves it's possible to make exceptional Barolos and Barbarescos mostly from purchased grapes. His secret: cherry-picking the finest sites for fruit. Portfolio highlights include the bright Arneis and the majestic Nebbiolo-based reds.

○ **Casa Vinicola Bruno Giacosa / 2010 / Roero Arneis / $$$**
It's worth seeking out Giacosa's terrific apricot- and citrus-inflected rendition of this ancient grape variety.

● **Azienda Agricola Falletto di Bruno Giacosa Falletto / 2007 / Barolo / $$$$** Giacosa's Falletto vineyard is the source of his most famous wines, including this coveted, collectible Barolo.

CERETTO

The vast size of this estate means that many of its wines are easier to find and more affordable than is often the case in Piedmont. Vintner Marcello Ceretto and his brother Bruno helped drive the craze for single-site Nebbiolos in the 1970s; today the next generation crafts wines in the same fruit-focused style.

○ **Ceretto Blangè / 2009 / Langhe Arneis / $$**
One of Piedmont's best-known Arneises, this features a slight effervescence and fresh peach and apple notes.

● **Bricco Rocche / 2007 / Barolo / $$$$**
Of the Cerettos' four single-vineyard Barolos, this is the best.

DOMENICO CLERICO

Domenico Clerico's seductive Barolos made him famous in the 1980s, when he became known as one of Piedmont's young rebels. Though Clerico uses modern techniques such as oak aging, his wines—with big tannins, graceful oak and deep fruit flavors— hew a middle ground between new and traditional winemaking styles. Don't overlook his terrific Barbera and Dolcetto.

- **Domenico Clerico Visadi / 2008 / Langhe Dolcetto / $$**
  Clerico makes this luscious, anise-accented red from prime vineyards in Dogliani and Alba.
- **Domenico Clerico Ciabot Mentin Ginestra / 2005 / Barolo / $$$$** A plush, powerful classic, filled out with notes of black cherries, violets, tar and earth.

ELIO ALTARE

One of the original "Barolo Boys," the youthful posse of winemakers who upended Piedmont's wine industry in the 1980s, Elio Altare is now a father figure to a new generation. He helped pioneer a fruitier, less tannic style for Barolo, and continues to make his revered boutique wines from the same 24 acres (12 owned, 12 rented). His Arborina cuvée is his most famous.

- **Elio Altare / 2009 / Barbera d'Alba / $$**
  A warmer-than-usual vintage is reflected in this wine's plush, sweet black plum flavors.
- **Elio Altare Vigneto Arborina / 2007 / Barolo / $$$$**
  This stunning single-vineyard red is a modern Barolo classic.

FONTANAFREDDA

Fontanafredda has long been known for making lots of good, but rarely great, wines that cover Piedmont's major bases: Barolos, Barberas, Barbarescos and Dolcettos plus whites and sparklers. But when entrepreneur Oscar Farinetti bought the estate with a partner in 2008, quality shot up. Today it's a winery to watch.

- **Fontanafredda Briccotondo Barbera / 2009 / Piedmont / $**
  One of Piedmont's most reliable bargains, this delivers loads of spicy, supple black cherry flavors.
- **Fontanafredda Serralunga d'Alba / 2006 / Barolo / $$$**
  Smoke, earth and spice inflect the winery's entry-level Barolo.

GIACOMO BORGOGNO & FIGLI

Borgogno has been known for its Barolos since the 1700s. Aged
in huge, old oak casks (which helps give Nebbiolos their longevity), Borgogno's reds are legendary; the Barbera is a true steal.
The estate's new owners, the Farinetti family (of Eataly food-
market fame), seem intent on preserving Borgogno's traditions.

● Borgogno / 2008 / Barbera d'Alba Superiore / $$
Aged in oak for a year—twice as long as Borgogno's regular
Barbera—this offers an affordable taste of the winery's style.
● Borgogno / 2005 / Barolo / $$$$
This famous multivineyard red is aged at least five years
before release: three in oak, two in bottle.

LA SCOLCA

La Scolca was one of the first wineries in Gavi to focus on quality
still wines from the local Cortese grape, which until the 1970s
was made chiefly into sparkling wine (most of it forgettable).
Owned by the Soldati family, the winery offers an exceptionally
tasty entry-level Gavi di Gavi, as well as other terrific cuvées.

○ La Scolca "White Label" / 2010 / Gavi di Gavi / $$
An always excellent bottling, this displays deep minerals,
lemony acidity and fragrant citrus notes.
● La Scolca Rosa Chiara / 2010 / Vino da Tavola / $$
A bold rosé with deliciously ripe, fresh strawberry flavors.

LA SPINETTA

The single-vineyard bottlings introduced by La Spinetta in 1978
redefined Moscato d'Asti. Since then, the Rivetti family has
rethought Barbera, Barbaresco and Barolo in a series of ambi-
tious cuvées. Today the Rivetti brothers are among Piedmont's
brightest stars. Low yields, oak aging and a focus on vineyards
is the Rivetti formula; showy, fruit-driven wines are the result.

● La Spinetta Vigneto Bordini / 2007 / Barbaresco / $$$$
Sweet cherry, leather and mint mingle in this structured
single-vineyard cuvée.
● La Spinetta Vigneto Garretti / 2006 / Barolo / $$$$
A new wine made from grapes that previously went into the
famous (and famously expensive) Campè bottling.

MARCHESI DI GRÉSY

Grapes have grown on the Di Grésy family's Martinenga estate in Langhe since antiquity. In 1973, Alberto di Grésy built a winery here to take advantage of the family's well-situated vineyards and soon began snapping up more top sites. Today Barbaresco is the winery's calling card, though winemaker Marco Dotta also has a deft hand with Barbera, Dolcetto and Sauvignon Blanc.

● **Marchesi di Grésy Monte Aribaldo** / 2008 / Dolcetto d'Alba / $$
This fresh, graceful wine comes from a vineyard that surrounds the Di Grésy family's hunting lodge.

● **Marchesi di Grésy Martinenga** / 2007 / Barbaresco / $$$
Aged first in French oak and then in Slavonian casks, this seamless, berry-rich red aims for elegance over power.

MASSOLINO

For generations the Massolino family has made well-regarded wines in Serralunga d'Alba, a small community known for its powerful Barolos. But it wasn't until after brothers Roberto and Franco Massolino began to take over the winery in the 1990s that this producer gained its buzzworthy status. Four ambitious single-vineyard Barolos top its varied estate-grown portfolio.

● **Massolino** / 2009 / Barbera d'Alba / $$
First made in 1896, this sophisticated, blackberry-inflected cuvée comes from top vineyards in Serralunga d'Alba.

● **Massolino** / 2009 / Dolcetto d'Alba / $$
This Dolcetto's deep black-plum flavors are silky and vibrant.

MICHELE CHIARLO

Michele Chiarlo made his name with ripe, oak-aged Barbera from his home turf in Asti. Today he's one of Piedmont's most important producers, making wines from nearly every major DOC. Chiarlo's single-vineyard Barolos attract collectors, while his introductory Barberas offer an affordable taste of his style.

● **Michele Chiarlo Le Orme** / 2008 / Barbera d'Asti Superiore / $
A great house red, with energetic cherry and licorice flavors.

● **Michele Chiarlo Tortoniano** / 2006 / Barolo / $$$
Blending fruit from several top vineyards creates this beautifully layered cuvée redolent of ripe red cherries and spice.

PIO CESARE

When Giuseppe Boffa took over Pio Cesare from his father-in-law in the 1940s, he began creating some of Piedmont's most prized Barolos. Boffa's son, Pio, is now the winemaker, and though he's added new cuvées, he has preserved the estate's structured style. He also uses obscure local grapes like Grignolino and Freisa; the wines are worth trying if you can find them.

● **Pio Cesare / 2009 / Dolcetto d'Alba / $$**
Earthy, herb-edged red cherry flavors and firm tannins mark this old-school Dolcetto.

● **Pio Cesare Ornato / 2006 / Barolo / $$$$**
The Ornato vineyard, in Serralunga d'Alba, yielded this powerful red layered with cherry, floral and spice notes.

PODERI LUIGI EINAUDI

Founded in 1897 by Luigi Einaudi, a future president of the Italian Republic, this estate is near Dogliani, a town known for its remarkable Dolcetto. Einaudi's versions are some of the finest, thanks to superb vineyards and, since the late '90s, the consulting help of Beppe Caviola. Caviola's influence has also brought new attention to Einaudi's three earthy, ripe yet firm Barolos.

● **Poderi Luigi Einaudi Vigna Tecc / 2008 / Dolcetto di Dogliani / $$** From a top Dolcetto zone, this exuberantly spicy bottling is both lush and vibrant.

● **Poderi Luigi Einaudi Costa Grimaldi / 2006 / Barolo / $$$$**
A seductively rich cuvée made from a selection of the best grapes in the Costa Grimaldi vineyard.

PRODUTTORI DEL BARBARESCO

Cooperative wineries are often known for tanker-loads of plonk, but Produttori del Barbaresco is a magnificent exception. This co-op not only makes some of Italy's best Barbarescos but also has helped drive Piedmont's trend toward site-specific winemaking. The winery's single-vineyard cuvées are outstanding, while a multivineyard Barbaresco and a basic Langhe red offer value.

● **Produttori del Barbaresco / 2006 / Barbaresco / $$$**
This velvety Barbaresco offers outstanding complexity, with layers of ripe red cherry, leather and sweet spice.

SANDRONE

Gifted winemaker and Piedmont upstart Luciano Sandrone began as a cellarhand but saved enough money to buy a piece of the famed Cannubi vineyard in 1970. Sandrone makes two magnificent Barolos, plus a Dolcetto and a Barbera that are among Piedmont's best. All his wines showcase a rich but refined style.

- ● **Sandrone / Dolcetto d'Alba / 2009 / $$**
  Get a taste of Sandrone's polished sensibility with this affordable unoaked wine.
- ● **Sandrone Cannubi Boschis / Barolo / 2007 / $$$$**
  Often sold out before it even arrives in the U.S., this great Barolo may be purchased online—albeit at a very high price.

VIETTI

Vietti is legendary for its traditionally styled single-vineyard Barolos. Beyond the top-end wines lies a compelling array of Piedmont classics, including a bright Arneis, the local white that owner Alfredo Currado rescued from near extinction in the 1960s. Son Luca Currado—an alumnus of California's Opus One and Bordeaux's Château Mouton Rothschild—helms the winery today.

- ○ **Vietti / 2010 / Roero Arneis / $$**
  A compulsively delicious, peach- and flower-inflected white.
- ● **Vietti Tre Vigne / 2008 / Barbera d'Alba / $$**
  Grapes from three top Alba vineyards yield a round Barbera redolent of plums and violets.
- ● **Vietti Castiglione / 2006 / Barolo / $$$**
  At about half the price of many top Barolos, this beautiful, densely layered bottling is a smart buy.

OTHER NORTHERN ITALIAN REGIONS

No region in Italy churns out more wine than the northeast. The Veneto makes oceans of industrial blends yet also produces a growing number of refined, well-priced wines. Sparkling Prosecco comes from vineyards near the Veneto coast. Farther north, bordering Slovenia, Austria and Switzerland, are the Friuli–Venezia Giulia and Trentino–Alto Adige regions. German is widely spoken in the latter (it's the majority language in Alto Adige), and the grapes and wines also reveal German influence. Friuli–Venezia Giulia grows many unusual native grape varieties.

💜 OTHER NORTHERN ITALIAN GRAPES & STYLES

Indigenous grapes form the backbone of the Veneto's best-known wines, lemony white Soave and popular red Valpolicella. At its best, well-crafted Valpolicella is one of Italy's great underrated reds, while luscious, powerful Amarone provides the Veneto's claim to world-class wine.

Whites dominate in the north, yet some firm reds are produced as well. Sauvignon Blanc and Merlot are gaining favor in Italy's northeast, where they are made into varietal wines and used to plump up native grapes in blends. Pinot Noir (known locally as Pinot Nero) makes racy, light wines throughout the north.

FRIULI–VENEZIA GIULIA The region is famous for high-quality whites that are aromatic and mineral-laden. Native white grapes include Friulano, Ribolla Gialla and Picolit; the region is also known for excellent Pinot Grigio, Pinot Bianco and Sauvignon Blanc. Its subregions Collio and Colli Orientali also produce a handful of reds, some from obscure native varieties.

TRENTINO–ALTO ADIGE Once focused mainly on red wines, Trentino–Alto Adige is now expanding plantings of its distinctive whites. The area's cool climate and sandy clay soils produce some of Italy's greatest Pinot Grigios, as well as whites from Germanic grapes such as Müller-Thurgau, Sylvaner, Riesling and Gewürztraminer and from the French native grape Pinot Blanc (Pinot Bianco). Other wines made from international grapes such as Chardonnay and Sauvignon Blanc (referred to here as just Sauvignon) can be excellent as well. The area has three red wines of note: light, simple Schiava, plus Lagrein and Teroldego, both of which are fuller-bodied and flavorful.

VENETO The indigenous Garganega grape gives the Veneto's Soave whites their lemon and almond flavors; look for bottles labeled *superiore*, which come from the *classico* zone. Valpolicella and its lighter sibling Bardolino are made from blends of native red varieties, chiefly Corvina, Molinara and Rondinella. Valpolicella contains more Corvina, which makes it richer. These red varieties also go into Amarone, an opulent wine made by drying grapes for several months before pressing out their juice. This process concentrates the grapes' sugars and turns the fruit halfway into raisins, resulting in high-alcohol reds with incredible depth and body. Most top Amarone producers make superior Valpolicella too, almost exclusively from the more prestigious *classico* zone. Recioto della Valpolicella is the sweet parent of Amarone, while *ripasso* styles seek a middle ground by infusing Valpolicella wine with leftover pressed Amarone grapes. The Veneto is also home to Prosecco, the popular sparkling white (see p. 267) made from the Glera grape (referred to as the Prosecco grape in many areas).

LOMBARDY The most famous wine district in Lombardy is Franciacorta, which makes Italy's best sparkling wines (see p. 267) using the same principal grape varieties—Chardonnay and Pinot Noir—and methods as in Champagne.

Producers/ Other Northern Italian Regions

ALLEGRINI

Following in the footsteps of his father, who reinvented Valpolicella at a time when most examples were charmless wines churned out in bulk, Franco Allegrini crafts reds that set the standard for the region. By limiting vineyard yields and exchanging traditional Slavonian casks for small French barrels, Allegrini creates intense, elegant Valpolicella. He lavishes the same kind of craftsmanship on his Amarone and Soave.

○ Allegrini / 2009 / Soave / $
  Citrusy and refreshing, this Soave boasts a round texture and loads of minerals on the finish.

● Allegrini / 2009 / Valpolicella Classico / $
  Aging in steel tanks keeps this bottling's juicy, supple red-fruit flavors bright—and the price reasonable.

● Allegrini / 2006 / Amarone della Valpolicella Classico / $$$$
  This seamless Amarone reveals voluptuous layers of plum, allspice and blackberry.

ALOIS LAGEDER

Fifth-generation owner Alois Lageder has made this Alto Adige winery one of Italy's most eco-friendly, building a carbon-neutral facility. Lageder and his brother-in-law, winemaker Luis von Dellemann, converted estate vineyards to biodynamic farming and created an organic label, Tenutæ Lageder. The wide portfolio includes crisp, mineral-laden whites and coolly refined reds.

○ **Tenutæ Lageder Löwengang Chardonnay** / 2007 / Alto Adige / $$$ Reminiscent of a white Burgundy, this has smoky mineral, apple and pastry crust notes.

● **Tenutæ Lageder Krafuss Pinot Noir** / 2007 / Alto Adige / $$$ Textbook Pinot, with plush raspberry flavors and fresh acidity.

BASTIANICH

Best known as the co-owner—with chef Mario Batali—of a small empire of restaurants, Joe Bastianich is also a partner in Manhattan's Italian megamarket Eataly as well as the author of two Italian-wine books. Bastianich's wine venture, which he owns with his mother, Lidia, focuses on small-lot Friuli wines.

○ **Bastianich Plus** / 2006 / Colli Orientali del Friuli / $$$ A peach-driven Friuliano of remarkable richness, from a single vineyard of 60-year-old vines.

○ **Bastianich Vespa Bianco** / 2008 / Colli Orientali del Friuli / $$$ Chardonnay adds creamy lushness and Sauvignon Blanc imparts crisp melon flavors to this balanced blend.

CANTINA ANDRIANO

Cantina Andriano (or Kellerei Andrian, as the winery is known in its mostly German-speaking slice of Italy) was one of Alto Adige's first wine cooperatives when it was founded in 1893. Located at the foot of a massive granite peak called Mount Gantkofel, it makes a wide range of wines, anchored by sleek, minerally whites.

○ **Kellerei Andrian Pinot Grigio** / 2010 / Alto Adige / $$ Zesty acidity and minerals course throughout this wine, nicely offsetting creamy stone-fruit and apple flavors.

● **Kellerei Andrian Tor di Lupo Lagrein Riserva** / 2008 / Alto Adige / $$$ Serve this Lagrein with food to best appreciate its juicy, angular structure and oak-aged cherry notes.

CANTINA TERLANO

Some of northern Italy's best whites come from this co-op founded in 1893. Paying growers based on the quality, not quantity, of their grapes is a key to Terlano's success. Another is its location in Alto Adige's Dolomite foothills, whose soils yield mineral-laden wines. Terlano's varied offerings range from Chardonnay to Lagrein, but vivid Pinot Biancos and Sauvignon Blancs are the stars.

○ **Kellerei Terlan Pinot Bianco** / 2010 / Alto Adige / $$
Reliably great, with penetrating fresh apple and pear flavors.

○ **Kellerei Terlan Quarz Sauvignon** / 2009 / Alto Adige / $$$
Luscious stone-fruit flavors nicely offset the flinty minerality in this wine, one of the region's most highly rated whites.

JERMANN

Born into a winemaking family in Collio, Silvio Jermann helped pioneer Friuli's Super-Whites—complex blends of French grapes along with native varieties such as Ribolla Gialla and Picolit. Jermann's flagship blend, Vintage Tunina, is one of the region's best; single-variety wines are delicious—and more affordable.

○ **Jermann Chardonnay** / 2009 / Collio / $$
Jermann's characteristic richness is on display here in the form of caramel-edged apple and warm spice flavors.

● **Jermann Red Angel on the Moonlight** / 2007 / Collio / $$$
Merlot adds a fruity quality to this spicy Pinot-based blend.

J. HOFSTÄTTER

One of the largest family wineries in Alto Adige, Hofstätter is the only one to own property on both sides of the Adige valley. Different growing conditions in their scattered vineyards allow the Foradori family to grow a range of grapes. Best-known bottlings include one of Italy's finest Pinot Noirs, the Barthenau Vigna San Urbano, and the prized Kolbenhof Gewürztraminer.

○ **Hofstätter Joseph Pinot Grigio** / 2010 / Alto Adige / $$
With floral-edged citrus and melon flavors and flinty minerality, this shows how compelling Pinot Grigio can be.

● **Hofstätter Joseph Lagrein** / 2009 / Alto Adige / $$
Vibrant, lightly earthy red plum and raspberry tones showcase Lagrein's supple, accessible side.

LIVIO FELLUGA

Livio Felluga's Colli Orientali winery has long been one of
northern Italy's most dynamic estates. His Terre Alte bottling—
a Super-White blend aged partly in French oak—helped define
Friuli's potential for world-class wine. Today Felluga's four children manage the 334-acre vineyard, which produces a lineup
of compelling wines made chiefly from traditional grapes.

○ **Livio Felluga Friulano** / 2010 / Colli Orientali del Friuli / $$
Creamy citrus, fig and mineral tones are beautifully balanced.

○ **Livio Felluga Terre Alte** / 2009 / Colli Orientali del Friuli / $$$$
This voluptuous, apple-inflected blend of Friulano, Pinot
Bianco and Sauvignon is one of Friuli's top whites.

MACULAN

Fausto Maculan turned his family winery into a Veneto power-
house by using French grapes and modern techniques and by
focusing intently on his vineyards. His wines range from aro-
matic, inexpensive rosés and white blends to luxury cuvées; the
Cabernet- and Merlot-based blends are among Italy's finest.

○ **Maculan Pino & Toi** / 2009 / Veneto / $
A peachy, floral blend of Tai (formerly known as Tocai), Pinot
Bianco and Pinot Grigio at a super price.

● **Maculan Brentino** / 2008 / Veneto / $$
Velvety black cherry, tobacco and herb notes define this
Bordeaux-inspired blend of Cabernet and Merlot.

MASI

Masi is one of the greatest names in Amarone. Responsible for
20 percent of the Veneto's Amarone output, this family winery
maintains high quality thanks to patriarch Sandro Boscaini's
fierce insistence on technical rigor. Also worth exploring are the
winery's non-Amarones, all made from local grapes.

● **Masi Campofiorin** / 2007 / Veronese / $$
A secondary fermentation using partially dried grapes adds
richness to this bottling's silky red-fruit flavors.

● **Serego Alighieri Vaio Armaron** / 2004 / Amarone della
Valpolicella Classico / $$$$ A polished, cherry-driven cuvée
from vineyards owned by descendants of the poet Dante.

PIEROPAN

Arguably Italy's master of Soave, Leonildo Pieropan resisted the Veneto trend toward mass-market wines in the 1980s as well as the push to plant international varieties. Pieropan uses only handpicked native grapes from organic vines; his reds and whites are beautifully structured and made in a classic style.

○ **Pieropan** / 2009 / **Soave Classico** / **$$**
Crisp and bold, with supple apple, quince and chalk flavors.
○ **Pieropan Calvarino** / 2008 / **Soave Classico** / **$$**
This single-vineyard, old-vine cuvée offers a lush, minerally mix of citrus and floral tones.

VILLA RUSSIZ

Friuli's Villa Russiz is famous for its lush, opulent whites, richer than most from the region. This quality-driven estate has been run for decades as a nonprofit foundation, its proceeds benefiting children in need. Winemaker Gianni Menotti crafts excellent entry-level wines as well as the acclaimed "de La Tour" cuvées.

○ **Villa Russiz Friulano** / 2008 / **Collio** / **$$$**
This wine's satiny layers of baked apple and spice finish dry.
○ **Villa Russiz Pinot Grigio** / 2008 / **Collio** / **$$$**
A coolish summer preserved acidity in this peachy white, which is expertly balanced between creamy and crisp.

TUSCANY

The Sangiovese grape is dominant in Tuscany. Although most Tuscan reds are Sangiovese-based, they range greatly in style. From regal Brunellos to suave Chianti Classicos, humble and juicy Morellinos to powerful Super-Tuscans, compelling wines are made throughout this art- and history-packed region.

TUSCANY: AN OVERVIEW

For centuries, the Chianti region, source of Tuscany's most famous wine, consisted of four neighboring villages, but the region's size grew in tandem with the fame of its wines. The original district is now called Chianti Classico and encompasses nine villages; it's located within the larger Chianti DOCG zone that includes seven other subzones. Of these, the subregion Chianti Rùfina makes wines to rival the finest of Chianti Classico.

Montalcino makes one of Italy's most esteemed wines from a local Sangiovese clone, Brunello. In Montepulciano, Sangiovese (called Prugnolo Gentile here) yields often excellent wines under the Vino Nobile di Montepulciano designation. The newer Bolgheri DOC was created for Super-Tuscans, premium wines made from grapes other than, or in addition to, Sangiovese (see opposite). The Carmignano DOCG and the Cortona DOC have been using Super-Tuscan grapes in wines across a wider price range.

❦ TUSCAN GRAPES & STYLES

Sangiovese yields cherry-inflected reds in a range of styles; all feature high acidity, which makes them very food-friendly. Winemakers often blend Sangiovese with various amounts of foreign and native grapes, depending on what part of Tuscany they're in. Cabernet, Merlot and Syrah are popular complements to Sangiovese in the coastal Maremma and Bolgheri regions. Native grapes include Canaiolo, Mammolo and Colorino.

Tuscany produces a fair amount of white wine, most of it based on the Trebbiano grape. But two other Tuscany whites are worth seeking out: crisp Vernaccia from San Gimignano and Vermentino, a wine full of minerality and zesty lime flavors.

CHIANTI Spurred by competition and regulation changes in the 1990s, Chianti's wines have been improving steadily. Sangiovese-based reds were once blended with white grapes, but the practice fell out of use and was officially prohibited in Chianti Classico as of the 2006 vintage. Flexibility in aging the wines has increased, and today winemakers often use small French barrels instead of large old casks. Most wineries use 100 percent Sangiovese, or blend it with up to 20 percent (in Chianti Classico; more is allowed in basic Chianti) Cabernet Sauvignon, Merlot or native grapes such as Canaiolo and Colorino. Generic Chianti, with no subzone on the label, is the simplest. *Riserva* Chiantis require at least two years of aging and are more powerful as a result.

MONTALCINO, MONTEPULCIANO & CORTONA Vineyards around the town of Montalcino make Tuscany's greatest wine, Brunello di Montalcino. The wines of nearby Montepulciano are lighter than Montalcino's and can include small amounts of other grapes along with Sangiovese. Vino Nobile di Montepulciano wines must be aged two years (three for *riservas*). Both regions release "baby brother" reds under *rosso* designations, Rosso di Montalcino and Rosso di Montepulciano—younger, lighter versions of their pricier siblings. Straddling Montepulciano is Cortona, a DOC devoted mostly to foreign grapes; Syrah thrives here.

CARMIGNANO & MORELLINO DI SCANSANO The town of Carmignano blends Sangiovese with Canaiolo and Cabernet (Sauvignon and/or Franc). The Carmignano DOCG zone tends to yield wines with lower acidity and firmer tannins than Chianti Classico. Morellino di Scansano is a mainly Sangiovese-based wine from southern Tuscany that has improved greatly in recent years.

SUPER-TUSCANS & OTHER TUSCAN REDS Super-Tuscans are reds dominated by Cabernet, Merlot and Syrah (though many include Sangiovese). The greatest are made within the Bolgheri and the single-estate Bolgheri Sassicaia DOC zones. Super-Tuscans are not an officially regulated category in Tuscany; the moniker originated when producers started using prohibited grape varieties to make quality wines. That's why Super-Tuscans from Chianti aren't called Chianti but instead are labeled *IGT Toscana* (see p. 69). Many other Sangiovese-based reds get the Tuscany designation but are made in a more traditional style.

Producers/ Tuscany

ALTESINO

Altesino's best-known Brunello, Montosoli, was one of the first single-vineyard Montalcino wines when it was introduced in 1975. Part of a vanguard of ambitious young wineries, Altesino helped elevate winemaking in Montalcino. The property has changed owners, but Claudio Basla is still making its bold, earthy reds.

● **Altesino / 2009 / Rosso di Montalcino / $$**
A fresh, berry-driven wine that shows Sangiovese's softer side.

● **Altesino Montosoli / 2005 / Brunello di Montalcino / $$$$**
The roughly 12-acre Montosoli vineyard is the source of this stunning Brunello, one of the region's most respected wines.

ANTINORI

The Antinori family have been making wine since the 14th century. While their empire now includes estates in nearly every Italian region (and winemaking partnerships around the world), Tuscany remains Antinori's center of gravity. For such a historic estate, the Antinoris make very modern wines; their Tignanello, for example, effectively created the Super-Tuscan category.

● **Antinori Pèppoli** / 2008 / Chianti Classico / $$
The Antinoris source this brisk, tart cherry-driven red from a medieval-era estate purchased in 1985.

● **Antinori Tignanello** / 2008 / Tuscany / $$$$
One of Italy's most famous wines, this blend combines Sangiovese, Cabernet Sauvignon and Cabernet Franc.

ARGIANO

Hans Vinding-Diers made wine on four continents before becoming head winemaker at this Montalcino estate in 2004. Breaking with house tradition, he ferments vineyard lots separately, then blends the best for Argiano's flagship Brunello. Also in the portfolio are a Super-Tuscan and a mini Super-Tuscan.

● **Argiano NC Non Confunditur** / 2008 / Tuscany / $$
An affordable version of a Super-Tuscan, this is a supple, cherry-rich blend of Cabernet, Sangiovese, Merlot and Syrah.

● **Argiano** / 2006 / Brunello di Montalcino / $$$
Aging in a combination of traditional Slavonian casks and French barrels yielded this especially silky red.

AVIGNONESI

Avignonesi is famous for its two Vini Nobili di Montepulciano and its Vin Santo Occhio di Pernice. But also worth weeking out are the nontraditional reds: Desiderio Merlot and 50&50, a Merlot-Sangiovese blend made with Chianti's Capanelle estate. The Rosso di Montepulciano and Toscana Rosso are great values.

● **Avignonesi** / 2009 / Rosso di Montepulciano / $$
Delivers loads of juicy, vibrant berry tones.

● **Avignonesi Desiderio Merlot** / 2007 / Cortona / $$$
Jam-packed with voluptuous blackberry flavors, this tasty red is made from grapes sourced from two hillside estates.

BADIA A COLTIBUONO

This thousand-year-old Chianti Classico estate was an abbey for centuries. The Stucchi Prinetti family bought it in 1846 and, more recently, converted the monastic quarters into a hotel and cooking school. Classic Sangiovese-based reds are the estate's focus, under the Badia a Coltibuono and Coltibuono labels.

- **Coltibuono Cetamura** / 2009 / Chianti / $
  Tangy berry flavors define this charming entry-level Sangiovese.
- **Badia a Coltibuono Sangioveto** / 2006 / Tuscany / $$$
  A spicy, cherry-flavored red that is made with handpicked grapes and aged for 18 to 20 months in French oak.

BIBI GRAETZ

Artist-turned-vintner Bibi Graetz is obsessed with old, native-variety vineyards that many elite Tuscan producers overlook. With his flagship Testamatta cuvée, first released in 2000, Graetz revived the winemaking reputation of Fiesole, a hill town near Florence. Graetz's offerings include the bargain Casamatta line and the midrange, Sangiovese-based Soffocone and Grilli reds.

- **Casamatta** / 2010 / Tuscany / $
  Made from Sangiovese, Graetz's entry-level red is a super value, with lush, energetic plum and cherry flavors.
- **Grilli del Testamatta** / 2008 / Tuscany / $$
  This baby brother to Graetz's flagship Testamatta perfectly balances fresh cherry flavors with a creamy, plush texture.

CASTELLO BANFI

The Mariani family had been importing Italian wine to the U.S. for 60 years when brothers John and Harry Mariani decided to become vintners in 1978 and established this Montalcino estate. Expansion into Piedmont brought the Vigne Regali estate into the fold, but Castello Banfi remains the mother ship, with 7,000 acres and a huge output of high-quality Tuscan bottlings.

- **Banfi Col di Sasso** / 2009 / Tuscany / $
  A well-priced, cherry-scented Cabernet-Sangiovese blend.
- **Castello Banfi** / 2006 / Brunello di Montalcino / $$$
  Grapes from premium sites among Banfi's vast acreage created this gorgeously fragrant, silky red.

CASTELLO DI AMA

Castello di Ama makes some of Tuscany's best, and most expensive, Chianti Classicos. Similarly renowned is its Merlot-based L'Apparita cuvée, from the winery's Gaiole estate. Winemaker Marco Pallanti also produces four more-modestly priced wines, including a Chianti Classico, a white blend and a rosé.

- **Castello di Ama** / 2007 / Chianti Classico / $$$
  This complex entry-level bottling could easily compete with most estates' top cuvées.
- **Castello di Ama L'Apparita** / 2007 / Tuscany / $$$$
  Merlot shines in this dark, concentrated Super-Tuscan.

CASTELLO DI FONTERUTOLI

Brothers Filippo and Francesco Mazzei are the 24th generation to run this Chianti Classico estate. In recent years, the family has expanded its vineyard holdings, built a cutting-edge winery and hired legendary winemaker Carlo Ferrini. They've also refocused Fonterutoli from Super-Tuscans to Chiantis (though the famous Sangiovese-Merlot blend Siepi remains).

- **Mazzei Badiola** / 2008 / Tuscany / $
  Don't let its peculiar orange cork deter you: This sturdy, raspberry-inflected blend is a terrific everyday-drinking wine.
- **Mazzei Castello di Fonterutoli Siepi** / 2006 / Tuscany / $$$$
  An international-style blend of Sangiovese and Merlot loaded with flashy black fruit and mocha layers.

CASTELLO DI MONSANTO

Castello di Monsanto's flagship wine, Il Poggio Riserva, was the original single-vineyard Chianti Classico, first made in 1962. It remains one of Tuscany's greatest wines. Proprietor Fabrizio Bianchi and daughter Laura, along with ex-Ornellaia winemaker Andrea Giovannini, also make a high-end Cabernet (called Nemo), a Chardonnay and a range of Sangiovese-based reds.

- **Monsanto Riserva** / 2007 / Chianti Classico / $$
  A classic *riserva* with a heady mix of rose, spice and cherry.
- **Monsanto Il Poggio Riserva** / 2006 / Chianti Classico / $$$
  This sumptuous, violet-edged single-vineyard bottling lives up to its famous reputation.

CASTELLO DI NIPOZZANO

The Frescobaldi family have been making wine in Tuscany for some 700 years. They own five top Tuscan estates, but Nipozzano, one of the oldest wineries in the Chianti Rùfina subzone, is arguably their best. The estate's wines include a cult 100 percent Sangiovese, Montesodi, plus the outstanding Mormoreto Super-Tuscan and a benchmark Chianti Rùfina.

- **Marchesi de' Frescobaldi Nipozzano Riserva** / **2007** / **Chianti Rùfina** / **$$** From the small, prestigious Rùfina subregion, this deeply flavored red offers impressive quality for the price.
- **Marchesi de' Frescobaldi Vigneto Montesodi** / **2007** / **Chianti Rùfina** / **$$$** The firmer tannins that come from Rùfina's higher altitude are on display in this elegant, spicy red.

COL D'ORCIA

Acquired by the Cinzano family (of vermouth fame) in 1973, this Montalcino winery built its reputation on traditionally styled Sangioveses. Its 12-wine portfolio includes cuvées from international grapes and a Super-Tuscan, but the Sangioveses are the stars; the Al Vento Brunello tops the list.

- **Col d'Orcia Banditella** / **2008** / **Rosso di Montalcino** / **$$$** Most of the Banditella vineyard's grapes go into the winery's expensive Brunello; the rest are used for this luscious bottling.
- **Col d'Orcia Riserva** / **2005** / **Brunello di Montalcino** / **$$$$** An earthy, creamy, less-expensive sibling to the Al Vento.

FATTORIA AMBRA

Ambra is a stellar winery in Carmignano, an often overlooked DOCG northwest of Florence where vintners have been blending Cabernet with native Sangiovese since the 1500s. Ambra's wines are softer than most Tuscan reds (an exception is the 90 percent Sangiovese Elzana cuvée). Thanks to its under-the-radar location, Ambra offers some of the best value in Tuscany.

- **Ambra** / **2009** / **Barco Reale di Carmignano** / **$$** An aromatic blend of Sangiovese, Canaiolo and Cabernet.
- **Ambra Elzana Riserva** / **2006** / **Carmignano** / **$$$** Two years of aging in oak softened the substantial tannins in this rich single-vineyard Carmignano.

FATTORIA DI FÈLSINA

Though Fèlsina has started planting French grapes and making wines approachable in their youth, it is still best known for structured reds of great longevity. Top cuvées such as Rància can require decades of aging. Fèlsina gained prominence in the early 1980s, when owner Domenico Poggiali's son-in-law, Giuseppe Mazzocolin, took over and hired winemaker Franco Barnebei.

● Fèlsina Berardenga / 2008 / Chianti Classico / $$
Juicy and ready to drink, with herb-edged red-fruit flavors.

● Fèlsina Berardenga Rància Riserva / 2007 / Chianti Classico / $$$ First made in 1983, this suave single-vineyard bottling features layers of rich, creamy cherry flavors.

FATTORIA LE PUPILLE

Superstar winemaker Christian Le Sommer, a veteran of Bordeaux's Château Latour, is the latest in a line of high-visibility consultants hired by Fattoria le Pupille. Owned by Elisabetta Geppetti, this is one of the top wineries in the Maremma's Morellino di Scanscano DOCG. Portfolio highlights include two Morellinos, a white blend and a lauded Super-Tuscan, Saffredi.

● Fattoria le Pupille / 2008 / Morellino di Scansano / $$
Sangioveses from Scansano, such as this winning example, are some of Tuscany's best values.

● Fattoria le Pupille Saffredi / 2007 / Maremma Toscana / $$$$
A stunning, seamless blend of Cabernet, Merlot and Alicante.

FATTORIA SELVAPIANA

Selvapiana's firm, ageworthy reds are classic examples of wines from Chianti Rùfina, a small subzone with high vineyards and cold nights. This microclimate allows proprietors Federico Giuntini and sister Silvia to create bold, expressive reds. With the help of famed consultant Franco Bernabei, Selvapiana makes two Sangiovese-based wines and two outstanding blends.

● Selvapiana / 2009 / Chianti Rùfina / $$
Deliciously fresh and balanced, with ripe fruit and floral notes.

● Selvapiana Vigneto Bucerchiale Riserva / 2007 / Chianti Rùfina / $$ This terrific single-vineyard *cru* offers astounding complexity given its low price.

FONTODI

The Manetti family used to make three Chianti Classicos at their Panzano winery, but a decade ago they dropped their *riserva* and now offer just two, one of which is the single-vineyard Vigna del Sorbo. The move bolstered quality across the board, and freed up juice for Flaccianello, Fontodi's blockbuster Sangiovese. Owner Giovanni Manetti and consulting enologist Franco Bernabei also make Syrah and Pinot Noir from Fontodi's organic vineyards.

- **Fontodi** / **2007** / **Chianti Classico** / **$$**
  Aging in French oak gives this *classico* a smooth texture.
- **Fontodi Flaccianello Della Pieve** / **2007** / **Colli della Toscana Centrale** / **$$$$** This coveted 100 percent Sangiovese is lavishly styled, with layers of dense, ripe fruit.

IL POGGIONE

This top producer has been owned by the Franceschi family since 1890 and is best known for its basic Brunello and its Vigna Paganelli *riserva*, made only in exceptional vintages. Located in Montalcino's hilly southwest subzone, Il Poggione's vineyards benefit from the area's cooler temperatures, which help create concentrated, ageworthy reds. The portfolio also includes a stellar Rosso di Montalcino and a Super-Tuscan blend.

- **Il Poggione** / **2008** / **Rosso di Montalcino** / **$$**
  A baby brother to the winery's star Brunellos, this *rosso* is spicy, impressively sleek and superdelicious.
- **Il Poggione** / **2006** / **Brunello di Montalcino** / **$$$**
  This is a consistently burly, muscular take on Brunello, thanks to the thick skins of high-altitude grapes.

ISOLE E OLENA

Isole e Olena owner Paolo de Marchi is a Sangiovese purist who makes his top cuvée, Cepparello, with Sangiovese alone (though it's an IGT Toscana). Monovariety Chianti was a radical notion when he introduced the wine in 1980; now it's a prized benchmark offering. Marchi bottles Syrah, Cabernet Sauvignon and Chardonnay on their own too, and they're consistently excellent.

- **Isole e Olena** / **2008** / **Chianti Classico** / **$$**
  One of Chianti's most reliably polished, well-made *classicos*.

LE MACCHIOLE

Unlike many Bolgheri estates, Le Macchiole was founded by a native of the coastal region, Eugenio Campolmi. Campolmi began working with consulting winemaker Luca d'Attoma in 1991, and their success with international varieties such as Merlot, Cabernet Franc and Syrah helped launch Le Macchiole into the ranks of Tuscany's elite modern estates. D'Attoma still helps craft the estate's wines—one charming white and four rich reds.

● **Le Macchiole Rosso** / 2008 / Bolgheri / $$
This Super-Tuscan blend offers a taste of the winery's opulent style at an accessible price.

● **Le Macchiole Messorio** / 2007 / Tuscany / $$$$
Collectors compete to snap up this ultra-rich Merlot—which explains its ultra-high price.

● **Le Macchiole Paleo** / 2007 / Tuscany / $$$$
This powerhouse red is entirely Cabernet Franc and shows off velvety, full-bodied layers of blackberry, herbs and smoke.

PODERI BOSCARELLI

Brunello specialist Boscarelli was founded by owner Paola de Ferrari Corradi's father in 1962. Thanks to the estate's location on one of Montepulciano's finest vineyards, Cervognano, Boscarelli's wines have excelled even in less-than-stellar vintages (such as 2008). Since coming on board in the mid-1980s, consulting winemaker Maurizio Castelli has helped put Boscarelli among Montepulciano's top properties.

● **Boscarelli** / 2007 / Vino Nobile di Montepulciano / $$$
A good introduction to the house style; full of generous oak, sweet red-fruit flavors and a silky texture.

QUERCIABELLA

Unusual for a Tuscan winery, one of Querciabella's best-known cuvées is a white wine, a luscious, toasty (and pricey) blend of Pinot Bianco and Chardonnay called Batàr. But it's the estate's reds that have made the winery's reputation, led by the stupendous Camartina Super-Tuscan. Forward-thinking proprietor Sebastiano Castiglioni, who took over the estate from his father in the early 1990s, adopted an organic—and later biodynamic—farming regime long before it became trendy.

○ **Agricola Querciabella Batàr** / 2008 / Tuscany / $$$$
Oak-aged Chardonnay and Pinot Bianco create a densely structured blend that's one of Tuscany's top whites.

● **Agricola Querciabella** / 2008 / Chianti Classico / $$
Mineral-laden cherry flavors mark this beautifully polished red.

RUFFINO

Ruffino is one of the most consistent large Chianti producers, turning out a vast selection of wines sourced from across Chianti and beyond, plus estate bottlings from farms in Chianti Classico, Montalcino and Montepulciano. Launched as a *négociant* business in 1877, the company is run by the Folonari family, who bought it in 1913 and turned it into one of Italy's megabrands.

○ **Ruffino Lumina Pinot Grigio** / 2010 / Venezia Giulia / $
A refreshing white with light-bodied apple and citrus flavors.

● **Ruffino Riserva Ducale Riserva** / 2007 / Chianti Classico / $$
Named for a 19th-century duke who was one of Ruffino's best customers, this bottling is plummy, velvety and ripe.

TENUTA DI CAPEZZANA

Though records of winemaking at this Carmignano estate date back 12 centuries, Tenuta di Capezzana is a very modern winery. Owners Count Ugo and Countess Lisa Contini Bonacossi promoted the use of Cabernet Sauvignon in Carmignano in the 1960s and later led the drive to establish the region as a DOCG. Today Capezzana is Carmignano's finest producer, with a lineup ranging from everyday reds to a muscular Super-Tuscan.

● **Capezzana** / 2008 / Barco Reale di Carmignano / $
A supple, invigorating blend of Sangiovese and Cabernet.

● **Capezzana Ghiaiedella Furba** / 2004 / Tuscany / $$$
This Super-Tuscan shows the benefit of some bottle aging, with leather and spice notes highlighting layers of ripe dark fruit.

OTHER CENTRAL ITALIAN REGIONS

There is much more to central Italy than just Tuscany. Savvy U.S. importers are cherry-picking the best wines from often overlooked zones in the regions immediately surrounding Tuscany, making it possible to find compelling central Italian bottles without the steep price tag of prestige.

❦ OTHER CENTRAL ITALIAN GRAPES & STYLES

The plummy, smoky Montepulciano grape makes some of central Italy's best reds. Umbria's indigenous Sagrantino variety yields one of Italy's most tannic, powerful and long-lived reds. Whites to look for include Le Marche's zesty Verdicchios and almond-edged blends made with Grechetto, a variety presumed to be native to Greece that's grown in Umbria.

ABRUZZO Refreshing, lovely Trebbiano d'Abruzzo is a white wine whose aromatic, expressive personality redeems the otherwise dull Trebbiano grape. This is also the most important region for the Montepulciano grape, which makes dark, spicy red wines. (Confusingly, the grape shares a name with the Tuscan town of Montepulciano, where the wines are made from Sangiovese.) Though typically a simple wine with nice berry flavors, Montepulciano d'Abruzzo can also be remarkably robust and tannic.

EMILIA-ROMAGNA Fizzy, red Lambrusco (made famous by the Riunite brand) is the region's most popular wine, but whites from Chardonnay and the Albana grape also shine. Albana takes well to a variety of styles, from dry to sweet. Sangiovese, Barbera and Cabernet Sauvignon make up most red wines.

LAZIO The region surrounding Rome provides the capital with white Frascati, a generally bland Trebbiano-and-Malvasia blend. Most Frascatis offer delicate, citrusy refreshment, though increasingly sophisticated offerings are becoming more common. Reds made from the Cesanese grape are gaining attention with the promotion of the Cesanese del Piglio zone to DOCG status.

LE MARCHE Look to Le Marche for value. The rich whites made from the Verdicchio grape are the signature wines of this underestimated region. The finest red is Rosso Conero, a bold, smoky wine made mostly with Montepulciano. From Ancona, Rosso Piceno is another well-made Sangiovese-Montepulciano blend.

UMBRIA This landlocked region is a fantastic source of crisp whites, of which Orvieto is the most important. Less interesting Orvietos are made from the Trebbiano grape alone; blends with the lively, lightly nutty Grechetto grape are far better. Umbria's Sagrantino di Montefalco is full-bodied, dark and complex.

Producers/ Other Central Italian Regions

ARNALDO CAPRAI

Marco Caprai and his late father, Arnaldo, gained fame for reviving Sagrantino, a red grape unique to Umbria. Sagrantino's firm tannins, plum flavors and food-friendly acidity are beautifully showcased in Caprai's benchmark wine, Sagrantino di Montefalco 25 Anni. Look also for the winery's more affordable Sangrantino offerings, all sourced from 336 acres of estate vines.

● **Arnaldo Caprai Montefalco Rosso / 2007 / Montefalco / $$** Caprai blends Sagrantino and Merlot with Sangiovese to create this ripe, silky, cherry-driven red.

● **Arnaldo Caprai Collepiano / 2005 / Montefalco Sagrantino / $$$$** This Sagrantino delivers nearly as much black fruit–filled pleasure as the 25 Anni, at about half the price.

CANTINE GIORGIO LUNGAROTTI

Giorgio Lungarotti established his eponymous winery in the Umbrian town of Torgiano in the early 1960s, betting on an innovative Sangiovese blend he called Rubesco Riserva. Its spectacular renown put Umbria on the wine world's radar. Today the winery, headed by daughters Teresa and Chiara, is the region's most prolific producer; the Vigna Monticchio and San Giorgio blends are its most famous (and most expensive) wines.

○ **Cantine Giorgio Lungarotti Torre di Giano Trebbiano-Grechetto / 2010 / Torgiano / $** A graceful, refreshing blend with floral, pear and apple tones and a subtle effervescence.

● **Cantine Giorgio Lungarotti Rubesco / 2008 / Torgiano / $$** Lungarotti's well-priced entry-level red (a Sangiovese-Canaiolo blend) delivers loads of velvety, spice-edged cherry flavors.

● **Lungarotti Rubesco Vigna Monticchio / 2005 / Torgiano Rosso Riserva / $$$** Umbria's most famous red, this single-vineyard blend gets its complexity from extended bottle aging.

CATALDI MADONNA

One reason this Abruzzo estate makes such terrific wines is its location. Situated in the high plains of the Aterno River valley, Cataldi Madonna's vines yield thick-skinned grapes that give its wines more structure than is usual in Abruzzo. Vintner and psychology professor Luigi Cataldi Madonna's portfolio includes outstanding Montepulcianos and unusually intense whites.

● **Cataldi Madonna** / 2008 / Montepulciano d'Abruzzo / $$
Winemaker Lorenzo Landi's basic Montepulciano is a reliable steal, with layers of dense dark-fruit and spice tones.

FALESCO

Winemaker Riccardo Cotarella consults for wineries around the world. But it's at his Umbrian estate, Falesco, that his passion for experimenting becomes clear: Cotarella and brother Renzo make Montiano, one of Italy's finest Merlots, as well as a compelling collection of wines based on French and obscure native varieties sourced from Umbria and neighboring Lazio.

● **Falesco Montiano** / 2007 / Lazio / $$$
The vineyards outside Rome are best known for whites, but this Merlot proves they can yield lush, plummy reds too.

FATTORIA LE TERRAZZE

Star consultants Attilio Pagli (winemaking) and Federico Curtaz (vineyards) work with winemaker Ettore Janni at this prominent Le Marche winery, helping to make it one of the region's very best. Owned by Georgina and Antonio Terni, whose family bought the estate in 1882, Le Terrazze turns out plummy, intense reds based on the Montepulciano grape.

● **Le Terrazze** / 2008 / Rosso Conero / $$
The Montepulciano grape yields broad, fruity reds with supple tannins—a description that fits this wine perfectly.

● **Le Terrazze Chaos** / 2005 / Marche Rosso / $$$
This soft, luscious blend of Merlot and Montepulciano bursts with ripe black fruit.

● **Le Terrazze Sassi Neri** / 2006 / Rosso Conero Riserva / $$$
Few Marche reds achieve the power and density of this velvety, black currant–infused bottling.

FONTANA CANDIDA

Fontana Candida is aiding in the revival of Frascati, the fragrant, soft white from the countryside outside Rome. Winemaker Mauro Merz selects vineyards for quality, not yields, and ferments grapes at cool temperatures to protect their delicate citrus flavors. Candida's two wines—a basic cuvée and a terrific reserve bottling, Luna Mater—exemplify Frascati's true charm.

○ **Fontana Candida / 2010 / Frascati / $**
Fresh and fragrant, with citrus, peach and floral flavors.
○ **Fontana Candida Luna Mater / 2009 / Frascati / $$**
A revelation for anyone who underestimates Frascati, this peach-driven white is minerally and complex.

MASCIARELLI

Founded on five vineyard acres in 1981, Masciarelli today encompasses 800 or so acres in four Abruzzo provinces. Gianni Masciarelli popularized modern winemaking in Abruzzo and drew international attention for the region with French-inspired bottlings, such as the iconic Montepulciano Villa Gemma.

○ **Marina Cvetic Trebbiano / 2008 / Trebbiano d'Abruzzo / $$$**
Invigorating acidity marks this lush, peach-inflected white.
○ **Masciarelli Castello di Semivicoli / 2008 / Trebbiano d'Abruzzo / $$$** The humble Trebbiano grape yielded this opulent white marked by baked apples and spice.
● **Marina Cvetic Montepulciano S. Martino Rosso / 2007 / Montepulciano d'Abruzzo / $$$** This dense red was aged for 36 months in French oak, just like the far pricier Villa Gemma.

VALLE REALE

Valle Reale's owners, the Pizzolo family, first bought property in Abruzzo's mountainous highlands as a site for trout farms. In the late 1990s, Giorgio Pizzolo acquired an old Montepulciano vineyard nearby, and nephew Leonardo created a winery. Today Valle Reale turns out delicious Montepulciano-based wines at affordable prices, plus a single-vineyard Trebbiano d'Abruzzo.

● **Valle Reale Vigneto Vigne Nuove / 2009 / Montepulciano d'Abruzzo / $** Made from young vines, this overachieving, unoaked red brims with juicy red fruit and food-friendly acidity.

VILLA BUCCI

Located in Le Marche's prestigious Castelli di Jesi subregion, where Verdicchio is the chief white grape, Villa Bucci produces two Verdicchios and two Rosso Piceno reds (blends of Montepulciano and Sangiovese), all shaped by the legendary Giorgio Grai, the winery's longtime consultant. The Verdicchio *riserva* is made only in excellent vintages, from the estate's oldest vineyards.

○ Bucci / 2009 / Verdicchio Classico dei Castelli di Jesi / $$
One of Italy's classic whites, this spicy, pear-driven bottling comes from Verdicchio's most prestigious subzone.

SOUTHERN ITALY

Once limited to selling grapes in bulk to industrial cooperatives, southern Italy's producers recently have transformed the lower part of the Italian boot and its neighboring islands into one of the wine world's star regions. They've succeeded in many cases by reviving ancient varieties and traditional farming methods.

SOUTHERN ITALY GRAPES & STYLES

Southern Italian white wines, including Falanghina, Fiano di Avellino and Greco di Tufo, share crisp floral and mineral flavors and are usually well priced. Aglianico is the leading red grape, grown in both Campania and Basilicata, where it yields smoky, dark and tannic wines; the best examples can age for decades.

APULIA Still known mainly for mass-produced, locally consumed wines, Apulia turns out an increasing number of high-quality reds. Look for jammy, fruity Primitivo, a relative of California's Zinfandel, as well as the spicy reds from Salice Salentino and Copertino, both made from the dark-skinned Negroamaro grape.

BASILICATA The aromatic, spicy, powerful Aglianico-based reds of Basilicata reflect the region's volcanic soils. Some Aglianico del Vulture can require a decade of aging. The newer DOCs Terre dell'Alta Val d'Agri and Matera produce reds, whites and rosés from blends based on grapes other than Aglianico.

CALABRIA On the toe of Italy's boot, Calabria is responsible for a lot of low-quality wine. An exception is the Gaglioppo-based red, Cirò, which is lightly tannic and flush with berry flavors.

CAMPANIA Campania has led southern Italy's native-grape revival. Its Aglianico-based red Taurasi, which requires at least three years of aging before release, has earned much acclaim since it achieved DOCG status in 1993. Also turning heads are Falanghina, the region's principal white wine, and whites made with lush, nutty Fiano di Avellino and floral, zesty Greco di Tufo.

SARDINIA Sardinia's best-known grape is Vermentino, a Spanish variety used to make the island's sole DOCG wine, intense and fresh Vermentino di Gallura. Look too for spicy, often rustic Cannonau (Grenache), which is showing up more often in the U.S.

SICILY Although Sicily still makes a lot of bulk wine, a small but growing number of producers are creating laudable wines. The best come from Mount Etna's volcanic slopes. Here, the native Carricante grape yields vivid, minerally whites. Reds—made chiefly from a blend of Nerello Mascalese and Nerello Cappuccio—offer rich berry and mineral flavors. Elsewhere in Sicily, the dominant red grape is Nero d'Avola, often blended with international varieties. Sicily makes bright, citrusy whites, usually with the Catarratto grape, and some complex whites with the local Grillo variety.

Producers/ Southern Italy

ARGIOLAS

Sardinia's most famous winery revitalized wine production on the island almost single-handedly. Longtime grape growers, the Argiolas family sold their fruit to bulk producers before brothers Franco and Giuseppe decided to make wine themselves. In 1989 they hired Mariano Murru, who along with consulting enologist Giacomo Tachis makes impressive wines from local grapes.

● **Argiolas Costera** / 2008 / Isola dei Nuraghi / $
Made mostly from Cannonau, this bursts with red-fruit flavors.

● **Argiolas Perdera** / 2009 / Isola dei Nuraghi / $
In the right hands, the Monica grape (which dominates this blend) yields sleek, juicy, raspberry-driven reds, like this one.

CANTINA SANTADI

Under the guidance of consultant Giacomo Tachis (of Sassicaia fame) and winemaker Davide Pera, this high-achieving Sardinian cooperative produces some of the world's most exciting versions of old-vine Carignane, a.k.a. Carignano, such as the rare, opulent Terre Brune. Other specialties include terrific Vermentino- and Cannonau-based blends.

○ **Cantina Santadi Villa Solais / 2009 / Vermentino di Sardegna /** $ A blend of 70 percent Vermentino and 30 percent Nuragus, this is sheer deliciousness, with crisp peach and orange flavors that are silky, ripe and vibrant.

● **Cantina Santadi Grotta Rossa / 2008 / Carignano del Sulcis /** $ The Carignane grape thrives in Sardinia, as this plush, sexy, cherry-infused wine shows.

● **Cantina Santadi Noras / 2008 / Cannonau di Sardegna / $$** An ultra-smooth Cannonau with a bit of Carignane, this is marked by anise, minerals and satiny red berry fruit.

CANTINE DEL NOTAIO

This cutting-edge producer is the undisputed wine leader of Basilicata, the mountainous region in the Italian boot's instep. Using fruit from biodynamically farmed vineyards on the slopes of the extinct Mount Vulture volcano, pioneering vintner Gerardo Guiratrabocchetti makes a handful of fragrant, powerful reds as well as a rosé and two sparkling wines, all from Aglianico.

● **Cantine del Notaio Il Repertorio / 2007 / Aglianico del Vulture /** $$ This minerally, blackberry-infused red is full-bodied and balanced and boasts a very reasonable price.

DI MAJO NORANTE

Delicious, affordable wines are the hallmark of Di Majo Norante, a family-owned estate that's drawing attention to the rising Molise region, south of Abruzzo. Unlike many modern Molise wineries, Di Majo Norante focuses on grapes traditional to the region, both red (Aglianico and Sangiovese) and white (Falanghina).

● **Di Majo Norante Sangiovese / 2009 / Terre degli Osci / $** This lush, dark and fruity red is packed with far more flavor and complexity than its price might suggest.

DONNAFUGATA

The Rallo family named their estate Donnafugata ("woman in flight" in Italian) after Queen Maria Carolina, who fled Naples in the early 1800s and took refuge near their estate vineyards in Sicily. For over a century, the Rallos used their grapes for fortified Marsala wines. Today it's Donnafugata's Nero d'Avola–based reds that have made this one of Sicily's leading estates.

● **Donnafugata Sedàra** / 2009 / Sicily / $
A bit of Syrah gives this Nero d'Avola–based blend a meaty edge.
● **Donnafugata Mille e Una Notte** / 2006 / Contessa Entellina / $$$$ Polished and muscular, the estate's top red showcases Nero d'Avola's spicy, tannic power.

FEUDI DI SAN GREGORIO

Though it has been around only since 1986, this Campania winery is already one of the region's most important producers. Founded by the Capaldo and Ercolino families, Feudi di San Gregorio turns out excellent wines with indigenous grapes, such as Falanghina and Aglianico, as well as a Merlot called Pàtrimo.

○ **Feudi di San Gregorio Falanghina** / 2009 / Sannio / $$
No oak aging results in fresh, perfumy white peach flavors.
● **Feudi di San Gregorio Rubrato Aglianico** / 2008 / Irpinia / $$
A complex, great-value red loaded with spicy, earthy black fruit.
● **Feudi di San Gregorio** / 2006 / Taurasi / $$$
Full-throttled Aglianico softenend by 18 months in French oak.

MASTROBERARDINO

Piero Mastroberardino is the latest in 10 generations of vintners to helm his family's Campania winery. Vast acreage, high-tech facilities and a commitment to native grapes make this quality-focused producer a go-to name for reds and whites up and down the price scale. Radici, a masterful Taurasi (a red wine made with Aglianico), is one of Italy's benchmark bottlings.

● **Mastroberardino Aglianico** / 2008 / Campania / $$
With exuberant, herb- and toast-inflected black cherry flavors, this serves as a terrific introduction to Aglianico.
● **Mastroberardino Radici Taurasi** / 2006 / Taurasi / $$$
Finesse tempers sheer power in this alluring Aglianico.

PLANETA

Francesca Planeta (daughter of Diego Planeta, president of Sicily's largest bulk-wine co-op) founded this winery with her cousins Alessio and Santi Planeta in the mid-1990s, building it into Sicily's largest and most dynamic quality-driven brand. Originally known for well-made Chardonnay and Merlot, Planeta has helped pioneer wines made from native grapes such as Nero d'Avola, Frappato and Grecanico.

WINE INTEL
At La Foresteria, Planeta's three-year-old hotel in Menfi, visitors can take Sicilian cooking classes, indulge in a four-course wine-and-food tasting menu and enjoy the pool.

○ **Planeta Cometa / 2009 / Sicily / $$$**
A perfect illustration of how compelling the Fiano grape can be, this offers rich tropical and peach flavors cut by crisp acidity.

● **Planeta / 2009 / Cerasuolo di Vittoria / $$**
With its sweet fruit, cream and vanilla notes, this juicy blend of Nero d'Avola and Frappato recalls a raspberry Creamsicle.

TASCA D'ALMERITA

When much of Sicily was churning out bulk wine, the Tasca d'Almerita family was making expressive reds and whites to rival Italy's best. Founded in 1830, this large, family-owned producer was among the first in Sicily to focus on fine wine. Its top wine is the legendary Rosso del Conte, a Nero d'Avola–based red.

○ **Tasca d'Almerita Regaleali Bianco / 2009 / Sicily / $**
Almerita's Regaleali estate turns out this fresh, floral-edged blend of three native grapes.

○ **Tasca d'Almerita Leone d'Almerita / 2009 / Sicily / $$**
Cool nights on mountain vineyards yielded this fabulously zesty, creamy, melon-inflected blend.

● **Tasca d'Almerita Regaleali Nero d'Avola / 2007 / Sicily / $**
This tasty, bold Nero d'Avola is an excellent value.

TENUTA DELLE TERRE NERE

Marco de Grazia, an Italian-American living in Florence, exports Italian wine for a living. But he and his wife became so enamored of wines from the lava-covered slopes of Sicily's Mount Etna that they started a winery there, naming it after the area's black earth (*terre nere*). Their whites made from Carricante and their Nerello-based reds are stars of Etna's emerging wine industry.

- **Tenuta delle Terre Nere Santo Spirito Rosso** / 2008 / Etna / $$$ From a small vineyard de Grazia bought in 2008, this blend of Nerello Mascalese and Nerello Cappuccio grapes offers spicy black cherry flavors and Etna's hallmark minerality.
- **Tenuta delle Terre Nere Prephylloxera La Vigna di Don Peppino Rosso** / 2008 / Etna / $$$$ The Nerello Mascalese grapes for this structured, herb-edged red came from a rare plot of very old vines that survived the phylloxera scourge.

TERREDORA

When a dispute divided Campania's famous Mastroberardino winemaking clan (see p. 99), Walter Mastroberardino gave up the right to make wine under the family name but kept most of the historic vineyards. His Terredora wines come from nearly 500 acres of estate vines, planted entirely with the region's native grapes. Ambitious and thoughtfully made, the wines are some of the most outstanding in the region.

- ○ **Terredora di Paolo Loggia della Serra** / 2009 / Greco di Tufo / $$ An opulent, peach-driven white from estate vineyards outside the hilltop town of Montefusco.

VILLA MATILDE

Naples attorney Francesco Paolo Avallone was a history and wine buff who founded Villa Matilde in the 1960s with a single goal: to reclaim Falerno, a red wine once popular with Roman emperors, from its reputation as cheap commercial plonk. Villa Matilde's success with Falerno—aided by consulting winemaker Riccardo Cotarella—has expanded to include other wines made from Campania's indigenous grapes, including top-notch Falanghina and Greco di Tufo.

- ○ **Villa Matilde Rocca dei Leoni Falanghina** / 2009 / Campania / $ This well-priced wine bursts with white peach and citrus notes.
- ○ **Villa Matilde Tenute di Altavilla** / 2009 / Greco di Tufo / $$ The Altavilla estate is rich in tuff, an ashy volcanic soil that gives this vibrant, peachy white its intensity.
- **Villa Matilde Tenute di San Castrese e Parco Nuovo Rosso** / 2008 / Falerno del Massico / $$ Villa Matilde's flagship red wine is a blend of Aglianico and Piedirosso grapes, inspired by the Falerno of Roman times.

Spain

Wine Region

Spanish wine is amazingly diverse. It's influenced by both the warm waters of the Mediterranean and the cool Atlantic; its winemaking can be deeply traditional or thrillingly avant-garde; and its bottles range from some of the world's greatest values to some of the world's most expensive. Home to ancient vineyards and architecturally groundbreaking wineries, Spain offers almost anything an adventurous wine lover could want.

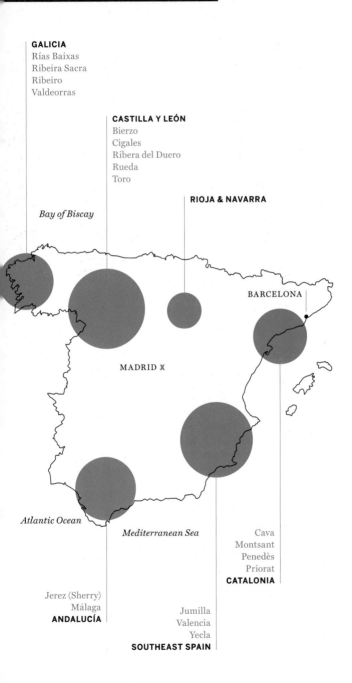

GALICIA
Rías Baixas
Ribeira Sacra
Ribeiro
Valdeorras

CASTILLA Y LEÓN
Bierzo
Cigales
Ribera del Duero
Rueda
Toro

RIOJA & NAVARRA

Bay of Biscay

BARCELONA

MADRID X

Atlantic Ocean

Mediterranean Sea

Cava
Montsant
Penedès
Priorat
CATALONIA

Jerez (Sherry)
Málaga
ANDALUCÍA

Jumilla
Valencia
Yecla
SOUTHEAST SPAIN

Spain

SPAIN'S MOUNTAIN RANGES divide the country into distinct viticultural areas. Albariño-based whites hail from the cool Atlantic region of Rías Baixas, in Galicia. In Castilla y León, to the east, Rueda produces zippier whites. Reds from Castilla y León's Ribera del Duero and Toro regions earn praise for their power. The renowned Rioja region, in north-central Spain, makes both modern and traditionally styled wines. Catalonia, in the northeast, is home to sparkling cavas, still wines from Penedès and robust reds from Priorat. Jerez, in southern Spain, is known for its fortified sherries (see p. 275).

SPANISH WINE LABELS

Spain's Denominación de Origen (DO) board determines a wine region's permitted grapes, harvest limits and vinification techniques and regulates wine labels. Spanish labels list the region and sometimes the grape variety. The *vino de la tierra* designation, like the French *vin de pays* category, is used for wines from designated zones that don't qualify for DO status. Terms such as *joven, crianza, reserva* and *gran reserva* indicate the amount of time a wine spent aging in barrel and bottle, though standards vary from region to region (see Rioja, opposite). Rioja and Priorat lay claim to the elite status of Denominación de Origen Calificada (DOCa).

RIOJA & NAVARRA

Rioja is Spain's most famous designated wine region. Many of Rioja's traditional reds historically lacked fruitiness thanks to years of oak aging. Contemporary tastes have driven vintners to make their wines differently, and modern Rioja reds display more-pronounced fruit flavors augmented by sweet spice and vanilla notes. Rioja whites, too, are now made in a fresher style (though some older-style whites are excellent). Rioja's neighbor Navarra has long been a source for *rosados* (rosé wines); it also has become a go-to region for great value reds.

❦ RIOJA & NAVARRA GRAPES & STYLES

If one grape is synonymous with Rioja, it is Tempranillo. Traditionally, it is blended with Garnacha (Grenache), Graciano and Mazuelo (the Rioja name for Carignane) and aged in American oak barrels. Cabernet Sauvignon is allowed in some vineyards. Rioja reds are given designations based on how much time they spent aging in barrel and bottle: *joven* wines spend little or no time in barrels; *crianza* reds must be aged a minimum of two years, one in barrel; *reservas* require three years total, one in oak; *gran reservas,* five years total, two in oak. A growing number of vintners in Spain, however, are now using subtler French oak barrels and aging their wines for shorter periods. Sometimes referred to as *alta expresión* (high expression), these wines have bold, fruit-forward flavors. Rioja's *rosado* wines are dry, with orange and red berry flavors. Traditional white wines from Rioja, made mostly with the Viura grape (the local name for Macabeo) and some Malvasia and Garnacha Blanca, are richly layered, barrel-aged and often intentionally oxidized. While this style still exists, the trend has been toward fresher wines. Rioja growers planted nonnative white varieties, including Chardonnay, Sauvignon Blanc and Verdejo, for the first time in 2007, and winemakers are now using them in blends.

In Navarra, Tempranillo has surpassed Garnacha, the traditional regional grape, in total vineyard plantings. Cabernet Sauvignon and/or Merlot often join these regional grapes in creative red blends. The region's *rosados* are excellent and widely exported. White grape varieties—primarily Chardonnay and Viura—account for only 5.5 percent of Navarra's vineyards, but these plantings have been increasing.

Producers/
Rioja & Navarra

BODEGAS CHIVITE

Now in the hands of winemaker Fernando Chivite, this family winery dates to 1647. More-recent acquisitions brought Viña Salceda (in Rioja), Señorío de Arínzano (in Navarra) and 50 acres of La Horra estate (in Ribera del Duero) into the Chivite fold. The Gran Feudo line, especially the tasty *rosado*, has many fans.

- ● Chivite Gran Feudo Rosado / 2010 / Navarra / $
  A bright, zesty rosé made primarily with Garnacha and full of graceful raspberry and cherry flavors.
- ● Chivite Gran Feudo Crianza / 2006 / Navarra / $
  Fruity Garnacha and bold Cabernet Sauvignon bolster juicy Tempranillo in this accessible blend.

BODEGAS NEKEAS

Established in 1989 by eight grape-growing families, Nekeas is a progressive, quality-focused cooperative that quickly became part of the vanguard of Navarra's new wine wave. Winemaker Concha Vecino has an adept hand with a wide range of local and international grape varieties, crafting juicy, modern wines that offer exceptional quality for the price.

- ○ Bodegas Nekeas Vega Sindoa Chardonnay / 2009 / Navarra / $
  Silky baked pear and stone fruit mark this great-value white.
- ● Bodegas Nekeas Vega Sindoa Tempranillo / 2009 / Navarra / $
  Juicy red-fruit flavors and a bit of spice make this delicious red perfect for barbecues.

BODEGAS RODA

Roda (a creative combination of the names of founders Mario Rotllant Solá and Carmen Daurella De Aguilera) is a full-century younger than most of its veteran Rioja neighbors. Prime contract vineyards contribute to a trio of concentrated, modern wines, while Roda's own estate vineyard is a repository of 552 different Tempranillo clones.

- **Bodegas Roda Roda Reserva** / 2006 / Rioja / $$$
  Small amounts of Garnacha and Graciano are added to this
  Tempranillo-based blend. Made with grapes from 17 vineyards,
  it has pronounced mushroom aromas and a smooth texture.
- **Bodegas Roda Cirsion** / 2006 / Rioja / $$$$
  A toasty, powerful, small-production red made with select
  bunches of Tempranillo from the best vineyard blocks.
- **Bodegas Roda Roda I Reserva** / 2005 / Rioja / $$$$
  Made only from Tempranillo and in a firmer style than the
  Roda Reserva, this offers layers of fragrant, spicy black fruit.

BODEGAS VALDEMAR

Although owner Jesús Martínez Bujanda comes from a long line
of grape growers, it was not until 1982 that his family launched
their winery. The entry-level Valdemar wines are fresh and
fruity, whereas the flagship Conde de Valdemar range includes
aged reds. The Inspiración Valdemar line, which often uses
experimental grapes in the blends, consistently impresses.

- **Conde de Valdemar Reserva** / 2004 / Rioja / $$
  A complex wine with a wonderfully low price, this is packed
  with supple, tobacco-inflected currant flavors.
- **Inspiración Valdemar** / 2006 / Rioja / $$
  Elegant and savory, with cedary oak and cherry tones.
- **Inspiración Valdemar Graciano** / 2005 / Rioja / $$$$
  A rare 100 percent Graciano, this showcases the grape's bold
  violet and black-fruit flavors.

FINCA ALLENDE

With a thoughtful focus on *terroir,* this boutique winery from
Miguel Angel de Gregorio is a fine example of the new face of
Rioja. All of Finca Allende's stellar wines, from the basic Allende
to the iconic Aurus and Calvario bottlings, defy Rioja tradition
with their concentrated flavors and use of mostly French oak.

- **Finca Allende Aurus** / 2005 / Rioja / $$$$
  Fans of muscular, modern-style Riojas will appreciate this
  blockbuster wine's dense, plummy flavors and brawny tannins.
- **Finca Allende Calvario** / 2005 / Rioja / $$$$
  Sourced from vines planted in 1945, this is worth the splurge;
  its cherry-liqueur notes are gracefully balanced with spice.

MARQUÉS DE CÁCERES

Founded in the late 1960s by Enrique Forner, with consulting help from Émile Peynaud, a former professor at the University of Bordeaux, Marqués de Cáceres was a pioneering bodega from the outset. Today Michel Rolland helps guide the winery, his hand evident in the stylish, small-production MC, made from Tempranillo. The Marqués de Cáceres Crianza remains the most widely available of the Cáceres wines in the U.S.

○ **Marqués de Cáceres White** / 2010 / Rioja / $
Stainless steel fermentation keeps this white Rioja's citrus flavors fresh and vibrant.

● **Marqués de Cáceres Rosé** / 2010 / Rioja / $
A hint of sweetness underscores this earthy, crisp rosé.

MARQUÉS DE MURRIETA

The focused portfolio here—a mere four wines—remains largely faithful to Murrieta's roots in traditional-style Rioja production. Founded by Peru native Luciano Francisco Ramón de Murrieta in 1852, the winery crafts two traditional reds and a white, Capellanía, using only estate fruit. The much pricier Dalmau represents a modern departure for the winery with its addition of Cabernet Sauvignon.

○ **Marqués de Murrieta Capellanía Blanco Reserva** / 2006 / Rioja / $$ This old-vine Viura, ready to drink right now, has luscious lemon-drop flavors that are very subtly sweet.

● **Marqués de Murrieta Reserva** / 2007 / Rioja / $$
Despite 22 months in oak barrels, this graceful red displays fresh, up-front blackberry flavors not dulled by wood.

● **Marqués de Murrieta Dalmau Reserva** / 2007 / Rioja / $$$$
Velvety and seductive, with beautifully balanced layers of black cherry, this stunning red justifies its high price.

MONTECILLO

Montecillo makes reliably good wines on a grand scale, thanks in large part to the talent and three-decade-long tenure of wine-maker María Martínez Sierra. Owned since 1973 by the Osborne Group, a privately held Spanish food-and-beverage company, Montecillo has the freedom, and the financial resources, to purchase the best grapes when the opportunity arises.

- **Montecillo Gran Reserva** / 2003 / Rioja / $$
  This offers good structure and classic Rioja flavors—fresh cherries, earth and spice—at a compelling price.
- **Montecillo Reserva** / 2003 / Rioja / $$
  A perfectly aged, affordable Rioja that's ready to drink now.

MUGA

Like most Rioja producers, Muga has a passion for barrels, but its diverse cellar—which includes French, American, Hungarian, Russian and Spanish oak—reveals the winery's experimental streak. Founded in 1932, Muga has always excelled with traditional red blends; prestige wines like Torre Muga and the recently introduced Aro show its skill with a more modern style.

- **Muga Rosado** / 2010 / Rioja / $
  This crisp, Garnacha-based rosé gets its appley edge from a touch of the white grape Viura.
- **Muga Reserva** / 2007 / Rioja / $$
  Made with Tempranillo, Garnacha and bits of Mazuelo and Graciano, this meaty, smoky *reserva* shows a mineral tang.

R. LÓPEZ DE HEREDIA
VIÑA TONDONIA

This family-owned Rioja winery hasn't changed much since it was founded in 1877. Now run by the fourth generation, the winery sources exclusively from hand-harvested estate vineyards and is one of the few in the world to maintain a working cooperage to craft its barrels. The red and white *gran reservas* are often released up to a decade later than most Rioja wines.

> **WINE INTEL**
> Architect Zaha Hadid designed López de Heredia's stunning tasting pavilion, part of a wave of new Rioja wineries dreamed up by modern masters such as Norman Foster and Frank Gehry.

- ○ **R. López de Heredia Viña Tondonia Blanco Reserva** / 1993 / Rioja Alta / $$$ A fascinating, orange-inflected white that's still fresh at nearly 20 years of age.
- **R. López de Heredia Viña Tondonia Reserva** / 2001 / Rioja Alta / $$$ Just hitting its stride, this polished, savory bottling comes from a terrific vintage.
- **Viña Bosconia Reserva** / 2003 / Rioja Alta / $$$
  Made with grapes from the acclaimed El Bosque vineyard, this currant-flavored red is supple and stylish.

SIERRA CANTABRIA

Sierra Cantabria is one of six wineries in the Eguren group today helmed by winemaker Marcos Eguren. Much of the fruit it uses, including the peculiar Tempranillo Peludo grape (literally, "hairy" Tempranillo), hails from the winery's hometown of San Vicente de la Sonsierra. In addition to a full line of Rioja reds, Cantabria is notable for a barrel-fermented white blend called Organza.

● **Sierra Cantabria Tinto** / 2009 / Rioja / $
A reliable value, the '09 vintage offers exuberant black-fruit flavors and a pleasant herbal cdgc.

● **Sierra Cantabria Amancio** / 2006 / Rioja / $$$$
Two years aging in new oak gives this famous, suavely structured red a smoky edge.

VIÑEDOS DEL CONTINO

Established in 1973, Viñedos del Contino is part of CVNE (the Spanish acronym for Wine Company of Northern Spain), which dates back to 1879 and is still owned by its founders' descendants. The modern-leaning Contino estate winery crafts bold (and pricey) wines such as Contino Graciano, while the original CVNE winery in Rioja Alta is known for traditional reds and whites.

○ **CVNE Monopole Blanc** / 2010 / Rioja Alta / $
Zippy acidity and ripe melon and citrus notes make this a textbook introduction to the Viura grape.

● **CVNE Imperial Gran Reserva** / 1999 / Rioja Alta / $$$
A classic, elegant Rioja with beautifully integrated red-fruit, spice and coconut flavors.

● **Contino Viña del Olivo** / 2007 / Rioja Alavesa / $$$$
This outstanding single-vineyard red will age well for years.

GALICIA

Rainy and green, Galicia is in Spain's northwestern corner, north of Portugal on the Atlantic Ocean. In the region's star DO, Rías Baixas (REE-ahs BYE-shuss), fronting both the Atlantic and the Miño River, white wine accounts for 99 percent of production. Since the denomination's official creation in 1988, Rías Baixas has earned Galicia a well-deserved reputation as a source for fresh, lively whites. The warmer Valdeorras and Ribeira Sacra subregions produce a small amount of interesting red wine.

GALICIA GRAPES & STYLES

Galicia's finest grape is Albariño, the white grape of Rías Baixas, which yields fresh, citrusy wines; it is sometimes blended with local grapes, such as Treixadura or Loureira. The Ribeiro region makes Albariño blends, although Treixadura is its leading grape. Quality has been improving in Galicia's inland Valdeorras and Ribeira Sacra subregions, where the Godello grape makes lush whites and Mencía, fruity reds. The Monterrei region produces mainly whites from Doña Blanca, Treixadura and Godello grapes.

Producers/ Galicia

ADEGA CONDES DE ALBAREI

This large co-op, with nearly 400 members, makes more than 1.5 million bottles of Albariño annually. The Condes de Albarei and Salneval lines are high quality and widely available, offering some of the region's best value. The winery itself was seized from a cocaine trafficker and purchased at auction by Albarei in 2008.

○ **Condes de Albarei Albariño** / 2010 / Rías Baixas / $
Its clean, minerally lemon-lime flavors are tangy and brisk.

○ **Salneval Albariño** / 2010 / Rías Baixas / $
An ideal summer sipper, this Albariño features light, zesty green apple notes and a salty kick.

BODEGAS DEL PALACIO DE FEFIÑANES

Dating to 1904, Fefiñanes is not only the oldest winery in the region, but it also was the first to bottle under the Rías Baixas DO, right after the *denominación* was created in 1988. Fefiñanes' super lineup of Albariños includes an unoaked version and the sherry barrel–aged 1583 bottling.

○ **Albariño de Fefiñanes** / 2010 / Rías Baixas / $$
Intense and pure, with sea salt, citrus and graphite flavors.

○ **Albariño de Fefiñanes 1583** / 2010 / Rías Baixas / $$$
Known for its lush complexity, the winery's premier cuvée is hard to find but worth the search.

BODEGAS MARTÍN CÓDAX

Since its founding as a co-op in 1986, Martín Códax has become one of the best-known wineries in Rías Baixas. In addition to a basic Albariño, Códax vintner and founding partner Luciano Amoedo crafts a range of distinctive, 100 percent Albariño wines, including lightly oaked Organistrum; slightly sweet Burgáns; and Lías, a modern, stainless steel–fermented interpretation.

○ **Martín Códax Albariño** / 2010 / Rías Baixas / $
This widely available bottling makes a great introduction to Albariño, with zesty lime and herb flavors and a hint of fizz.

FILLABOA

This winery is owned by the Masaveus, a historic winemaking family that returned to the business by acquiring wineries in Rioja and Navarra, followed by the purchase of Fillaboa ("good daughter" in Galician) in Rías Baixas in 2000. Of Fillaboa's two Albariños, the Selección Finca Monte Alto is one of the region's few single-vineyard estate wines.

○ **Fillaboa Albariño** / 2010 / Rías Baixas / $$
This herb-edged white is made with estate-grown grapes and offers expressive mineral flavors.
○ **Fillaboa Selección Finca Monte Alto** / 2009 / Rías Baixas / $$
From the highest vineyard on the Masaveu estate, this Albariño is lean and salty, with bright floral and citrus notes.

TERRAS GAUDA

Founded in 1990, Gauda was born of the merger of the Viñedos do Rosal and Adegas das Eiras wineries. Given its large production, Gauda surprises with both innovation (by tinkering with sparkling wine, for example) and high quality. The flagship Terras Gauda bottling is a blend of Albariño, Loureira and Caiño Blanco, while the Black Label version spends time in oak.

○ **Terras Gauda Abadia de San Campio** / 2010 / Rías Baixas / $$
Albariño's sea-salty, citrusy side is clearly evident in this delicious single-vineyard wine.
○ **Terras Gauda O Rosal** / 2010 / Rías Baixas / $$
The winery's top offering, this blend of three local grapes (including Albariño) is a racy, unusually generous cuvée.

VIÑA MEÍN

Javier Alén started Viña Meín with the help of friends and rela-tives in 1988 by replanting about 40 acres with traditional Ribeiro varieties. Both of his excellent white blends have the Treixadura grape at their heart, securing Alén's legacy as the variety's greatest champion. The white wines are joined by a much smaller-production *tinto* (red wine), blended from the Mencía, Caiño Longo and Ferrón grapes.

○ Viña Mein / 2010 / Ribeiro / $$
The fragrant Treixadura grape gives this light-bodied white its zippy apple and citrus notes.

SOUTHEASTERN SPAIN

The Valencia and Murcia regions occupy much of Spain's south-east; offshore lie the Balearic Islands, of which only Mallorca produces a significant amount of wine. Long a source of olives, almonds, citrus and bulk wine, this area is still developing as a quality wine region. Many vineyards in Murcia's Jumilla region were destroyed by phylloxera in 1989, a full century after most of Europe's vineyards recovered. The plague was something of a blessing, however, as it spurred necessary replanting. Still remain-ing, however, are some vineyards full of ancient Monastrell (Mourvèdre) vines, which escaped unscathed.

SOUTHEASTERN SPAIN GRAPES & STYLES

Though still a source of bulk wine, the Jumilla region is getting deserved attention for its inky, ripe reds based on the Monastrell grape. Monastrell also stars in the quality wines of the adjacent Murcia DO Yecla, a small area of just 11 wineries. The larger Valencia DO utilizes a vast mix of grapes to make wine, yet little is high quality. The primary white grape of Valencia is Mer-seguera, and Tempranillo is becoming a more important red. Bobal is the region's most distinctive native grape, yielding dark, brooding reds. Utiel-Requena is the finest denomination for the grape—Bobal accounts for 80 percent of its total production. The DOs Binissalem Mallorca and Pla i Llevant are the best regions on Mallorca, although in 2007 the entire island became eligible for the Vinos de la Tierra de Mallorca quality designation. While white wine is made throughout southeastern Spain, most of it is unremarkable, and very little of it is imported to the U.S.

Producers/ Southeastern Spain

BODEGAS CASTAÑO

This dynamic winery has had a prominent role in transforming the Yecla region—once known for bulk wine—into an exciting zone for quality reds. Founder Ramón Castaño Santa started bottling his own wine in 1980; today his three sons run the estate. Their Monastrell-centric bottlings are perennial values.

- **Castaño Monastrell** / 2009 / Yecla / $
Fresh-cracked black pepper notes spice up this plummy, plush, incredibly low-priced Monastrell.

BODEGAS JUAN GIL

The Jumilla estate founded by Juan Gil Giménez in 1916 is now run by his great-grandchildren. In recent years they have built a new winery, partnered with famed importer Jorge Ordóñez and seen their wines take off in the U.S. Made with old-vine Monastrell, Juan Gil's inky reds offer lots of power for the price.

- **Bodegas Hijos de Juan Gil Juan Gil** / 2008 / Jumilla / $
A fleshy, international style of Monastrell with rich flavors and ample mocha and oak notes.

BODEGAS LUZÓN

One of the largest wineries of DO Jumilla, turning out more than nine million bottles a year, Bodegas Luzón has modernized and upgraded since joining the agricultural group Fuertes in 2005. The winery crafts delicious Monastrell-based reds; its affordable Luzón Verde wines are made with organic grapes.

- **Luzón Verde** / 2010 / Jumilla / $
Aging without oak keeps the bold red berry flavors in this organic Monastrell center stage—and the price low.
- **Alma de Luzón** / 2005 / Jumilla / $$$
One of the benchmark bottlings of Jumilla, it has impressive density, thanks to its 50-year-old source vines.

OLD WORLD / SPAIN / SOUTHEASTERN

CASA DE LA ERMITA

In addition to the region's signature grape, Monastrell, Ermita grows Petit Verdot, Merlot, Syrah and Cabernet. Jumilla native Marcial Martínez Cruz has made wine throughout Spain for more than two decades; he brings his talents home to craft Ermita's core range, Casa de la Ermita, which includes red blends and wines from organically grown Monastrell.

● **Casa de la Ermita Roble** / 2010 / Jumilla / $
A touch of Petit Verdot adds firmness to the finish of this grapey, juicy Monastrell blend.

● **Casa de la Ermita Crianza** / 2008 / Jumilla / $$
The savory, herb-inflected flavors in this structured Monastrell blend need food to tame their tannic edge.

OLIVARES

Having first made the transition from bulk wine to quality bottled wine in 1998, Olivares is still realizing the full potential of its heritage vineyards: more than 300 acres of ungrafted vines in the coolest area of Jumilla. Olivares offers its debut wine—the single-vineyard, old-vine, wild yeast–fermented red Altos de la Hoya—at an astonishingly low price.

● **Olivares Altos de la Hoya** / 2009 / Jumilla / $
Made from ungrafted old vines, this great-value Monastrell-Garnacha blend is loaded with berry and mineral flavors.

SEÑORÍO DE BARAHONDA

Bodegas Antonio Candela was established in 1925; in 2005, the Candela family constructed this impressively high-tech Yecla winery. They focus on reds made with Monastrell across their extensive and growing portfolio of brands, which include Barahonda Summum, Bellum, Heredad Candela and Carro.

● **Barahonda Barrica** / 2009 / Yecla / $
A muscular Syrah-Monastrell blend with exotic spice notes.

● **Barahonda Monastrell** / 2009 / Yecla / $
Made *sin madera* (without oak), this delivers the burly, earthy intensity of a more expensive red.

● **Nabuko** / 2009 / Yecla / $
Another amazing value, with meaty spice and chocolate notes.

VINOS SIN-LEY

Launched in 2003 by Emili Esteve and Manuel Martínez, this innovative project—whose name translates as "wines without law"—eschews various winemaking regulations. Along with guest winemakers, Esteve and Martínez offer the G (Garnacha) and M (Monastrell) lines, and red blends dubbed Zestos.

● **Vinos Sin Ley Puerta Bonita G5 / 2010 / Vinos de Madrid / $**
This terrific old-vine Garnacha features ultra-ripe and chewy raspberry flavors laced with minerals.

CATALONIA

The Catalonia region is in Spain's northeastern corner. Priorat, which joins the ranks of Rioja with a superior DOCa designation, garners international attention for its reds. Production of sparkling cava is centered in Penedès (see p. 269). The vast DO of Catalonia serves as the generic designation for regional wines.

CATALONIA GRAPES & STYLES

Catalonia is largely planted with Garnacha, much of it old-vine. Cariñena (Carignane) and Garnacha compose the heart of Priorat's reds. Some vintners blend in Cabernet or Syrah. Softer reds hail from the DO of Montsant, formally established in 2001. Spain's sparkling wine DO Cava encompasses several regions across the country. The largest is Penedès, in Catalonia, where the traditional cava grapes—Macabeo, Parellada and Xarel-lo—as well as Chardonnay are also used to make still whites. Penedès reds are often blends of local grapes and Tempranillo or Monastrell.

Producers/ Catalonia

ÁLVARO PALACIOS

Applying his Bordeaux training to Priorat Garnacha, Álvaro Palacios created a wine in 1993 that would become a modern icon of Spain: L'Ermita. That, along with his first wine, Finca Dofí, established him as one of Spain's great stars. Today Palacios also crafts affordable high-quality wines, such as Camins del Priorat.

- **Álvaro Palacios Camins del Priorat** / 2008 / Priorat / $$
  A supple Cariñena-based blend with cherry-rich intensity.
- **Álvaro Palacios Les Terrasses Velles Vinyes** / 2008 / Priorat /
  $$$ From some of Priorat's oldest, steepest vineyards, this
  dark fruit–flavored blend is beautifully polished.

CELLER DE CAPÇANES

Five families came together to create this Montsant winery in
1933. Kosher bottlings have been an important part of their
portfolio since 1995, when they began making wines for Barcelona's Jewish community. Today the co-op's range includes the
entry-level Mas Donís and the powerful Cabrida wines, made
only with Garnacha. The top red, Peraj Ha'Abib, is also kosher.

- **Capçanes Mas Donís Rosat** / 2009 / Montsant / $
  Made from mostly Garnacha, this is juicy and fresh, with ripe
  cherry flavors and a savory mix of herbs.

CELLERS JOAN D'ANGUERA

Though the Anguera family had been making wine since the
1820s, they produced it in bulk and sold it locally. In 1984 Joan
bottled the first Joan d'Anguera wines, focusing on estate-grown
Syrah. Their wild success, now shepherded by sons Joan and
Josep, helped transform the once little-known Montsant region.

- **Joan d'Anguera Finca L'Argatà** / 2008 / Montsant / $$
  A spicy, deeply fruity blend of Syrah, Garnacha and Cabernet
  Sauvignon from a single vineyard.

CELLER VALL LLACH

Spanish singer Lluís Llach founded this Priorat winery with
partner Enric Costain in the 1990s, supplementing the 60- to
90-year-old Cariñena and Garnacha vineyards with new plant-
ings. The winery's premier red, simply called Vall Llach, is fol-
lowed by Idus de Vall Llach and entry-level Embruix de Vall Llach.

- **Embruix de Vall Llach** / 2007 / Priorat / $$
  This brawny, raspberry-driven blend is a great value.
- **Vall Llach** / 2007 / Priorat / $$$$
  A full-throttle Priorat built for the long haul, it has savory,
  herb-infused black-fruit flavors.

MAS IGNEUS

A pioneer in making wine with organic grapes since 1996, Mas Igneus draws upon three estates as well as contract farmers for its red and white Priorat wines. The seemingly cryptic names of some of the wines refer to the type of oak, age of barrels and months spent in barrel. For example, FA206 was aged in French Allier oak and spent six months in two-year-old barrels.

● **Mas Igneus Barranc dels Closos / 2008 / Priorat / $$**
A flashy, boldly structured blend of 80 percent Garnacha and 20 percent Cariñena with dried-cherry and licorice flavors.

● **Mas Igneus Vinyes de Coster FA112 / 2002 / Priorat / $$$**
This violet-scented red gets its intense minerality and gripping tannins from very old vines.

TORRES

Although the newest Torres wines include Celeste (Ribera del Duero) and Ibéricos (Rioja), this venerable family winery is firmly rooted in Catalonia. Its Sangre de Toro line, with its famous plastic-bull bottle ornament, was launched in 1954; the Coronas label recently marked its centenary. Today the winery continues to expand its range under a fifth generation of the Torres family.

○ **Torres Viña Esmeralda / 2010 / Catalonia / $**
This perfumed, light-bodied blend of Moscatel and Gewürztraminer showcases lime and sweet orange blossom notes.

● **Torres Salmos / 2008 / Priorat / $$$**
A firmly structured and concentrated Rhône-style blend.

● **Torres Mas La Plana / 2007 / Penedès / $$$$**
This famous single-vineyard Cabernet offers mineral-laden black currant flavors that show great depth and polish.

CASTILLA Y LEÓN

Castilla y León, in north-central Spain, encompasses several diverse wine regions. Foremost is Ribera del Duero, which owes much of its original fame to one producer, Vega Sicilia, and its legendary Unico, a Tempranillo-Cabernet blend renowned for its longevity—and exorbitant price. Not until the debut in the 1980s of Alejandro Fernández's Pesquera (a relative bargain) did interest in Ribera del Duero increase in a major way. As a whole, Castilla y León has many new wineries these days, and if there is a prevailing winemaking style, it's an emphasis on power, especially in Ribera del Duero and Toro. Cigales DO *rosados* have become better and fresher, and the region is making more bold reds. Long underrated, Rueda shines as a source of crisp whites, with red wine production now permitted there as well.

❧ CASTILLA Y LEÓN GRAPES & STYLES

Tempranillo (known locally as Tinto Fino or Tinta del País) is Castilla y León's star grape. In Ribera del Duero, most wines are pure Tempranillo, although small amounts of Cabernet, Merlot and Malbec are permitted. The aging regulations for reds are the same as in Rioja (see p. 105). Rueda is an anomaly in this red wine–dominated region, creating citrusy whites, the best of which use the Verdejo grape, although Viura and recently introduced Sauvignon Blanc are often added. The pure Tempranillo wines of Toro (where the grape's local version is called Tinta de Toro) are full-bodied and dense, usually made to be consumed earlier than those of Ribera. The northerly Bierzo DO makes mostly reds from the Mencía grape and a few whites from Godello.

Producers/ Castilla y León

ABADÍA RETUERTA

Because this sprawling 15-year-old estate technically lies just outside the borders of the prestigious Ribera del Duero DO, its wines are labeled with the humble *vino de la tierra* status. But don't let that deter you: The supertalented Ángel Anocíbar makes Abadía Retuerta's wines, which include Tempranillo-based blends, single-vineyard wines and a handful of bottlings made with other grapes, such as Cabernet Sauvignon and Syrah.

- Abadía Retuerta Selección Especial / 2008 / Vino de la Tierra de Castilla y León / $$ Eighteen months in new oak barrels give this juicy Tempranillo-based red its smoky cedar notes.
- Abadía Retuerta Pago Negralada / 2006 / Vino de la Tierra de Castilla y León / $$$$ From a single vineyard (*pago*), this stylish Tempranillo is impressively refined.

BODEGAS ALEJANDRO FERNÁNDEZ/ TINTO PESQUERA

Until Alejandro Fernández's powerhouse Tempranillo, Pesquera, came along, Ribera del Duero had only one superstar winery— Vega Sicilia. Pesquera's wild acclaim helped galvanize the region's quality revolution, and Fernández went on to create a mini dynasty of four wineries in emerging regions throughout Spain: Pesquera and Condado de Haza in Ribera del Duero; Dehesa la Granja in Castilla y León; and El Vínculo in La Mancha.

- ● Alejandro Fernández Dehesa la Granja / 2004 / Vino de la Tierra de Castilla y León / $$ A few years of bottle aging have brought out this chewy red's savory olive and spice tones.
- ● Condado de Haza / 2008 / Ribera del Duero / $$
  This tightly wound Tempranillo opens up after a bit of time in the glass to reveal meaty, smoke-edged berry flavors.
- ● Tinto Pesquera Reserva / 2007 / Ribera del Duero / $$$
  One of four Pesquera wines, this powerful, lightly gamey red is a step up from the entry-level *crianza*.

BODEGAS ÁNGEL RODRÍGUEZ VIDAL

The very existence of Verdejo in Rueda can be credited to wine-maker Ángel Rodríguez, who used clippings from his tiny ancient plot to propagate a 25-acre vineyard, saving the grape from extinction. Both the ancient vines and their progeny contribute to a single wine, Martínsancho Verdejo, made at the Marqués de Riscal facilities in limited quantities.

- ○ Martínsancho Verdejo / 2010 / Rueda / $$
  Adding a portion of grapes from very old vines gives this stellar white a terrific concentration; refreshing citrus tones have an exotic tropical edge on the palate.

BODEGAS EMILIO MORO

This family-owned Ribera del Duero producer draws upon more than 200 acres of old family vineyards, the earliest dating back to 1932, to craft a portfolio of five Tempranillo wines that together reflect the breadth of vineyard age: The youngest fruit goes to the affordably priced Finca Resalso, while the oldest vines are dedicated to the top cuvées, including the revered Malleolus de Valderramiro.

- **Emilio Moro Finca Resalso** / 2009 / Ribera del Duero / $
  An earthy red whose firm tannins, spice and acidity make it
  ideal for burgers, lamb or steak.
- **Emilio Moro** / 2007 / Ribera del Duero / $$
  Textbook Tempranillo, packing an abundance of ripe, spicy
  cherry, crisp acidity and fine-grained tannins.
- **Malleolus** / 2008 / Ribera del Duero / $$$$
  Sourced from vines between 25 and 75 years old, this is a
  beautifully refined Tempranillo with seamless sour cherry
  and black licorice notes.

DESCENDIENTES DE J. PALACIOS

Álvaro Palacios (see p. 116) partnered with his nephew Ricardo
Pérez Palacios in 1999 to make red wines in the Bierzo DO. Rely-
ing on Mencía grapes from old vines planted on steep hillsides,
the pair offer their entry-level Pétalos del Bierzo, the higher-end
Corullón (sourced from the nearby town of the same name) and
a handful of single-vineyard wines in select vintages.

- **Descendientes de J. Palacios Pétalos** / 2008 / Bierzo / $$
  Fragrant, complex, silky-smooth raspberry flavors make this
  Bierzo red a terrific value.
- **Descendientes de J. Palacios Villa de Corullón** / 2008 /
  Bierzo / $$$ Mencía's leafy freshness takes on a spicy, darkly
  fruity intensity in this old-vine cuvée.

NUMANTHIA

Created in 1998 by the Eguren family (see p. 110), Numanthia
had fast become a rising star in Toro even before luxury-goods
group LVMH acquired it 10 years later. Manuel Louzada, previ-
ously of Argentina's Bodegas Chandon, now manages opera-
tions. Tinta de Toro, the local vesion of Tempranillo, contributes
to Numanthia's three wines, which vary widely in price yet are
consistently outstanding.

- **Numanthia Termes** / 2008 / Toro / $$
  An ageworthy red at an affordable price, with brooding
  black-fruit, spice and game flavors.
- **Numanthia** / 2008 / Toro / $$$
  Ancient vines yield a very modern wine, with concentrated
  black cherry, mocha and chalk tones.

Portugal

Wine Region

The relative obscurity of Portugal's table wines—as opposed to port, the well-known, fortified, sweet wine of the Douro Valley—means that they're often overlooked and, equally as often, underpriced. Produced mostly from native varieties and often from very old vines, Portuguese reds are spicy, sultry and full of character, while the country's whites are vibrant and incredibly refreshing.

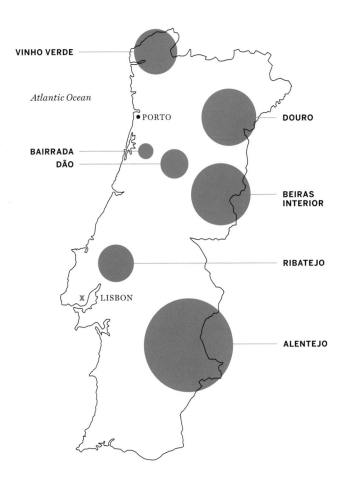

VINHO VERDE

Atlantic Ocean

● PORTO

DOURO

BAIRRADA

DÃO

BEIRAS INTERIOR

RIBATEJO

X LISBON

ALENTEJO

Portugal

PORTUGAL'S DOURO VALLEY was designated an official wine region in 1756, yet only now is it getting into table-wine production at a high-quality level. For centuries, most of the Douro's wine grapes were used to make sweet, fortified ports, a profitable industry controlled by large companies. A change in law in 1986, when Portugal entered the European Union, allowed small producers to bottle and export their own wines. Since then, outside investment has enabled vintners to vastly improve quality, and the results have been dramatic, particularly in the Douro region. Winemakers are turning out compelling dry reds, nearly always crafted with the same grapes used to make port. Outside the Douro, structured, spicy reds are made in Alentejo, Bairrada and Dão. Look to Lisboa (until recently known as Estremadura), Tejo and Terras do Sado, near Lisbon, for value reds, and to Vinho Verde, in the northwest, for zesty whites.

 PORTUGUESE GRAPES & STYLES

Portugal is primarily a country of blends, most made with native grapes such as Touriga Nacional, Tinta Roriz (Tempranillo) and Touriga Franca. The country's best reds come from the Douro, where the arid climate yields firm, spicy wines with dark-fruit flavors. Bairrada and Dão are both Denominação de Origem

Controlada (DOC) zones of the Beiras region; the former has a reputation for tannic and fruity reds (usually based on the Baga grape), whereas Dão's wines are softer blends.

Portugal's white wines are improving rapidly. The country's long Atlantic coastline yields a range of fish-friendly whites—chief among them crisp, bright Vinho Verde (green wine), which has powerful acidity, slight effervescence and low alcohol. Many versions of this widely popular, affordable wine are tart and simple. Yet a growing number of complex, fuller-bodied Vinhos Verdes are being made today, typically from the Alvarinho and Loureiro grapes. Vinho Verde is meant to be drunk when young and fresh, so look for the most recent vintage when shopping. Whites from Alentejo, Dão, the Douro, Bairrada and Bucelas, among other areas, are worth seeking out too.

PORTUGUESE WINE LABELS

Most Portuguese wines are labeled by region. Wines labeled *reserva* must be at least half a percent higher in alcohol than the DOC-established minimum. Wines labeled by variety must include at least 85 percent of the specified grape.

Producers/ Portugal

AVELEDA

Aveleda's delicious Vinhos Verdes are among Portugal's best-known wines. This large, family-owned winery is both innovative and prolific: It was one of the first to exploit the Douro's potential for table wine and to focus on Vinho Verde's best grapes. At its Quinta da Aguieira property, the family hired star French consultant Denis Dubourdieu to create ambitious reds.

○ Aveleda Follies Alvarinho-Loureiro / 2010 / Minho / $
Loaded with bright, zippy lemon and green pear flavors, this refreshing white is a terrific value.

○ Aveleda Fonte / 2010 / Vinho Verde / $
A blend of Trajadura, Loureiro, Arinto and Azal Branco grapes, this is bracing, with citrus and green apple notes.

CARM

The Madeira family's farm (CARM is its acronym) was an olive plantation long before Rui Madeira convinced his relatives to grow grapes. Since 1995, the Madeiras have practiced organic viticulture as well, an approach aided by the dry climate of the rugged Douro Superior hills. The family's stylish wines have put them at the forefront of Portugal's up-and-coming producers.

● **CARM Reserva Red** / 2008 / Douro / $$
There's an elegant balance to the mocha and plum flavors in this ripe blend of traditional Portuguese varieties.

● **CARM Grande Reserva Red** / 2007 / Douro / $$$
A gripping, concentrated, cedar-tinged red made with grapes sourced from the winery's top vineyards.

HERDADE DO ESPORÃO

Alentejo, in Portugal's south-central section, is one of Europe's most exciting emerging wine regions, and Herdade do Esporão is one of its leading producers. At the helm since 1992, Australian winemaker David Baverstock deserves much of the credit: He makes modern, bold wines with native and French grapes.

○ **Herdade do Esporão Esporão Reserva White** / 2009 / Alentejo / $$ This lush, peachy blend of three native varieties (Antão Vaz, Arinto, Roupeiro) is nicely framed by toasty oak.

● **Herdade do Esporão Defesa Tinto** / 2009 / Alentejano / $$
Touriga Nacional and Syrah make up this muscular, herb- and ripe fruit–infused red.

JOÃO PORTUGAL RAMOS

Influential Alentejo winemaker João Portugal Ramos first gained fame in the 1980s when he helped build Quinta do Carmo into one of the area's finest estates. Ramos then planted vineyards and built his own winery in 1997. His well-structured wines are made from both local and international grapes.

○ **Loios Vinho White** / 2009 / Alentejano / $
This is pleasantly austere, with tart lemon and mineral flavors.

● **Loios Vinho Tinto** / 2009 / Alentejano / $
An appealing, herb-laden red blend of the indigenous Aragónez, Trincadeira and Castelão varieties.

JOSÉ MARIA DA FONSECA

Not to be confused with the port house Fonseca, this old-school winery became famous—or perhaps infamous—in the U.S. in the 1960s for turning out oceans of Lancers, a spritzy rosé. Now, J.M. Fonseca's production (led by California-educated wine-maker Domingos Soares Franco) mirrors Portugal's wine revolution, with a well-crafted portfolio that represents great value.

● **Periquita Reserva / 2008 / Setúbal / $**
From an emerging coastal region, this cherry-driven blend of Castelão, Touriga Nacional and Touriga Franca is very fresh.

LUIS PATO

The Bairrada region got little notice as a quality wine district until Luis Pato started making headlines at his family estate in the 1980s. Pato adopted modern techniques (destemming grapes and using French barrels, for example) to refine wines made from local grapes such as Baga. Today Pato is a godfather to a generation of quality-minded Bairrada producers, and the estate is known for both soulful reds and expressive whites.

○ **Luis Pato Maria Gomes White / 2010 / Beiras / $**
Fragrant pear and nectarine flavors have a mineral-rich finish in this blend of Maria Gomes and Arinto grapes.

NIEPOORT

Dirk Niepoort is a revolutionary in Portuguese wine. The descendant of a centuries-old Dutch port-producing family, Niepoort is a leader of the collective that makes the Lavradores de Feitoria table wines, as well as the producer of two of Portugal's greatest reds: Batuta and Charme. His lower-priced Vertente blends and white wines are equally impressive.

WINE INTEL
One of Dirk Niepoort's many side projects is an intriguing collaboration in Austria called Muhr-van der Niepoort, where he's making silky, bold and spicy Blaufränkisch.

● **Niepoort Twisted Tinto / 2008 / Douro / $$**
An excellent value, this has a chewy texture and blackberry, herb and earth tones.
● **Niepoort Vertente Tinto / 2008 / Douro / $$**
This fresh, streamlined blend of several indigenous varieties is loaded with flavors of herbs and black fruit.

PRATS & SYMINGTON

This high-profile winery represents a joint venture between Bruno Prats, formerly of Bordeaux's Château Cos d'Estournel, and the famed Symington family, owners of port brands such as Graham's and Warre. Prats creates the polished Chryseia red blend as well as a second wine called Post Scriptum. In 2009 the Symingtons acquired part of Quinta de Roriz, adding the Prazo de Roriz red wine and a port to the company's lineup.

● **Post Scriptum de Chryseia** / 2007 / Douro / $$
Supple and intense, with a great balance of spice and cherries.
● **Chryseia** / 2008 / Douro / $$$$
Touriga Nacional and Touriga Franca yield a wine that's equal parts power and finesse, packed with dried-black-fruit flavors.

QUINTA DO CRASTO

Perched on a ridiculously steep mountain jutting out over the Douro's banks, this well-known winery branched out from port to nonfortified wines in 1994. Under the direction of the Roquette family, Crasto has been incredibly successful—thanks to a focus on quality plus a wealth of well-situated vineyards, many of them old (the best lots go into the winery's stunning *reserva*). Don't overlook Crasto's value-priced white blend.

○ **Quinta do Crasto White** / 2009 / Douro / $$
This blend of three obscure native grapes (Gouveio, Roupeiro and Rabigato) is zippy and medium-bodied, with lovely tangerine and juicy cantaloupe notes.
● **Quinta do Crasto Flor** / 2008 / Douro / $
A great everyday wine with appealing plum and herb flavors.
● **Quinta do Crasto Superior** / 2008 / Douro Superior / $$
Polished flavors of blackberry and black currant are laced with minerals in this smooth red.

QUINTA DO VALLADO

When Quinta do Vallado's sixth-generation owner Francisco Ferreira decided to make table wines from his family's port vineyards, he asked his cousin Francisco "Xito" Olazabal, one of the Douro's greatest young talents, to helm the cellar. With prime Douro vineyards and a modern, gravity-flow winery, Vallado is a source of consistently terrific wines, both red and white.

● **Quinta do Vallado Vinho Tinto** / 2008 / Douro / $$
A reliable bargain, this entry-level red blend of Touriga Nacional, Tinta Roriz and Sousão offers herb-inflected plum and strawberry flavors backed by firm tannins.

● **Quinta do Vallado Reserva** / 2008 / Douro / $$$
Flashy black cherry and licorice flavors are round and rich, thanks to careful selection from old vines.

● **Quinta do Vallado Touriga Nacional** / 2008 / Douro / $$$
The Touriga Nacional grape can make stellar wines on its own, unblended, as this powerful, spicy red proves.

RAMOS PINTO

Founded in 1880 and owned for the past 22 years by French Champagne house Roederer, Ramos Pinto was a pioneer of single-variety viticulture—a huge shift for a country in which different grapes traditionally had been planted together. Its four estates—two in the upper Douro Valley and two in the middle Douro (Cima Corgo)—provide grapes for an array of affordable wines, including the Duas Quintas and Collection labels.

● **DQ** / 2008 / Douro / $
This peppery, layered blend of Touriga Franca, Tinta Roriz and Touriga Nacional offers excellent value.

SOGRAPE

Like many of Portugal's large wine companies, Sogrape spent the past few decades reinventing itself. It built a fortune selling zillions of bottles of Mateus rosé and, more recently, Sandeman and Ferreira ports. But it now owns wineries across Portugal that produce terrific nonfortified, nonpink wines. They range from low-priced bottlings such as the Callabriga wines to the iconic, $200 Barca-Velha red from Casa Ferreirinha.

● **Callabriga** / 2008 / Douro / $
A blend of Tinta Roriz, Touriga Franca and Touriga Nacional, this plum-driven red is always delicious.

● **Casa Ferreirinha Vinha Grande** / 2006 / Douro / $$
The entry-level blend from one of Portugal's oldest houses offers ample chocolate and blueberry flavors woven with mint.

Germany

Wine Region

Germany is the source of most of the world's greatest Rieslings. That, if nothing else, should make it indispensable to wine lovers. But Germany also produces a surprising number of other delicious and compelling wines at reasonable prices. Plus, the country's wine-makers increasingly are starting to make drier, fuller-bodied styles of Riesling, broadening the scope of Germany's already versatile and food-friendly wines.

MOSEL-SAAR-RUWER

RHEINGAU

RHEINHESSEN

MUNICH •

NAHE

PFALZ

Germany

GERMANY'S COOL CLIMATE makes it white wine territory, and Riesling is its king. Red grapes do grow here, but most varieties need more heat and sun than this northern country can provide. To make the most of the available sunshine, many of the best vineyards cling to steep, south-facing slopes along the river valleys of the Rhine and Mosel and the Mosel's Saar and Ruwer tributaries. The slate-soil vineyards of the Mosel-Saar-Ruwer and Rheingau regions produce Rieslings with a purity and intensity rarely equaled elsewhere. Rieslings from the Mosel tend to be delicate and mineral-laden; those from the Rheingau are usually drier and fuller-bodied. The hilly terrain of the Rheinhessen region yields many low-quality sweet wines, but excellent bargains lurk among the bulk offerings. Some of the best Scheurebes and Silvaners—two other German white varietals—are made here, particularly in the Rheinterrasse subregion. The relatively warmer Pfalz, Nahe and Baden regions produce lusher Rieslings, as well as a range of interesting wines from other grapes, including Pinot Gris (Grauburgunder) and Gewürztraminer. Some of Germany's best Pinot Blanc (Weissburgunder) wines come from Baden and Pfalz. Baden also stands out as a red wine area; this southern zone produces most of the country's Pinot Noir (Spätburgunder).

Most of Germany's winemaking sites have been cultivated for centuries—the oldest, since Roman times. Battered in the 1970s and '80s by the dominance of big commercial bottlers, Germany's wine industry has strengthened over the past 20 years, stoked by a renewed focus on quality and by the energy of the newest generation of vintners. All over Germany, Jungwinzer (young winemaker) associations have popped up, fostering community through social-networking websites such as Facebook and Flickr. Germany also has benefited from a string of exceptionally warm vintages; on average, Germany's vineyards have warmed up by nearly 2 degrees Fahrenheit during the past 25 years. Though that may not sound like much, the effects in vineyards have been dramatic, with white grapes ripening more easily and red varieties growing much more successfully.

❖ GERMAN GRAPES & STYLES

The stereotypical German white wine is unoaked, aromatic and fruity, with low alcohol and a degree of sweetness to balance its generous acidity. But taste an assortment of German whites—especially bottlings of Riesling, the country's most widely planted and prestigious grape—and a vast stylistic range becomes clear. German white styles range from bracingly dry to unctuously sweet, light to powerful, fruity and floral to mineral.

Other noteworthy white grapes include two members of the Pinot family, Pinot Gris and Pinot Blanc. The former goes by the name Grauburgunder when made in a crisp, dry style; in sweeter versions it's sometimes called Ruländer. Pinot Blanc generally is made in a dry style in Germany, but sweeter examples are not uncommon. Gewürztraminer and Muscat (Muskateller) make intensely fragrant whites, whereas the widely planted Silvaner is used mainly in blends (though it can yield sleek, exciting whites in the Franken and Rheinhessen regions). The white Scheurebe variety, often used for dessert wines, displays a distinctive black currant aroma and citrusy flavors. Even though it is Germany's second most widely planted grape after Riesling, Müller-Thurgau (Rivaner) is used mostly for forgettable blends and doesn't appear much in the U.S.

Red wine now accounts for 36 percent of vineyard acreage in Germany, a huge increase from the past, driven mostly by the wild popularity of Pinot Noir. Germany is now the world's third-largest producer of Pinot Noir, though little of it is exported to the U.S. Nevertheless, these wines are well worth seeking out for their delicate, fresh cherry flavors. Dornfelder, a grape that was first cultivated in 1979 and makes juicy, deeply colored reds, is also catching on in Germany.

GERMAN WINE LABELS

The exacting specificity of German wine labels can make them hard to decipher, yet it's incredibly helpful once you've cracked the code. German labels offer more information than most, including not just the producer and geographic origin but also wine-making details such as grape ripeness. Labels usually list grapes, though in regions like the Rheingau, Riesling is assumed.

The vast majority of German wine qualifies for one of two "quality" designations, most of it falling into the Qualitätswein (Qualitätswein bestimmter Anbaugebiete, or QbA) category. This includes everything from bulk wines such as Liebfraumilch, the sweet blend that tarnished Germany's reputation in the 1980s, to solidly made value bottlings. Qualitätswein mit Prädikat (QmP) wines, a big step up from QbAs, are held to higher quality standards; they are ranked by the grapes' sugar levels, or ripeness, at harvest, from Kabinett (the least ripe) to Spätlese, Auslese and Beerenauslese (BA) all the way up to incredibly ripe, and sweet, Trockenbeerenauslese (TBA). In theory, grapes with higher sugar levels have the potential to make sweeter wines. Yet in practice, perceived sweetness depends more on the balance between acidity and sugar or the amount of natural grape sugar allowed to ferment into alcohol—which means, essentially, that a Kabinett wine is usually drier than an Auslese wine, but there are no guarantees. Watch for the words *trocken* (dry) or *halbtrocken* (off-dry) on labels, which vintners use to help clarify how sweet a wine tastes. *Spätlese trocken*, for example, means the wine is dry in style yet made from grapes picked at Spätlese levels of ripeness.

Classic and *Selection* on labels denote wines that are high quality and dry. Classic wines are usually made with a single variety and bear the name of the producer but not the vineyard. Selection wines are higher in quality; they must be made from hand-harvested grapes and list the producer and vineyard.

A recent trend has been for producers to add more consumer-friendly proprietary names to some quality wines, such as S.A. Prüm's "Essence" Rieslings or Dr. Loosen's "Dr. L" Riesling.

Producers/ Germany

DÖNNHOFF

The much respected Helmut Dönnhoff creates masterfully balanced wines—both dry and sweet—that are some of Germany's most sought-after bottlings and command a cultlike devotion from fans. The estate is not in the prestigious Mosel region but in the less heralded Nahe zone, where the slightly warmer climate works to Dönnhoff's advantage by giving its sweet Rieslings their famous opulence.

○ **Dönnhoff Tonschiefer Dry Slate Riesling Trocken** / 2009 / Nahe / \$\$ An emphasis on *terroir* is a Dönnhoff hallmark, exemplified by this peachy, stony Riesling.

○ **Dönnhoff Hermannshöhle Grosses Gewächs Riesling** / 2009 / Nahe / \$\$\$ Savory, fragrant and complex, this is an ideal expression of a Grosses Gewächs, or first-growth, site.

DR. LOOSEN

Every wine region needs someone like Ernst Loosen, an ebullient, charismatic risk taker who helped revolutionize German winemaking. Loosen had intended to become an archaeologist but ended up in 1987 taking over his family's Mosel estate, where he focused his efforts on old, ungrafted vines and low yields. His powerful single-vineyard Rieslings epitomize site-specific winemaking; his more affordable wines are made mostly from purchased grapes under the Dr. L label.

> **WINE INTEL**
> Winemaker Erni Loosen's experimental drive extends to the U.S. too: He collaborates with Washington's Chateau Ste. Michelle to make Eroica, a stellar Riesling that's always among the country's best.

○ **Dr. Loosen Blue Slate Riesling Kabinett** / 2009 / Mosel / \$\$ Citrusy acidity nicely balances this wine's dense apple flavors.

○ **Dr. Loosen Wehlener Sonnenuhr Riesling Auslese** / 2009 / Mosel / \$\$\$\$ A warm, sunny autumn and botrytis-affected grapes (used for the first time this vintage) imparted tremendous intensity to this spicy, peach-laden Auslese.

JOH. JOS. CHRISTOFFEL ERBEN

One of the great names in Riesling, the Christoffel estate is located in the Middle Mosel town of Ürzig, best known for the legendary Würzgarten (literally, spice garden) vineyard, which yields wines of profound depth and distinctive spiciness. Since 2001, Robert Eymael of Weingut Mönchhof has leased the Christoffel vineyards and made the wines, hewing closely to the Christoffel style of pure, racy Rieslings.

○ **Joh. Jos. Christoffel Erben Ürziger Würzgarten Riesling Spätlese / 2009 / Mosel / $$$** Made in a lush, very pure and bright style, this Riesling reveals silky fig and raspberry notes.

JOH. JOS. PRÜM

The eldest of three daughters, 31-year-old Katharina Prüm has been apprenticing with her famous winemaker father, Manfred, for half a decade and will soon become the latest in a line of famous Prüms to helm this renowned Mosel estate. The family's Rieslings are built for the long haul, with tight, mineral-laden flavors that expand after a few years of aging and can continue to gain complexity for decades after release.

○ **Joh. Jos. Prüm Bernkasteler Badstube Riesling Kabinett / 2008 / Mosel / $$$** A mineral-rich, pleasantly lean wine, with a bright beam of green apple and slate tones.

○ **Joh. Jos. Prüm Wehlener Sonnenuhr Riesling Kabinett / 2009 / Mosel / $$$** From a famed Middle Mosel site comes this sophisticated Kabinett with tangy peach and lime flavors.

○ **Joh. Jos. Prüm Wehlener Sonnenuhr Riesling Spätlese / 2009 / Mosel / $$$** This exceptionally refined Riesling shows creamy apple tones that linger in the mineral-rich finish.

MAXIMIN GRÜNHAUS/
SCHLOSSKELLEREI C. VON SCHUBERT

The Maximin Grünhaus estate consists of three esteemed and extremely old vineyards in the tiny Ruwer valley region. Romans first planted grape vines here; the vineyards were later farmed by monks and finally purchased by ancestors of the current owner, Dr. Carl von Schubert, in 1882. Today von Schubert farms naturally; winemaker Stefan Kraml, who arrived in 2004, turns the estate's grapes into outstanding, expressive Rieslings.

○ **Maximin Grünhäuser Abtsberg Riesling Kabinett** / 2009 / Mosel / $$$ Juicy and streamlined, with nuances of vibrant strawberry, peach and slate woven throughout.

○ **Maximin Grünhäuser Herrenberg Riesling Spätlese** / 2009 / Mosel / $$$ This peachy, tropical Riesling is made from low-yielding vines in the estate's Herrenberg vineyard.

○ **Maximin Grünhäuser Herrenberg Superior Riesling** / 2009 / Mosel / $$$$ An impressive intensity marks this steely, apple- and peach-flavored Riesling.

MÜLLER-CATOIR

This Pfalz winery shook up the German wine world in the 1980s by producing stellar dry whites from unfashionable grapes. Thanks to the brilliant, influential cellarmaster Hans-Günther Schwarz, Müller-Catoir became known for extraordinary wines made from Pinot Gris, Scheurebe and Rieslaner as well as Riesling. Winemaker Martin Franzen continues the tradition today, and all farming is now organic.

○ **Müller-Catoir Riesling Trocken** / 2009 / Pfalz / $$ A mix of loamy gravel and clay soils yields this zippy, bone-dry wine with grassy citrus and apple notes and a slight spritz.

REICHSGRAF VON KESSELSTATT

Manager Annegret Reh-Gartner and winemaker Wolfgang Mertes can afford to be choosy about which vineyards they showcase in single-site cuvées: With nearly 90 acres of vines in enviable locations along the Mosel, Saar and Ruwer rivers, this is one of the largest of Germany's top wine estates. Their single-vineyard wines offer compelling individuality, whereas blends from multiple vineyards deliver terrific quality for the price.

○ **Reichsgraf von Kesselstatt Josephshöfer Riesling Kabinett** / 2009 / Mosel / $$ A light, minerally, herb-inflected wine with peach flavors that stop just shy of sweet.

○ **Reichsgraf von Kesselstatt Piesporter Goldtröpfchen Riesling Kabinett** / 2009 / Mosel / $$ A warm vintage added extra ripeness and spice to this graphite- and slate-flavored wine.

○ **Reichsgraf von Kesselstatt Scharzhofberger Riesling Spätlese** / 2009 / Mosel / $$$ Its rich flavors of candied strawberry and peach linger on the palate.

SCHLOSS JOHANNISBERG

This historic Rheingau estate produces some of the world's longest-lived Rieslings. Founded around 1100, Schloss Johannisberg was given to the famed diplomat Prince Klemens von Metternich by Emperor Franz I of Austria in 1816. The estate remained in the Metternich family until 2006, when it was sold to the Oetker family, German packaged-food magnates.

○ **Schloss Johannisberger Erstes Gewächs Silberlack Riesling** / 2009 / Rheingau / $$$$ This first-growth (or Erstes Gewächs, as it's called in Rheingau) wine is intense and vibrant, with a broad palate of apple, quince and minerals.

○ **Schloss Johannisberger Riesling Spätlese** / 2009 / Rheingau / $$$$ Nicknamed Grünlack (green label), this amazingly complex, creamy-textured wine brims with flavors of orange, stone and flowers.

SELBACH-OSTER

This famous Mosel estate was founded in 1961 by Hans Selbach, whose family runs a well-known *négociant* firm and has been making wine since the 1600s. His small winery initially relied on a historic five-acre estate vineyard, but today son Johannes works with nearly 46 acres of superlative, steeply terraced estate vines—including legendary sites such as the Sonnenuhr in both Zeltingen and Wehlen—to make his masterful Rieslings.

○ **Selbach-Oster Riesling Kabinett** / 2009 / Mosel / $$ Impressively graceful and bright, with a slaty minerality accenting ripe, juicy apple notes.

○ **Selbach-Oster Zeltinger Sonnenuhr Riesling Spätlese** / 2009 / Mosel / $$ This truly opulent wine from a famous Mosel vineyard shows bold fruit offset by minerals.

WEINGUT JOSEF LEITZ

Josef Leitz got his winemaking start working out of a cellar attached to his family's home in suburban Rüdesheim (an old Rheingau wine town). His stunning Rieslings quickly made him one of the brightest stars of the modern German wine industry. Now installed in a sparkling-new facility, Leitz turns out a range of Rheingau Rieslings offering both terrific value (the Eins Zwei Dry bottling, for one) and extraordinary quality.

○ **Leitz Dragonstone Riesling** / 2010 / Rheingau / $$
Full of slightly sweet lemon chiffon and cherry flavors.
○ **Leitz Eins Zwei Dry 3 Riesling** / 2009 / Rheingau / $$
A consistent value from the stellar Geisenheimer Rothenberg
vineyard, this is bursting with grapefruit and floral aromas.
○ **Weingut Leitz Rüdesheimer Klosterlay Riesling Kabinett** /
2010 / Rheingau / $$ This wine's fragrant melon, strawberry
and crushed-stone flavors are succulent and intense.

WEINGUT REICHSRAT VON BUHL

The Reichsrat von Buhl estate landed in capable hands when
businessman Achim Niederberger bought it in 2005—a lucky
break for a winery that's one of the most historic names in the
Pfalz. An expert team is making the most of von Buhl's 150
acres, which include some prime Pfalz sites. Now organically
farmed, the estate is a fine source for Riesling.

○ **Reichsrat von Buhl Armand Riesling Kabinett** / 2009 / Pfalz /
$$ Juicy, with mouthwatering acidity firming up peach, yellow
apple and mineral flavors.
○ **Reichsrat von Buhl Maria Schneider Jazz Riesling** / 2009 /
Pfalz / $$ Its hint of sweetness is perfectly balanced, filled out
with tangy peach, lime and mineral layers.

WEINGUT ROBERT WEIL

Star Rheingau winemaker Wilhelm Weil made radical changes
when he took over his family's estate in 1987, like picking a
vineyard 17 separate times in order to harvest only perfectly ripe
grapes. The resulting wines are some of Germany's most prized.
His finest come from three superb vineyards near the town of
Kiedrich; grapes from other sites go into two entry-level blends.

○ **Weingut Robert Weil Riesling Trocken** / 2008 / Rheingau / $$
Full of crisp yet slightly sweet lime and green apple flavors.
○ **Weingut Robert Weil Kiedrich Turmberg Riesling Trocken** /
2009 / Rheingau / $$$ An excellent growing site yields the
small, intensely flavored grapes that give this bone-dry Riesling
its bold apple and grapefruit flavors and complex minerality.
○ **Weingut Robert Weil Kiedrich Gräfenberg Riesling Spätlese** /
2008 / Rheingau / $$$$ An incredibly ripe Spätlese with
succulent layers of strawberry and peach.

Austria
Wine Region

Austria's superb wines are now
well known, thanks to the success
of Grüner Veltliner, the country's
leading white. Grüner's fresh
citrus and peppery flavors and its
versatility with food have made
it a staple on top restaurant lists
across the U.S. Austria's finest reds,
Zweigelt and Blaufränkisch, are
more obscure, but they shouldn't be:
Supple and fruity, with juicy
acidity, they're much easier to drink
than to pronounce.

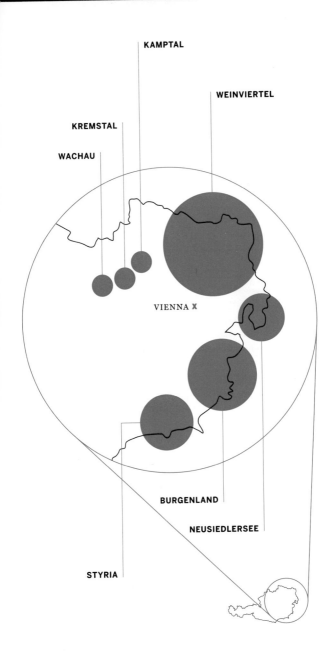

KAMPTAL

WEINVIERTEL

KREMSTAL

WACHAU

VIENNA

BURGENLAND

NEUSIEDLERSEE

STYRIA

Austria

AUSTRIA'S GREAT WHITE wines come mainly from the province of Lower Austria (Niederösterreich), where the small Wachau region is responsible for most of the country's richest Grüner Veltliners and Rieslings. The neighboring Kremstal area also makes stellar examples. For similar wines at more-modest prices, look to Kamptal. One of Austria's warmest areas, Burgenland produces most of the country's reds (and many great dessert wines). Styria (Steiermark) makes vivid whites from Sauvignon Blanc, Chardonnay and Welschriesling.

AUSTRIAN GRAPES & STYLES

High in minerals and acidity and full of expressive fruit flavors, Austrian whites are among the world's most exciting wines. The nation's signature grape is Grüner Veltliner, a crisp, peppery white (often called simply Grüner in the U.S.). Its finest examples improve over time, gaining notes of honey and smoke.

Riesling is Austria's second most important quality white grape. Austrian Rieslings tend to be drier and fuller-bodied than those of Germany and fruitier than Alsatian versions. Welschriesling (not related to Riesling) makes simple whites; Müller-Thurgau (Rivaner) makes mostly bulk wines. Of the international grapes, Chardonnay, sometimes called Morillon here, has had the most success, though Sauvignon Blanc (Muskat-Sylvaner) plantings are increasing. Pinot Blanc (Weissburgunder) makes many of Burgenland's dessert wines and some great dry wines. The rare Gelber Muskateller is wonderfully floral.

While most Austrian wines feature a single variety, some vintners craft traditional field blends (*gemischter satz*). For these cuvées, winemakers grow and ferment different grape varieties together, rather than blending them after fermentation.

Red wines are gaining ground in Austria. Juicy, cherry-tinged Zweigelt is by far the most well known, followed by Blaufränkisch, which makes spicy, medium-bodied wines. Bottlings of the lush, smoky St-Laurent variety are also worth seeking out.

AUSTRIAN WINE LABELS

Most Austrian wines list grape and region and use a quality system similar to Germany's Qualitätswein (see p. 134), although Austrian standards are often higher. The Wachau area uses its own classification: Steinfeder are light wines, Federspiel are heavier and Smaragd are capable of long aging. Other common words include *weingut* (winery) and *ried* (vineyard). Austria recently introduced the Districtus Austria Controllatus (DAC) system; DAC wines are thought to represent the unique styles of their regions, and today there are seven appellations.

Producers/ Austria

DOMÄNE WACHAU

Domäne Wachau is one of those rare large cooperatives known for quality. Members farm one-third of the vineyards in the Wachau (nearly 1,100 acres). Prime grapes go into Domäne Wachau's accessibly priced Terrassen and Einzellagen tiers; the best of these wines are on a par with the Wachau's finest.

○ **Domäne Wachau Terrassen Grüner Veltliner Federspiel** / 2010 / Wachau / $ Terrassen bottlings come from terraced vineyards, which yield intense, focused wines, like this citrusy example.

F.X. PICHLER

F.X. Pichler's Rieslings and Grüner Veltliners inspire cultlike devotion, thanks to their phenomenal depth, concentration and penetrating minerality. Pichler's top wines come from Austria's most famous vineyards and are snapped up by collectors around the world. Easier to find are the fresh, enticing Federspiel cuvées. All are made by Lucas Pichler, son of the eponymous Franz Xaver.

○ **F.X. Pichler Urgestein Terrassen Grüner Veltliner Smaragd /
2009 / Wachau / $$$** Savory and mineral-laden, with a lemon-curd richness, prickly acidity and a silky texture.

○ **F.X. Pichler Loibner Steinertal Riesling Smaragd / 2009 /
Wachau / $$$$** From a small vineyard on the Wachau's eastern end, this shows bold floral, slate and peach flavors.

LOIMER

Among Austria's most progressive vintners, Fred Loimer crafts single-vineyard wines that are some of Kamptal's best, plus four affordable bottlings made from purchased grapes under the Fred Loimer label. Specializing in Riesling and Grüner Veltliner, Loimer recently made the switch to biodynamic farming.

○ **Fred Loimer Lenz Riesling / 2009 / Kamptal / $$**
This fresh, apple-inflected white is a perfect summer sipper.

○ **Loimer Grüner Veltliner / 2009 / Kamptal / $$**
A satiny, herbal, citrusy wine that offers a taste of Loimer's refined style at an affordable price.

NIKOLAIHOF-WACHAU

This acclaimed Wachau estate was officially founded in AD 985, and its wine cellar was once a Roman crypt. The Saahs family's methods have changed little in the two centuries or so since they purchased it from the Catholic Church. Their outstanding small-lot cuvées are made from old vines and display terrific purity.

○ **Nikolaihof Hefeabzug Grüner Veltliner / 2009 / Wachau / $$**
Aging on its lees gives this white a creamy texture that is nicely offset by crisp, spicy citrus notes.

○ **Nikolaihof Vom Stein Riesling Smaragd / 2008 /
Wachau / $$$$** Vom Stein cuvées come from select parcels chosen for their intense stone-fruit and rich mineral flavors.

RUDI PICHLER

Since taking over his family's winery in 1997, Rudi Pichler has steadily transformed it into one of the Wachau's very best. A signature and somewhat unorthodox technique he uses is letting freshly pressed grape juice macerate with the skins after crushing. It gives his savory, minerally Rieslings and Grüner Veltliners complex aromatics and a characteristic firmness.

O **Rudi Pichler Wösendorfer Kollmütz Grüner Veltliner Smaragd / 2008 / Wachau / $$$** The grapes for this extremely fine Grüner hail from a rocky, terraced site that imparts pronounced mineral flavors and a distinctive smokiness.

SALOMON UNDHOF

Situated along the Danube in Kremstal, this legendary winery was a medieval monastery called Undhof. The Salomon family purchased it in 1792, and they were among the first in the region to bottle their own wines and to focus on dry whites. Today their offerings include the fruity, accessible Sal'mon tier and benchmark cuvées from such top vineyards as Pfaffenberg and Kögl.

O **Salomon Undhof Lindberg Erste Lage Reserve Grüner Veltliner / 2009 / Kremstal / $$$** This dense first-growth (*erste lage*) cuvée offers white pepper and grapefruit notes.

O **Salomon Undhof Steiner Kögl Erste Lage Reserve Riesling / 2009 / Kremstal / $$$** Old vines are behind this Riesling's especially concentrated peach and citrus flavors.

SCHLOSS GOBELSBURG

Former hotelier Michael Moosbrugger partnered with star winemaker Willi Bründlmayer (see p. 146) in 1996 to lease Schloss Gobelsburg, a Kamptal farm with many old vineyards. Bründlmayer is no longer involved day-to-day, but Moosbrugger learned well from his mentor: Schloss Gobelsburg is a source of some of Austria's most brilliant white and red wines.

O **Weingut Schloss Gobelsburg Lamm Erste Lage Reserve Grüner Veltliner / 2009 / Kamptal / $$$** A rich, structured bottling with robust tropical flavors and a spicy finish.

● **Gobelsburger Cistercien Rosé / 2010 / Kamptal / $$** A crisp, cherry-flavored blend of Zweigelt and St-Laurent.

WEINBAU HEIDI SCHRÖCK

The Burgenland town of Rüst is famous for its sumptuous sweet wines, called Rüster Ausbruch. Vintner Heidi Schröck produces some of the best examples of these at her small estate. But it's her fabulous dry cuvées that have vaulted her to stardom; made with grapes such as Weissburgunder and Grauburgunder (Pinot Gris), they expertly balance silkiness and spice, delicacy and lushness.

○ **Heidi Schroeck Weissburgunder / 2009 / Burgenland / $$**
Made entirely with Pinot Blanc, this elegant wine has a creamy texture offset by chalky minerality.

WEINGUT BRÜNDLMAYER

Willi Bründlmayer has run this organically farmed 200-acre Kamptal estate for the past three decades. Seven Grüner Veltliners and five Rieslings form the core of the magnificent portfolio; some of Bründlmayer's reds are aged in acacia, a practice championed by him that is becoming increasingly common.

○ **Weingut Bründlmayer Kamptaler Terrassen Grüner Veltliner / 2009 / Kamptal / $$** A zesty, citrus-inflected white marked by delicate notes of stone and spice.

○ **Weingut Bründlmayer Käferberg Erste Lage Reserve Grüner Veltliner / 2009 / Kamptal / $$$$** Käferberg's famous south-facing vineyard yields ripe, deeply flavored grapes, on display in this brilliant, apple-inflected offering.

● **Weingut Bründlmayer Langenloiser Zweigelt Rosé / 2010 / Kamptal / $$** A juicy, dry rosé with graceful strawberry and watermelon flavors that are bright and refreshing.

WEINGUT ERICH & MICHAELA BERGER

Erich and Michaela Berger specialize in charming, affordable Grüner Veltliners. Based just east of the town of Krems, they farm 44 acres of vines planted mainly in terraces of loess, a fine, loose gray soil that's ideal for bringing out Grüner's expressive flavors. Their basic offerings—sold in liter bottles with crown caps—are always delicious, but the trade up to their small-lot cuvées is worth the jump in price.

○ **Berger Grüner Veltliner** / 2010 / **Niederösterreich** / $
(1L) Sealed with an easy-to-pop crown cap, this zesty one-liter bottling makes a great summer white.

○ **Berger Gebling Reserve Grüner Veltliner** / 2009 / **Kremstal** / $$
This is a gorgeously balanced Grüner, with satiny layers of mineral-tinged ripe apple flavors.

WEINGUT HIRSCH

Johannes Hirsch started helping run his family's Kamptal winery when he was in his 20s and promptly ripped out every red variety growing in their vineyards—never mind that Hirsch's reds counted among the region's best. Unafraid to innovate, he converted to biodynamic farming and was the first Austrian to use screw caps for his entire portfolio, which now consists of compelling, wonderfully pure Grüner Veltliners and Rieslings.

○ **Hirsch Heiligenstein Grüner Veltliner** / 2009 / **Kamptal** / $$
An especially vivid Grüner Veltliner, packed with apple and pear flavors and a hint of gingersnap.

○ **Hirsch Veltliner #1** / 2009 / **Kamptal** / $$
Easily spotted by its quirky reindeer label, Hirsch's basic Grüner is fragrant, juicy and squeaky clean.

○ **Hirsch Lamm Grüner Veltliner** / 2009 / **Kamptal** / $$$
Voluptuously styled, this features enough acidity to keep its lush pear and citrus flavors fresh.

WEINGUT PRAGER

Ilse Prager's husband, Vienna-born biologist-turned-winemaker Toni Bodenstein, has made Prager into one of the Wachau's most sought-after names. The estate's flagship bottlings come from the Achleiten vineyard, a revered ancient site planted with Riesling and Grüner Veltliner. Its newest vineyards are in far cooler, high-elevation sites—conditions that help preserve the wines' bright flavors and acidity.

○ **Prager Achleiten Grüner Veltliner Smaragd** / 2009 / **Wachau** / $$$ The Achleiten vineyard is known for yielding mineral-rich whites; this stunning wine is no exception.

○ **Prager Klaus Riesling Smaragd** / 2009 / **Wachau** / $$$$
Power and sophistication are the hallmarks of this exceptional grapefruit- and mineral-flavored wine.

Greece / Wine Region

Greek wines are finally starting to receive the critical acclaim they deserve. There are thousands of years of winemaking history here, but radical quality improvements over the past few decades have transformed Greece's wines. Now, citrusy, mineral-laden white wines and distinctive, food-friendly reds—most made with indigenous grape varieties—have propelled Greece to the front ranks of the world's up-and-coming wine-producing regions.

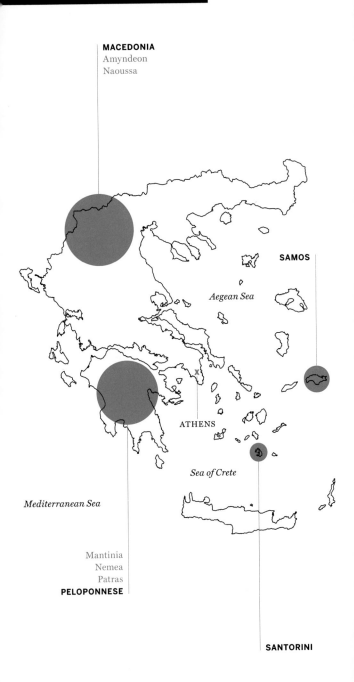

MACEDONIA
Amyndeon
Naoussa

SAMOS

Aegean Sea

ATHENS

Sea of Crete

Mediterranean Sea

Mantinia
Nemea
Patras
PELOPONNESE

SANTORINI

Greece

ALTHOUGH GREECE HAS been producing wine for 4,000 years, decades of churning out forgettable, resin-flavored wines damaged its modern reputation. Fortunately, Greece is once again focused on quality, an effort aided by the country's admission to the European Union in 1981. Today Greece makes incredibly good wine, most of it crafted economically from grape varieties native to this sun-drenched country.

Top-notch regions include the Peloponnese, the go-to zone for aromatic red wines made from Agiorgitiko and for fresh, floral whites. The Nemea subregion makes great reds; Mantinia is known for whites. Volcanic Santorini island makes the nation's finest whites—complex, mineral-laden bottlings. In northern Greece, Macedonia turns out young and fruity reds as well as tannic, ageworthy examples; look for wines from Naoussa, the region's finest appellation, and from neighboring Amyndeon.

GREEK GRAPES & STYLES

Of the hundreds of grapes cultivated in Greece, the Assyrtiko grape is one of the best. A Santorini native, it yields bone-dry, mineral-rich whites. Peloponnesian Moscofilero stands out for crisp, low-alcohol white and rosé wines with floral, slightly spicy qualities reminiscent of the Alsace Gewurztraminer variety.

Other whites worth mentioning include Athiri, which yields succulent, citrusy wines; Robola, the same grape as Friuli's Ribolla Gialla; Malagousia, a recently revived variety that makes satiny, peachy whites; and Roditis, which, while used chiefly in bulk wine, produces charming, floral whites in the Peloponnese's Patras appellation. The most widely planted grape is Savatiano, used to make the well-known pine resin–flavored retsina.

Many of the best reds are made from Agiorgitiko (also called St. George), which offers a lush texture and juicy cherry flavors. Styles range from fresh rosés and elegant dry reds to wines with richness and depth of fruit. Bigger, bolder reds come from Macedonia's tannic Xinomavro grape. Sauvignon Blanc, Chardonnay, Merlot and Cabernet Sauvignon appear in Greece, but vintners typically use them in blends with their prized native grapes.

GREEK WINE LABELS

Regions typically take priority over the grape names on most labels. Naoussa reds are required to be made from the Xinomavro grape, and those from Nemea are produced with Agiorgitiko. Mantinia wines must be at least 85 percent Moscofilero, whereas Santorini's wines are dominated by Assyrtiko.

Producers/ Greece

ARGYROS

Exhilarating Assyrtikos and lusciously sweet Vinsantos are the hallmarks of this Santorini estate. Current proprietor Yiannis Argyros inherited his family's winery in the 1970s and turned it into one of Greece's best. The entry-level Atlantis line includes an Assyrtiko, a rosé and a silky red from the Mandelaria grape.

○ **Estate Argyros Assyrtiko** / 2010 / Santorini / $$
Old vines provide the mouthwatering intensity in this white's mineral-inflected apple and anise flavors.

○ **Estate Argyros Atlantis White** / 2010 / Cyclades / $$
Made mostly from the Assyrtiko grape, this crisp, citrusy blend gets a floral hint from a bit of Athiri.

BOUTARI

A progressive, family-owned company, Boutari was founded in Naoussa in 1879. Its portfolio, which features wines from the best wine regions all over Greece, offers a snapshot of the country's phenomenal diversity. The winery's flagship bottling, the Grande Reserve Naoussa, is Greece's most famous example of the Xinomavro grape. Look also for Boutari's fresh, sunny Santorini white and its plummy Nemea red.

● **Boutari Grande Reserve Naoussa / 2004 / Naoussa / $$**
Just beginning to integrate its firm tannins and earthy licorice and cherry tones, this will benefit from more age.

DOMAINE GEROVASSILIOU

One of Greece's most respected vintners, Evangelos Gerovassiliou studied winemaking in Bordeaux in the 1970s and became a protégé of wine guru Émile Peynaud. In the 1980s Gerovassiliou helped launch Greece's wine revolution with his Macedonia estate. Though he has always grown some French varieties, Gerovassiliou has been instrumental in demonstrating the potential of native varieties.

> **WINE INTEL**
> The Malagousia grape was nearly extinct when Gerovassiliou started reviving it 30 years ago. It's now the source of many deliciously silky peach- and spice-flavored white wines.

○ **Domaine Gerovassiliou Malagousia / 2009 / Epanomi / $$**
This shows fragrant honeysuckle and lush peach flavors.

○ **Domaine Gerovassiliou Fumé Sauvignon Blanc / 2009 / Epanomi / $$$** Made in an ambitious, concentrated style, it has creamy oak and crisp, tropical fruit notes.

● **Domaine Gerovassiliou Avaton / 2005 / Epanomi / $$$**
A muscular, leathery blend of three indigenous Greek varieties: Limnio, Mavroudi and Mavrotragano.

DOMAINE SIGALAS

A mathematician, Santorini vintner Paris Sigalas started his winery in 1992 as a hobby. It's now one of the country's leading estates, famous for its incredibly focused, minerally Assyrtikos and elegant red wines made from indigenous grapes. Domaine Sigalas boasts very old vines, all of which are organically farmed and woven into round tangles resembling birds' nests (the shape protects the vines from the island's high winds).

○ **Sigalas Asirtiko-Athiri / 2010 / Santorini / $$**
This delicious lemon- and kiwi-inflected blend offers lovely weight and a crisp, minerally freshness.

○ **Sigalas Assyrtiko / 2010 / Santorini / $$**
Dense yet not heavy, this zippy Assyrtiko has a chalky minerality and savory lemon flavors that linger on the palate.

DOMAINE SKOURAS

Trained in France, George Skouras was among the first in Greece to blend the plush Agiorgitiko grape with Cabernet Sauvignon. The result, an elegant red that Skouras baptized Megas Oenos (great wine), has lived up to its name, becoming one of the definitive bottlings of the current Greek wine renaissance. Based in Nemea, Skouras works with both native and French grapes and turns out many top-quality, affordable wines.

○ **Domaine Skouras Moscofilero / 2010 / Peloponnese / $**
An expressive honeysuckle nose and zesty citrus palate define this charming, summer-perfect white.

● **Domaine Skouras Red St. George–Cabernet Sauvignon / 2009 / Peloponnese / $** This shows Beaujolais-like fresh cherry flavors. (St. George is an anglicization of Agiorgitiko.)

● **Domaine Skouras Megas Oenos / 2007 / Peloponnese / $$**
An elegant, violet-scented blend of Agiorgitiko and Cabernet.

GAIA WINES

Yiannis Paraskevopoulos was working for Boutari when he was sent to Santorini to research vineyards. A Bordeaux-trained vintner with a PhD in enology, Paraskevopoulos then founded Gaia with another vineyard expert, Leon Karatsalos. Their expressive Assyrtikos made the brand an instant success. Today they're even better known for refined Agiorgitikos from Nemea.

○ **Gai'a Wild Ferment Assyrtiko / 2010 / Santorini / $$$**
Concentrated and infused with ripe melon flavors, this rich Assyrtiko is made with fruit from 80-year-old vines.

● **Agiorgitiko by Gai'a / 2008 / Nemea / $$**
Its berry, grapefruit and cedar flavors are bold yet balanced.

● **Gaia Estate / 2006 / Nemea / $$$**
The winery's top cuvée, this beautiful red offers velvety plum and herb notes woven with a chalky minerality.

NEW
WOR

United
States/
Australia/
New
Zealand/
Argentina/
Chile/
South
Africa

156
UNITED
STATES

236
ARGENTINA

LD

210 AUSTRALIA

226 NEW ZEALAND

244 CHILE

252 SOUTH AFRICA

United States

Wine Region

The United States has now surpassed France as the world's largest consumer of wine. That's especially significant for American winemakers, since over 65 percent of what we drink in the U.S. comes from our own vineyards. California still far outstrips the rest of the nation in terms of production, but wine lovers these days are delving into wines from other states as well. Oregon and Washington are chief among these.

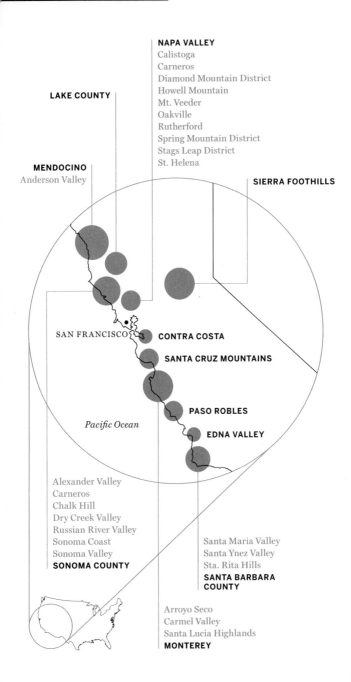

NAPA VALLEY
Calistoga
Carneros
Diamond Mountain District
Howell Mountain
Mt. Veeder
Oakville
Rutherford
Spring Mountain District
Stags Leap District
St. Helena

LAKE COUNTY

MENDOCINO
Anderson Valley

SIERRA FOOTHILLS

SAN FRANCISCO

CONTRA COSTA

SANTA CRUZ MOUNTAINS

Pacific Ocean

PASO ROBLES

EDNA VALLEY

Alexander Valley
Carneros
Chalk Hill
Dry Creek Valley
Russian River Valley
Sonoma Coast
Sonoma Valley
SONOMA COUNTY

Santa Maria Valley
Santa Ynez Valley
Sta. Rita Hills
**SANTA BARBARA
COUNTY**

Arroyo Seco
Carmel Valley
Santa Lucia Highlands
MONTEREY

United States

CALIFORNIA REMAINS AMERICA'S viticultural powerhouse, producing about 90 percent of the nation's wine, with Washington, New York and Oregon accounting for most of the rest. The temperate West Coast makes fine wine from European *Vitis vinifera* varieties (grapes such as Chardonnay, Cabernet Sauvignon, Pinot Noir). Other parts of the country with cold, harsh winters once grew only the hardier native American *Vitis labrusca* varieties but have since switched to European varieties and hybrids; winemakers in New York and Virginia have been leading the way. The classic American style, which often emphasizes bold flavors over subtlety, with ripe fruit and the generous use of oak, is also changing: Many of today's American wines are exhibiting more nuance and *terroir*.

UNITED STATES WINE LABELS

Most U.S. labels list the winery name, vintage, grape and official wine region, or AVA (American Viticultural Area). Unlike some European designations, AVAs don't stipulate how a wine must be made, which grapes may be used or the maximum yields allowed per vineyard. Rather, U.S. law dictates that a wine labeled with an AVA must contain at least 85 percent grapes from that region. If an AVA wine lists a vintage date, 95 percent of the fruit must be from that year's harvest. Wines with the name of one grape, often called varietal wines, must contain 75 percent of that variety. Some states go beyond these requirements. Oregon, for example, mandates a higher minimum percentage for most varietal wines and for geographic designations.

The labels of some of the best U.S. wines, however, don't indicate any variety. Blends of various Bordeaux grapes sometimes carry the legally recognized moniker Meritage (pronounced like "heritage"), although many producers use a proprietary name instead—for instance, Mondavi's "Opus One." The term *reserve* has no legal definition but generally connotes wines of higher quality. There is no official meaning for the phrase *old vines*, which is seen most often on California Zinfandel.

CALIFORNIA

California sunshine is a mixed blessing for viticulture. Producers struggle to find areas that are cool enough to keep grapes from ripening too fast and thus ensure proper flavor development. Some of the best wines are made in coastal regions tempered by Pacific breezes, as well as in high-elevation vineyards. California happens to have a bounty of such areas all along its coast.

CALIFORNIA: AN OVERVIEW

The northernmost of California's important wine regions is the North Coast, which includes Napa, Sonoma, Mendocino and Lake counties. Mendocino's Anderson Valley provides the perfect climate for Chardonnay and Pinot Noir as well as for high-quality sparkling wines (see p. 270). In Sonoma, the legendary Alexander, Russian River and Dry Creek valleys are home to elegant Chardonnays, spicy Zinfandels and fruity Sauvignon Blancs. East of Sonoma is the smaller yet more renowned Napa Valley, where the country's greatest Cabernets and Bordeaux-style blends are made. Nearby, Carneros makes great Chardonnays, Pinot Noirs and sparkling wines. The vast Central Coast region grows a range of grapes. Generally speaking, Pinot Noir and Chardonnay do well throughout this area; Zinfandel and France's Rhône grapes—Syrah, Grenache, Mourvèdre and Viognier—also produce some superb wines here. Farther inland, east of San Francisco Bay, Lodi, in the Central Valley, and the Sierra Foothills region are famous for old-vine Zinfandels.

❦ CALIFORNIA GRAPES & STYLES

California's diverse terrain gives its winemakers the freedom to grow an array of grapes and to craft wines in many styles. Chardonnay, the state's most planted grape, makes wines that range from rich and heavily oaked to refreshing and mineral-laden.

Sauvignon Blanc in California shows tropical fruit and citrus flavors that distinguish it from grassier New Zealand versions. And Pinot Grigio, grown throughout the state, produces some delicious, citrusy wines, particularly from cooler regions. Rhône varieties include Viognier and, in small amounts, Marsanne and Roussanne. The most widely planted white grape after Chardonnay is actually French Colombard, used mostly in bulk wine.

As for rosé, California turns out plenty of sweet blush wines mostly made from the red Zinfandel grape. Today more quality-focused producers are turning their attention to classically styled dry rosé, often crafted from Grenache, Syrah or Pinot Noir.

Cabernet Sauvignon put California on the international map back in the 1970s and it remains the state's iconic wine, with complex, ageworthy examples from Napa Valley setting the standard. Merlot, hurt by massive overproduction in the late 1990s, has bounced back in quality and, less quickly, prestige—which means shrewd shoppers can find great Merlots that are less expensive than Cabernets but no less sophisticated.

Rhône reds, led by Syrah and often blended with Grenache and/or Mourvèdre, thrive in the California sun, particularly in the so-called Rhône Zone around Paso Robles, in California's Central Coast. Syrah's style follows the climate, with taut, elegant versions coming out of cooler regions like Santa Barbara and lush, fruitier bottlings hailing from warmer areas such as Paso Robles. Petite Sirah can also do well, although winemakers use it mostly to add color and tannin to blends.

The best Pinot Noirs come from the state's cool coastal regions, including western Sonoma, the Anderson Valley and Santa Barbara County. And although Zinfandel is not a native grape (it's an obscure Croatian grape), its long-established relationship with the state gives it a unique American identity. Sonoma's Dry Creek Valley produces spicy, jammy examples.

California today is a hotbed of experimentation. A small number of vintners are working with Italian grapes such as Sangiovese, Barbera, Dolcetto and Malvasia Bianca. Tempranillo, Spain's calling-card variety, also has been finding adherents.

Producers/ California

AU BON CLIMAT WINERY

Jim Clendenen's minerally, elegant Pinot Noir and Chardonnay wines helped earn wider recognition for Santa Barbara back when the area was best known as a setting for daytime soap operas and vacationing presidents (Ronald Reagan). Grapes for his Au Bon Climat bottlings come mostly from Bien Nacido, a famous vineyard in the Central Coast's breezy Santa Maria Valley subregion. Clendenen Family Vintners, his second label, includes small-production wines from estate-grown grapes.

- ○ **Au Bon Climat Hildegard / 2007 / Santa Maria Valley / $$$** Mostly Pinot Gris and Pinot Blanc, this luscious, melony white is named after Charlemagne's wife.
- ● **Au Bon Climat Knox Alexander Pinot Noir / 2008 / Santa Maria Valley / $$$** This soft, herb-accented Pinot comes from the famed Bien Nacido Vineyard.
- ● **Clendenen Family Vineyards Bien Nacido Estate Plantings Petit Verdot / 2005 / Santa Maria Valley / $$$** A minor Bordeaux blending grape gets a starring role in this firmly tannic, blueberry-inflected red.

BEAULIEU VINEYARD

This historic winery produces one of California's iconic Cabernet Sauvignons, Georges de Latour Private Reserve. One of California's largest-volume producers, Beaulieu is again among the greats, thanks to winemaker Jeffrey Stambor's renewed focus on quality. Beaulieu's Reserve line and Appellation-tier bottlings offer good quality at reasonable prices.

- ○ **Beaulieu Vineyard Chardonnay / 2009 / Carneros / $$** Made in a toasty, ripe style, this Chardonnay is part of Beaulieu's Napa Valley Collection.
- ● **Beaulieu Vineyard Cabernet Sauvignon / 2007 / Rutherford / $$** Firm and earthy, with leather and meat flavors, BV's 2007 Cabernet is drinking beautifully right now.

BECKMEN VINEYARDS

Most of Beckmen's Rhône-style wines come from one spectacular vineyard on Purisima Mountain, in Santa Ynez Valley. Planted by Tom Beckmen in 1996, the vineyard is now farmed biodynamically. Tom's winemaker son Steve and his team (led by Mikael Sigouin) offer fascinating varietal wines and Rhône-style blends.

● **Beckmen Vineyards Purisima Mountain Vineyard Clone #1 Syrah / 2008 / Santa Ynez Valley / $$$** Limestone soils impart minerality to this burly, concentrated red.

● **Beckman Vineyards Purisima Mountain Vineyard Syrah / 2008 / Santa Ynez Valley / $$$** Packed with the spicy dark fruit and bold structure typical of mountain-grown Syrah.

BERINGER VINEYARDS

Founded in 1876, Beringer is the oldest continuously operating winery in Napa Valley. Today's Beringer wines owe much to the 25-year tenure of winemaker Ed Sbragia. Protégé Laurie Hook now oversees the portfolio, which delivers quality across a broad spectrum, from blush wine to the storied Beringer Private Reserve.

○ **Beringer Alluvium Blanc White Wine / 2009 / Knights Valley / $$** Sauvignon Blanc and Sémillon make up the bulk of this richly textured citrus- and melon-flavored white.

● **Beringer Private Reserve Cabernet Sauvignon / 2007 / Napa Valley / $$$$** Powerful but refined, the 2007 Private Reserve shows decadent layers of ripe blackberries and cedar.

BERNARDUS WINERY

Former Olympic skeet shooter and race-car driver Bernardus Pon embraces traditional winemaking techniques such as fermenting in oak tanks at this Carmel Valley winery. The Bordeaux-style blend Marinus is the producer's showpiece; the basic Monterey County Chardonnay and Pinot Noir are great values.

○ **Bernardus Griva Vineyard Sauvignon Blanc / 2009 / Arroyo Seco / $$** Bright citrus and fresh grass flavors are countered by a tropical richness in this balanced white.

● **Bernardus Marinus / 2007 / Carmel Valley / $$** This muscular Bordeaux-style blend shows loads of cedary oak, dark fruit and lingering herb notes.

BONNY DOON VINEYARD

Iconoclastic Central Coast vintner Randall Grahm sold his high-volume brands back in 2006. Since then he has returned to his roots, focusing on the Rhône varieties that first made Bonny Doon's reputation in the 1980s. He has continued his foray into Italian and Spanish grapes at the Ca' del Solo estate vineyard.

> **WINE INTEL**
> Randall Grahm consulted with neighbor and Michelin-starred chef David Kinch for the menu at Bonny Doon's terrific café and tasting room, in Santa Cruz, which opened in 2009.

○ **Bonny Doon Vineyard Ca' del Solo Estate Albariño** / 2009 / Monterey / $$ An unusual almond-scented white made with biodynamic grapes.

● **Bonny Doon Vineyard Le Cigare Volant** / 2007 / Central Coast / $$$ A terrifically ripe Grenache-based red, this offers a mix of black cherry, chocolate and dried-herb notes.

BONTERRA VINEYARDS

A leader in eco-friendly farming, midsize Bonterra has been turning out wine made entirely from organic grapes since 1992. Crafted from vineyards in Mendocino and Lake counties, winemaker Bob Blue's wines deliver terrific bang for the buck. The McNabb and Butler biodynamic blends command a premium.

○ **Bonterra Riesling** / 2009 / Lake and Mendocino counties / $ Tangy and fresh, with subtly sweet apple and citrus notes.

● **Bonterra Merlot** / 2008 / Mendocino County / $$ This is a supple, juicy and bright Merlot filled out with herb-infused black currant flavors.

BUENA VISTA WINERY

California's oldest premium winery—founded in 1857 by a Hungarian count—has had its ups and downs over the years, but Buena Vista is on an upswing now, with a range of quality single-vineyard Chardonnay and Pinot Noir wines from the cool Carneros region and an ambitious new owner, Boisset Family Estates.

○ **Buena Vista Carneros Ramal Vineyard Chardonnay** / 2007 / Carneros / $$$ A lemony undertone nicely balances the ripe pear flavors and oak nuances in this delicious Chardonnay.

● **Buena Vista Carneros Pinot Noir** / 2007 / Carneros / $$ Svelte cherry notes mark this engaging entry-level offering.

CAKEBREAD CELLARS

Jack Cakebread launched his winery with the release of a 1973 Napa Valley Chardonnay. The runaway success of that ripe, full-bodied wine fueled Cakebread's growth. Today 450 acres of estate vineyards contribute to a broad range of reds and whites, and though Chardonnay remains a star, winemaker Julianne Laks also has a deft hand with Cabernet and red blends.

○ **Cakebread Cellars Sauvignon Blanc / 2009 / Napa Valley / $$**
Perennially delicious, with a taste of crisp green apple and lime.

● **Cakebread Cellars Dancing Bear Ranch / 2007 / Howell Mountain / $$$$** A streamlined and superbly crafted Cabernet blend grounded with firm black fruit.

CALERA WINE COMPANY

Established 40 miles southeast of Santa Cruz in 1975, Josh Jensen's Calera was named for the remnants of a limestone kiln (*calera* in Spanish) on the vineyard site. Limestone-loving Burgundian grape varieties and Viognier are Calera's specialties, and its pricey Mt. Harlan Chardonnays and Pinot Noirs have made Jensen one of California's most respected vintners. His Central Coast wines, made with purchased fruit, offer terrific value.

● **Calera de Villiers Vineyard Pinot Noir / 2008 / Mt. Harlan / $$$**
The second vintage of this wine is spicy and structured, with ripe cherry and cedary oak.

● **Calera Ryan Vineyard Pinot Noir / 2008 / Mt. Harlan / $$$**
From Calera's highest-altitude vineyard block, this is fragrant and sleek, with tobacco, mineral and red-fruit notes.

CASTLE ROCK WINERY

Founded in 1994, Castle Rock has become one of the most successful U.S. *négociant* brands, thanks to a reputation for great wine at very fair prices. Consultant August "Joe" Briggs (ex–La Crema) helps craft a portfolio that focuses on regional wines from California, Washington and Oregon. Best known for Pinot Noir, Castle Rock also makes a range of other varietal wines.

● **Castle Rock Pinot Noir / 2009 / Mendocino County / $**
Making decent, value-priced Pinot Noir is almost impossible, but Castle Rock pulls it off with this bright, plummy wine.

CAYMUS VINEYARDS

Caymus's flagship wine, a Napa Valley Cabernet called Special Selection that was first produced in 1975, was one of the first cult California Cabs; it remains among the country's benchmark reds, along with Caymus's other Napa Valley Cabernet offering. Chuck Wagner, son of the founders, directs this Rutherford winery, which continues to concentrate on Cabernet Sauvignon.

● Caymus Vineyards Cabernet Sauvignon / 2008 / Napa Valley / $$$$ Dense waves of caramel-tinged oak and black cherries come together in this concentrated Cabernet.

● Caymus Vineyards Special Selection Cabernet Sauvignon / 2008 / Napa Valley / $$$$ This is the first vintage to contain Merlot, which adds a lushness to smoky black cherry flavors.

CHALK HILL ESTATE VINEYARDS & WINERY

This vast Sonoma County estate—home to a winery, a hospitality center, guesthouses and stables—is the most prominent label of Sonoma County's Chalk Hill subregion. Coastal fogs make the area prime territory for such cool-climate grapes as Chardonnay and Sauvignon Blanc, both specialties of the winery. Longtime viticulturist Mark Lingenfelder works with 300 acres of estate vines, the exclusive source for Chalk Hill wines.

○ Chalk Hill Sauvignon Blanc / 2010 / Chalk Hill / $$$
Barrel fermentation contributes weight and vanilla notes to this mouth-filling, melony white.

● Chalk Hill Estate Red / 2007 / Chalk Hill / $$$$
This outstanding Bordeaux-style blend proves the winery has a talent for red wines, not just whites.

CHALONE VINEYARDS

Visionary winemaker Dick Graff made Chalone's first commercial vintage in 1966: the Chardonnay that became the winery's signature. Today alluring Pinot Noir and small amounts of Pinot Blanc, Chenin Blanc and Syrah join the Chardonnay. Chalone is part of Monterey County but has its own Chalone AVA, thanks to its distinctively cool and sunny microclimate.

● Chalone Vineyard Estate Grown Syrah / 2008 / Chalone / $$
A classic Syrah with vibrant red-fruit and peppery notes.

CHAPPELLET VINEYARD & WINERY

Founded by Donn and Molly Chappellet in 1967, this winery was one of the first to focus on Napa Valley's mountain terrain. Grapes come mainly from 100 acres of vines on Pritchard Hill. The cellar-worthy Napa Valley Pritchard Hill bottling is a star; the Chardonnay and Mountain Cuvée red are also highlights.

- **Chappellet "Signature" Cabernet Sauvignon / 2008 / Napa Valley / $$$** Muscular tannins and intense black cherry notes mark this flagship bottling.
- **Chappellet Pritchard Hill Cabernet Sauvignon / 2008 / Napa Valley / $$$$** Concentrated black fruit and chewy tannins give this formidable Cabernet its ability to age.

CHATEAU MONTELENA WINERY

Chateau Montelena vaulted to stardom when its 1973 Napa Valley Chardonnay famously bested prestigious white Burgundies in a 1976 tasting in Paris. It was only the second vintage for the historic Calistoga estate, which had been bought and rehabilitated by Jim Barrett. Son and winemaker Bo Barrett, who is at the helm today, displays a similarly delicate hand with oak.

- ○ **Chateau Montelena Potter Valley Riesling / 2010 / Potter Valley / $$** This lime- and melon-inflected Riesling is the stealth choice in Montelena's Cabernet-driven portfolio.
- **Chateau Montelena Estate Cabernet Sauvignon / 2007 / Calistoga / $$$$** The winery's top offering is this elegant, layered red from estate-owned vineyards in Calistoga.

CHATEAU ST. JEAN

Founded near the town of Kenwood in 1973, Chateau St. Jean turns out a range of wines from across Sonoma County. Winemaker Margo Van Staaveren is especially skilled with Fumé Blanc and Chardonnay. The Sonoma County Chardonnay is a reliable value; the top red is Cinq Cépages, a fine Bordeaux-style blend.

- ○ **Chateau St. Jean Chardonnay / 2009 / Sonoma County / $** A weighty white full of apple, vanilla and tropical flavors.
- ○ **Chateau St. Jean Robert Young Vineyard Chardonnay / 2008 / Alexander Valley / $$** This single-vineyard bottling affirms the site's reputation for elegant, plush, peachy Chardonnays.

CLIFF LEDE VINEYARDS

Canadian Cliff Lede's high-end winery has been getting a lot of attention ever since it was established in Napa's Stags Leap District in 2002. Lede enlisted French winemaker Philippe Melka and equally renowned viticulturalist David Abreu for his all-star team. Together they produce a lively, delicious Sauvignon Blanc and a range of ambitious Cabernet Sauvignons.

● **Cliff Lede Cabernet Sauvignon** / 2008 / Stags Leap District / $$$ Dense, rich blackberry and espresso plus youthful tannin equal the perfect steak wine.
● **Poetry Cabernet Sauvignon** / 2007 / Stags Leap District / $$$$ Sourced from vineyard blocks named after rock songs, this is intensely flavorful and seamlessly rich.

CLINE CELLARS

Exuberant, reasonably priced Zinfandels and Rhône-inspired wines have made this Carneros-based winery a source for value. Owner Fred Cline has access to a large cache of old vines scattered across obscure corners of California, such as in Contra Costa County. Look also for Cline's blends under the Oakley label.

● **Cline Ancient Vines Zinfandel** / 2009 / California / $ A supple, juicy Zin with expressive root beer and red plum flavors layered with notes of oak.
● **Cline Cashmere** / 2009 / California / $ Mourvèdre, Grenache and Syrah yield chocolate and cherry flavors in this lush Rhône-style blend.

CLOS DU BOIS

This Sonoma County–based brand made its name with high-quality, easy-to-love Merlot. Its portfolio today—representing more than a million cases of wine each year—includes the Classic series, the Sonoma-focused Reserves and limited-production offerings such as Marlstone, an elegant Bordeaux-style blend.

○ **Clos du Bois Chardonnay** / 2009 / North Coast / $ Reliably graceful, with bright vanilla, apple and pear tones.
● **Clos du Bois Merlot** / 2007 / North Coast / $ Clos du Bois helped popularize Merlot in the 1980s with plummy, herb-accented bottlings like this one.

CONTINUUM ESTATE

Tim Mondavi, who directed winemaking for his family's legendary Napa Valley winery until its sale, works today with his sister Marcia to oversee Continuum, a superpremium project consisting of a single Cabernet-based red. Grapes come mainly from a prized estate vineyard high on Napa's Pritchard Hill.

● **Continuum / 2008 / Napa Valley / $$$$**
A dark, brooding, well-knit and monumentally structured Bordeaux-style blend that will age beautifully for decades.

COPAIN WINE CELLARS

Copain's winemaker and co-founder, Wells Guthrie, apprenticed with Rhône vintner Michel Chapoutier, which may explain the French sensibility at this Russian River Valley winery. Pinot Noir and Syrah are the focus, and although collectors snatch up its single-vineyard offerings, Copain's Les Voisins and Tous Ensemble bottlings are easier to find—and easier on the wallet.

● **Copain Tous Ensemble Pinot Noir / 2009 / Anderson Valley / $$** A food-friendly Pinot with minerally berry flavors.
● **Copain Tous Ensemble Syrah / 2009 / Mendocino County / $$** Guthrie's entry-level Syrah delivers velvety dark-fruit and sassafras notes edged in white pepper.
● **Copain Les Voisins Pinot Noir / 2009 / Anderson Valley / $$$** A crisp, cherry- and spice-inflected blend of fruit from vineyards in southern Mendocino County.

CUVAISON ESTATE WINES

This eco-friendly, family-owned winery is justly famous for its terrific Chardonnay, sourced from estate vineyards on the Napa side of the Carneros region. Winemaker Steven Rogstad works in a solar-powered facility built in the middle of the vineyard; a Mount Veeder vineyard provides fruit for two Cabernets.

○ **Cuvaison Chardonnay / 2009 / Carneros / $$**
This lush Chardonnay's peach and pear flavors are ripe and nicely balanced, with a touch of vanilla oak.
● **Cuvaison Pinot Noir / 2009 / Carneros / $$$**
Eleven months in oak barrels helped soften this impressively dense and aromatic Pinot.

DANCING BULL WINERY

Part of E & J Gallo Winery, Dancing Bull made its mark by bringing tasty and affordable Zinfandel to the masses. Much credit goes to winemaker Eric Cinnamon, who originally launched the brand under the Rancho Zabaco label. That tier has since evolved to include other red varietals, and white wines have emerged as an important strength for Dancing Bull.

○ **Dancing Bull Chardonnay** / 2009 / California / $
An appealing everyday Chardonnay with ample yellow apple flavors that have just a hint of sweetness.
○ **Dancing Bull Sauvignon Blanc** / 2009 / California / $
Terrific acidity and herb notes define this fresh, citrusy white.

DASHE CELLARS

Winemakers Michael and Anne Dashe founded Dashe Cellars in 1996, the year they married. Their passion is small-lot, single-vineyard Zinfandel, joined by the occasional Grenache, Cabernet and Riesling. Wines under their Les Enfants Terribles label have subtle oak and lower alcohol levels.

○ **Dashe McFadden Farm Riesling** / 2009 / Potter Valley / $$
Subtly sweet with a juicy mix of flowers, apples and citrus.
● **Dashe Todd Brothers Ranch Old Vines Zinfandel** / 2008 / Alexander Valley / $$$ From gnarled, hillside vines near Geyserville, this offers exuberant berry, plum and spice flavors.

DELOACH VINEYARDS

Cecil DeLoach's winery helped pioneer Sonoma Pinot Noir in the 1970s. In 2003 Burgundy's Boisset family purchased the Russian River Valley estate, switching to biodynamic farming and hiring winemaking luminary Greg Lafolette. His protégé, rising star Brian Maloney, now heads the cellar, turning out a range of wines, though Burgundian varietals remain the focus.

○ **DeLoach Chardonnay** / 2009 / Russian River Valley / $$
Maloney aged only about a third of this wine in oak, giving its green apple, lemon and pear tones brightness and precision.
● **DeLoach OFS Pinot Noir** / 2009 / Russian River Valley / $$$
OFS stands for "Our Finest Selection"; here it features alluring spice and berry flavors.

DON SEBASTIANI & SONS

Don Sebastiani's Sonoma *négociant* firm was founded only in 2001, but its high-quality, affordable brands soon became ubiquitous. These include Smoking Loon, SKN (a screw-cap-topped wine) and the new Pepperwood Grove line of 3-liter box wines.

- **Pepperwood Grove Wines The Big Green Box Old Vine Zinfandel / NV / California / $** (3L) This delicious Zin comes in an eco-friendly 3-liter box (the same as four bottles).
- **Project Paso Zinfandel / 2009 / Paso Robles / $** A terrific value, with loads of zippy berries and judicious oak.
- **SKN Merlot / 2008 / Napa Valley / $** This plum-rich Merlot is particularly lush and enjoyable.

DRY CREEK VINEYARD

David Stare set up shop in Sonoma's Dry Creek Valley in 1972, determined to make Loire-inspired wines. Two Loire varieties, Chenin Blanc and Sauvignon Blanc, are used to make the most popular wines in Dry Creek Vineyard's lineup. Zinfandel, including single-vineyard and old-vine bottlings, is also a specialty.

- ○ **Dry Creek Vineyard Dry Chenin Blanc / 2009 / Clarksburg / $** Made with grapes from a vineyard located in the Sacramento–San Joaquin Delta, this features lively citrus tones.
- ○ **Dry Creek Vineyard Foggy Oaks Chardonnay / 2008 / Russian River Valley / $$** Although this Chardonnay spent 14 months in French oak, it is fresh and graceful, with citrusy apple notes.

DUCKHORN VINEYARDS

Rich, layered Napa Valley Merlot and Cabernet are the best-known wines from this estate, established by Dan and Margaret Duckhorn in 1976. Spin-off brands such as Goldeneye and Migration offer Pinot Noir at lower prices. Paraduxx concentrates on unique red blends; affordable varietal wines go by Decoy.

- ○ **Duckhorn Vineyards Sauvignon Blanc / 2009 / Napa Valley / $$** The addition of 25 percent Sémillon adds a waxy richness to this fleshy, tropical white.
- **Duckhorn Vineyards Cabernet Sauvignon / 2007 / Napa Valley / $$$$** About 20 percent of this tobacco- and cherry-flavored Cab is actually Merlot, enhancing its plush texture.

EDMEADES

Dr. Donald Edmeades's neighbors thought he was crazy to plant vines in Anderson Valley in 1963, but the former cardiologist was sure the region could produce spectacular wines. In 1988, he sold his successful winery to Jackson Family Wines. Today this Zinfandel-only label offers powerful cuvées from remarkable sites, such as the 138-year-old Ciapusci Vineyard, as well as an affordable Mendocino bottling.

● **Edmeades Zinfandel / 2008 / Mendocino County / $$**
Winemaker David Ready, Jr., adds some Petite Sirah and Syrah to give this racy, berry-driven Zin its oomph.

● **Edmeades Ciapusci Vineyard Zinfandel / 2007 / Mendocino Ridge / $$$** Terrifically juicy, with energetic plum and licorice flavors and sweet vanilla oak.

EDNA VALLEY VINEYARD

A good part of the vine acreage in the Edna Valley appellation—a cool, green corridor running inland from the Central Coast—belongs to Edna Valley Vineyard. That kind of control over farming gives winemaking team Harry Hansen and Josh Baker a quality edge that shows in their wines, particularly some of their succulent small-lot Chardonnays.

○ **Edna Valley Vineyard Paragon Chardonnay / 2009 / San Luis Obispo County / $** A great everyday white, bursting with refreshing green apple and citrus notes.

● **Edna Valley Vineyard Pinot Noir / 2009 / Edna Valley / $$**
Up-front cherry flavors are layered with herb nuances.

ESSER VINEYARDS

Following his success as the head of a wine-import company as well as of Napa's Cuvaison winery (see p. 168), Manfred Esser established this value-focused label in 2002. Esser's winemaking team often blends different varieties and includes grapes from multiple sources in the wines, which adds complexity to the easy-drinking lineup.

● **Esser Vineyards Cabernet Sauvignon / 2009 / California / $**
A dash of peppery Petite Sirah adds a bit of firmness to this supple, berry-driven Cabernet.

ETUDE WINES

Tony Soter founded Etude with the aim of making great Pinot Noir; he planted eight different clones and eight low-yielding heirloom varieties at this Carneros estate. Now owned by Treasury Wine Estates, Etude is still known as a Pinot Noir powerhouse, though its Cabernets and whites are sought after as well.

- ● **Etude Pinot Noir Rosé** / 2010 / Carneros / $$
  Made in a dry, crisp style, this lovely rosé offers fragrant strawberry and herb notes.
- ● **Etude Pinot Noir** / 2008 / Carneros / $$$
  Seductively smooth, Etude's entry-level Pinot melds sweet red cherry with savory cedar and olives.

FAR NIENTE

The late Gil Nickel and his wife, Beth, bought this run-down pre-Prohibition winery in 1979 and beautifully restored it. Lavish gardens and vintage cars offer pleasant distractions, but the wines are the real draw. Far Niente's Chardonnay and Cabernet earn high marks—and command high prices—every vintage.

- ○ **Far Niente Chardonnay** / 2009 / Napa Valley / $$$
  French oak imparts creamy vanilla nuances to this rich white.
- ● **Far Niente Cabernet Sauvignon** / 2008 / Oakville / $$$$
  Its rich black currant flavors are impressively concentrated and linger beautifully on the palate.

FERRARI-CARANO VINEYARDS AND WINERY

With 1,400 acres of estate vineyards across five appellations, Ferrari-Carano has come a long way since its modest beginnings in 1981. The consistently first-rate white wines are made at the Dry Creek Valley winery, where the tasting room is located; reds, including top cuvées called PreVail, are produced at Ferrari-Carano's Mountain Winery Estate, in Alexander Valley.

- ○ **Ferrari-Carano Tré Terre Chardonnay** / 2008 / Russian River Valley / $$ Seven different clones of Chardonnay give layered depth to this creamy, pear-driven white.
- ● **Ferrari-Carano PreVail West Face** / 2007 / Alexander Valley / $$$ A substantial, weighty blend of Cabernet and Syrah with outstanding density.

FESS PARKER VINEYARD & WINERY

Baby boomers recognize Fess Parker as the man who portrayed Davy Crockett and Daniel Boone, but for a new generation of wine drinkers the name conjures terrific Santa Barbara County wine. The single-vineyard Pinot Noir, Syrah and Chardonnay are well made and fairly priced. Winemaker Blair Fox also crafts a fine entry-level blend of red Rhône varieties, Frontier Red.

○ **Fess Parker Chardonnay** / 2009 / Santa Barbara County / $$
Generous apple flavors are woven with oak and lemon notes.

● **Fess Parker Rodney's Vineyard Syrah** / 2007 / Santa Barbara County / $$$ From a site named for Parker's late son-in-law, this is a serious, ageworthy—and delicious—red.

FOLEY ESTATES

Along with Santa Barbara's Lincourt winery, Foley Estates was an early cornerstone of Foley Family Wines, Fortune 500–company chairman and vintner Bill Foley's portfolio of premier vineyards and wineries. Leslie Mead Renaud crafts Foley's richly flavored Santa Rita Hills Chardonnays and Pinots in tiny quantities.

○ **Foley Rancho Santa Rosa Chardonnay** / 2008 / Sta. Rita Hills / $$ This opulent, vanilla-edged white comes from a vineyard planted on a former horse farm.

● **Foley Rancho Santa Rosa Pinot Noir** / 2008 / Sta. Rita Hills / $$$ Twenty months in French oak add spice and cedar to this Pinot's overtones of ripe cherry.

FOXEN VINEYARD & WINERY

Bill Wathen and Dick Doré founded Foxen Winery 27 years ago in Santa Maria Valley on land once owned by Doré's great-great-grandfather William Benjamin Foxen. It's ideal territory for cool-climate Pinot Noir, Chardonnay and Syrah, which Wathen, Foxen's winemaker, uses for his eclectic range of small-lot wines.

○ **Foxen Bien Nacido Vineyard Block UU Chardonnay** / 2009 / Santa Maria Valley / $$$ Racy acidity and zesty grapefruit and green apple course through this vibrant wine.

● **Foxen Pinot Noir** / 2009 / Santa Maria Valley / $$$
A layered, berry-driven blend of four different clones of Pinot Noir from five separate vineyard blocks.

FOXGLOVE

Co-owners Bob (the winemaker) and Jim Varner make tiny
quantities of their cult-worthy Santa Cruz Mountain Chardonnay
and Pinot Noir under their prestigious Varner and Neely labels,
respectively. The brothers also use their deft touch to produce
the Foxglove line of affordable wines, which offer far more pleasure and complexity than one would expect for the price.

○ **Foxglove Chardonnay** / 2009 / **Central Coast** / $
The prestigious Santa Barbara region is the main source of
the grapes used in this zesty, unoaked white.

● **Foxglove Zinfandel** / 2009 / **Paso Robles** / $
The juicy wild berry and herb flavors in this great-value
Zinfandel finish with tart acidity.

FRANCISCAN ESTATE

At this popular Napa winery, Janet Myers is the latest in a line
of well-known winemakers, following Chilean vintner Agustin
Huneeus, Justin Meyer and, most recently, Greg Upton. A quartet of mid-priced Napa Valley bottlings offer reliable quality,
and the Sauvignon Blanc is excellent. The premium offerings,
including the red Bordeaux-variety blend Magnificat and the
Cuvée Sauvage Chardonnay, can dazzle.

○ **Franciscan Sauvignon Blanc** / 2009 / **Napa Valley** / $$
Invigorating citrus and fig flavors have a tropical accent.

○ **Franciscan Cuvée Sauvage Chardonnay** / 2007 / **Carneros** /
$$$ Made with wild yeasts, this luscious, pear-driven white is
wonderfully complex.

FRANCIS FORD COPPOLA WINERY/ INGLENOOK

These wineries have little in common except
their owner, film director Francis Ford Coppola. Napa's Inglenook (until 2011 called Rubicon Estate) represents the rebirth of a historic
winery, newly invigorated by the arrival of ex–
Château Margaux winemaker Philippe Bas-
caules. Sonoma's Francis Ford Coppola Winery
offers affordable wines sourced from the valley's diverse subzones and beyond.

WINE INTEL
Sonoma County is
buzzing about the
Francis Ford
Coppola Winery's
newest amenities:
an upscale
restaurant, called
Rustic, Francis's
Favorites; a
huge, resortlike
swimming pool;
and a bocce court.

○ **Francis Ford Coppola Director's Cut Chardonnay** / 2009 / **Russian River Valley** / $$ Lively and fresh, with apple, green pear and vibrant citrus tones.

● **Francis Ford Coppola Director's Cut Pinot Noir** / 2009 / **Sonoma Coast** / $$ A cool coastal climate gives this raspberry-infused Pinor Noir a bright spine of acidity.

● **Rubicon** / 2007 / **Rutherford** / $$$$
From organically farmed estate vineyards, this Cabernet-based flagship bottling is firm and structured, with sweet black fruit and polished tannins.

FREI BROTHERS RESERVE

This green, eco-minded Sonoma-based winery works to preserve its natural resources without compromising the quality of the wine. Its six wines, all reserves, offer a tour of Sonoma's subregions: Cool-climate varietals (Chardonnay, Sauvignon Blanc, Pinot Noir) come from the Russian River Valley, Cabernet Sauvignon from Alexander Valley, and Merlot and Zinfandel from the Dry Creek region.

○ **Frei Brothers Reserve Sauvignon Blanc** / 2009 / **Russian River Valley** / $$ Made with just a touch of Sémillon, this is loaded with round, supple flavors of lime, passion fruit and grass.

GALLO FAMILY VINEYARDS

Third-generation winemaker Gina Gallo proves that she has the talent and the resources to produce world-class wines bearing the well-known Gallo name. The Sonoma Reserve bottlings are well-made, large-production red and white wines, with the Chardonnay an exceptional offering. And the much more limited single-vineyard wines—especially the Chardonnay from Two Rock and reds from Frei Ranch Vineyard, which was planted in the 1880s—really impress.

○ **Gallo Family Vineyards Two Rock Vineyard Chardonnay** / 2008 / **Sonoma Coast** / $$ Fermenting this mostly in steel tanks keeps its juicy pear and citrus flavors pure and fresh.

● **Gallo Family Vineyards Frei Ranch Vineyard Zinfandel** / 2008 / **Dry Creek Valley** / $$ Frei Ranch is located in a cooler section of Sonoma's warm Dry Creek Valley, which makes for a Zin with loads of bold, plummy flavor and terrific balance.

GEYSER PEAK WINERY

The original Geyser Peak facility, built in 1882, looked out on the geothermal steam bursting from Alexander Valley's Geyser Peak Mountain. Winemaker Ondine Chattan continues the Sonoma stalwart's track record of producing stellar wines. Its widely available Varietal line offers great value; the Block Collection is a step up in complexity and price.

○ **Geyser Peak Winery Sauvignon Blanc** / 2009 / California / $
This zesty, always delicious white offers exuberant lime, sweet melon and grass flavors.

● **Geyser Peak Winery Cabernet Sauvignon** / 2007 / Alexander Valley / $$ Velvety tannins underpin black currant and malt flavors in this great-value red.

HALL WINES

Dedicated to crafting top-notch Napa Valley Cabernet, Kathryn and Craig Hall purchased the acclaimed Sacrashe vineyard in the hills of Rutherford in 1995. Under winemaker Steve Leveque, the winery excels with Bordeaux varieties, including a crisp Sauvignon Blanc, the iconic flagship Kathryn Hall Cabernet and a bounty of collectible wines called the Artisan series.

● **Hall Cabernet Sauvignon** / 2008 / Napa Valley / $$$
A flashy, intense Cabernet brimming with black cherry fruit and sourced mainly from an estate site in Rutherford.

● **Kathryn Hall Cabernet Sauvignon** / 2008 / Napa Valley / $$$$
Chocolaty black cherry flavors mark this lavishly oaked red.

HANNA WINERY & VINEYARDS

Many hobbyist winemakers dream of going pro, but Dr. Elias Hanna, a cardiac surgeon, made it happen: He grew his 12-acre vineyard in the Russian River Valley into a thriving winery with more than 600 Sonoma acres. Daughter Christine Hanna is the second-generation owner, and Jeff Hinchliffe is winemaker.

○ **Hanna Chardonnay** / 2009 / Russian River Valley / $$
A lemony tartness nicely balances this rich Chardonnay's tropical, vanilla-edged notes.

● **Hanna Cabernet Sauvignon** / 2007 / Alexander Valley / $$
Pair this savory, herb-inflected Cabernet with a juicy steak.

THE HESS COLLECTION

Switzerland's Hess family has been in the beverage business since 1844, starting with beer. Donald Hess added bottled water and finally wine to the lineup, purchasing vineyards on Napa's Mount Veeder in 1978. The three wine tiers include the Hess Collection, sourced from Mount Veeder, followed by the mid-range Napa Series and the entry-level Hess Select line.

○ **Hess Collection Chardonnay** / 2009 / Napa Valley / $$
An elegant white with modest oak and lemony verve.

● **Hess Collection Cabernet Sauvignon** / 2007 / Mt. Veeder / $$$
Mount Veeder's steep slopes and thin soil amp up the tannin and concentration of this muscular Cabernet.

HIRSCH VINEYARDS

David Hirsch sold his grapes to an impressive list of Sonoma cult-wine makers before he got into the wine business himself in 2002. He has spent nearly three decades decoding the wild jumble of soils in his extraordinary Sonoma Coast vineyard, an experience that has made the winery's site-specific cuvées—sumptuous Pinot Noirs and a Chardonnay—world famous.

● **Hirsch Vineyards San Andreas Fault Pinot Noir** / 2009 / Sonoma Coast / $$$ Definitive Sonoma Coast Pinot, with a minerally depth to its vivid berry and cherry fruit.

● **Hirsch Vineyards Reserve Pinot Noir** / 2009 / Sonoma Coast / $$$$ With seamless waves of velvety raspberry and currant, this is one of California's most compelling Pinots.

HONIG VINEYARD & WINERY

In 1964, Louis Honig bought a 68-acre ranch in Napa Valley and planted grapes. He never made wine, but future generations started to. As Michael Honig, Louis's grandson, took control of the winery in the '80s, the crisp Sauvignon Blanc made the brand a favorite—but the Cabernet is arguably even better.

○ **Honig Sauvignon Blanc** / 2010 / Napa Valley / $$
A bit of effervescence adds freshness to citrus and grass notes.

● **Honig Cabernet Sauvignon** / 2008 / Napa Valley / $$$
Small berries from a small crop resulted in this brawny, firmly tannic, currant-flavored red.

HUNDRED ACRE WINERY/LAYER CAKE WINES

Jayson Woodbridge's fearless confidence made him a successful investment banker; it's also what allowed him to plunge into the high-end wine business in 2000 with zero experience. Woodbridge's Hundred Acre reds—three Napa Valley Cabernets and a Barossa Shiraz—are hard-to-find and expensive cult classics. His Layer Cake wines are compelling and wonderfully low-priced.

- **Layer Cake Cabernet Sauvignon / 2009 / California / $$**
  Aging in used Hundred Acre barrels gives this red's luscious blackberry flavors a gentle cedar note.
- **Hundred Acre Kayli Morgan Vineyard Cabernet Sauvignon / 2008 / Napa Valley / $$$$** This stunning, violet-scented Cab is suave and satiny, with velvety tannins and effortless depth.

JORDAN VINEYARD & WINERY

In the 1970s, oil-and-gas entrepreneur Tom Jordan created this Sonoma brand, which turns out a single Cabernet and Chardonnay each year. Winemaker Rob Davis worked with the legendary André Tchelistcheff to produce Jordan's first Cabernet in 1976; more than 30 years later, Davis still makes this wine in an old-school style. The vibrant Chardonnay is also not to be missed.

- ○ **Jordan Chardonnay / 2009 / Russian River Valley / $$**
  A refined wine with bright acidity offsetting rich, ripe pear.
- **Jordan Cabernet Sauvignon / 2007 / Alexander Valley / $$$**
  Decant this powerful Cabernet to allow its layers of decadent black currant flavors to fully emerge.

JOSEPH PHELPS VINEYARDS

Joe Phelps's Insignia red, first produced in 1974, helped bring Bordeaux-style blends to prominence in California and remains a standard-bearer for the entire state. Helmed today by son Bill Phelps and winemakers Damian Parker and Ashley Hepworth, the winery remains focused on Bordeaux varieties and Syrah.

- ○ **Joseph Phelps Vineyards Sauvignon Blanc / 2009 / St. Helena / $$$** Appealingly tart, with apple and citrus.
- **Joseph Phelps Insignia / 2007 / Napa Valley / $$$$**
  A Cabernet-based blend with a magnificent balance of power and finesse; its ripe, firm tannins frame currant and herb notes.

JUSTIN VINEYARDS & WINERY

A revelatory sip of Bordeaux led ex-banker Justin Baldwin to found his winery, specializing in estate-made Bordeaux blends, in 1981 near Paso Robles. The now midsize winery's offerings include the flagship Isosceles bottling and a new high-end Syrah blend, Focus. Baldwin recently sold the winery to FIJI Water, but he and winemaker Fred Holloway remain on board.

● **Justin Vineyards & Winery Justification** / 2008 / Paso Robles / $$$ A Cabernet Franc–Merlot blend, this weaves savory, earthy complexity with ripe kirsch flavors.

● **Justin Vineyards & Winery Isosceles** / 2008 / Paso Robles / $$$$ This Bordeaux-style blend is rich, luscious and packed with sweet black fruit.

KENDALL-JACKSON

Based in Sonoma Valley, Kendall-Jackson is a megabrand that maintains impressive consistency and quality despite its huge size. Almost all its grapes come from 14,000 acres of estate vineyards amassed by the company's late founder, Jess Jackson. The KJ portfolio, best known for its Vintner's Reserve Chardonnay, includes Highland Estates single-vineyard offerings.

○ **Kendall-Jackson Vintner's Reserve Chardonnay** / 2009 / California / $ Straightforward citrus flavors are rich yet focused in this tasty KJ white.

● **Kendall-Jackson Vintner's Reserve Cabernet Sauvignon** / 2008 / Sonoma and Napa counties / $$ Small amounts of Cabernet Franc, Merlot and others add to this red's complexity.

KENWOOD VINEYARDS

Kenwood Vineyards sources grapes from all over Sonoma's diverse subregions. Entry-level wines carry the Sonoma County appellation, whereas reserves come from prime subregions. The top Cabernet barrels are destined for the flagship Artist Series.

○ **Kenwood Vineyards Sauvignon Blanc** / 2009 / Sonoma County / $ This always-appealing wine features a crisp mix of refreshing lemon-lime flavors.

● **Kenwood Vineyards Zinfandel** / 2008 / Sonoma County / $ A bit of Petite Sirah adds heft to briary berry and vanilla.

KUNDE FAMILY ESTATE

The Kunde estate spreads across nearly 2,000 acres in Sonoma Valley. Planted with vines since the 1870s and purchased in 1904 by German immigrant Louis Kunde, the property today specializes in estate-grown and reasonably priced wines; its three reserve bottlings include a complex old-vine Zin.

○ **Kunde Family Estate Chardonnay / 2009 / Sonoma Valley / $**
Refreshing lemon and green apple flavors have a floral accent.

● **Kunde Family Estate Reserve Century Vines Zinfandel / 2008 / Sonoma Valley / $$** Grapes from 126-year-old vines give this bold, darkly fruity Zin its notable tannins.

LA CREMA

Elizabeth Grant-Douglas worked under the talented Melissa Stackhouse before taking over her boss's job as La Crema's winemaker in 2010. Under Stackhouse, La Crema's reputation for producing high-quality Chardonnay and Pinot Noir soared. Grapes come from Northern California's cool coastal regions.

● **La Crema Pinot Noir / 2009 / Monterey / $$**
This wild strawberry–infused red shows an appealing liveliness compared with most California Pinot Noirs.

● **La Crema Pinot Noir / 2009 / Sonoma Coast / $$**
There's a great acidic verve in this Pinot, which gives lift to bright cherry, raspberry and earth flavors.

LANDMARK VINEYARDS

In the past decade, this Sonoma winery has introduced a series of small-lot wines from high-profile vineyards. These wines have joined other well-known bottlings in Landmark's portfolio, such as the Overlook Chardonnay and Grand Detour Pinot Noir. Founded in Sonoma Valley in 1974 and known primarily for Burgundian varietals, Landmark has, under owners Michael and Mary Colhoun, expanded into Rhône varietals.

○ **Landmark Overlook Chardonnay / 2009 / Sonoma County / $$**
Elegant pear and toasty oak are balanced by lemony acidity.

○ **Landmark Damaris Reserve Chardonnay / 2008 / Sonoma Coast and Carneros / $$$** This satiny Chardonnay comes from the acclaimed Flocchini and Sangiacomo vineyards.

LOUIS M. MARTINI WINERY

Founded in 1933, this Cabernet-focused Napa winery was purchased by Gallo in 2002, but the company left Michael Martini in charge of winemaking. Thanks to his talent and Gallo's deep pockets, quality continues to improve and the top wines—such as the Lot No. 1 and Monte Rosso Cabernets—are world-class.

● Louis M. Martini Lot No. 1 Cabernet Sauvignon / 2007 / Napa Valley / $$$$ Sweet cassis aromas lead to a silky licorice- and spice-inflected palate in this lovely, concentrated red.

MACMURRAY RANCH

MacMurray Ranch takes its name from a stunning western swath of the Russian River Valley that was once owned by actor Fred MacMurray (of *My Three Sons* fame). On the renowned Westside Road, the ranch, now owned by Gallo, provides a portion of the grapes for its Pinot-focused portfolio, which includes bottlings from some of California's top Pinot regions and Oregon's Willamette Valley plus cool-climate whites, too.

○ MacMurray Ranch Chardonnay / 2009 / Sonoma Coast / $$
Round and beautifully fleshed out with a combination of lemon zest, vanilla and pear flavors.

● MacMurray Ranch Pinot Noir / 2008 / Santa Lucia Highlands / $$$ From a single estate vineyard, this Pinot offers flavors of roasted black cherry and warm spice.

MERRY EDWARDS WINERY

Since 1997, when she first made wine under her own name, Merry Edwards has focused her skills on small-lot, cool-climate Pinot Noir and a single Sauvignon Blanc. Edwards has honed her craft for nearly 40 California vintages, with early experience at such pioneering wineries as Mount Eden and Matanzas Creek, and it shows in her bold, expertly balanced wines.

● Merry Edwards Meredith Estate Pinot Noir / 2008 / Russian River Valley / $$$ Cola and supple cherry notes reveal a terrific minerality woven throughout.

● Merry Edwards Pinot Noir / 2008 / Sonoma Coast / $$$
A sleek, vibrant combination of red currant, berry and dried-herb flavors makes this a stellar Pinot.

MERRYVALE

Located in a 1930s building along a narrow stretch of Napa Valley's famed Highway 29, this lauded winery has been owned since the mid-'90s by the Schlatter family. Merryvale's affordable Starmont label became so successful that it's now its own brand, produced at a newish facility in Carneros; the winery's prestigious Profile bottling sits at the top of the portfolio.

- **Merryvale Pinot Noir** / 2009 / Carneros / $$$
  A refreshing Pinot, with berry, cherry and cola flavors.
- **Merryvale Cabernet Sauvignon** / 2007 / Napa Valley / $$$$
  Made in the same ripe, heavyweight style as the Profile, this red has a lot of the same complexity, yet a lower price tag.
- **Merryvale Profile** / 2007 / Napa Valley / $$$$
  Superripe black cherry and tobacco flavors mark this powerful, mouth-coating Bordeaux-style blend.

MORGAN WINERY

One of the leading wineries in the cool coastal Monterey County region, Morgan Winery is known for its Pinot Noir and Chardonnay. Founders Dan Morgan Lee and wife Donna source fruit from some of the best vineyards in the Santa Lucia Highlands as well as from their own Double L organic vineyard.

- ○ **Morgan Highland Chardonnay** / 2009 / Santa Lucia Highlands / $$ Made with organically grown grapes, this is creamy and full-bodied yet vibrant.
- ● **Morgan Twelve Clones Pinot Noir** / 2009 / Santa Lucia Highlands / $$$ This Santa Lucia Pinot shows savory highlights amid red fruit and cedary oak.

NAVARRO VINEYARDS

Navarro sells most of its wine to fans directly and to savvy tourists who make the trek to its tasting room in Mendocino County. But it's a brand worth seeking out: Navarro produces remarkably elegant, affordable Pinot Noir and a variety of fresh whites.

- ○ **Navarro Vineyards Pinot Gris** / 2009 / Anderson Valley / $$
  Almond, quince and honey flavors have a lime-infused finish.
- ● **Navarro Vineyards Rosé of Pinot Noir** / 2010 / Anderson Valley / $$ This appealing rosé offers crisp strawberry flavors.

NEW WORLD / UNITED STATES / CALIFORNIA

THE OJAI VINEYARD

Instead of owning vineyards, winemaker Adam Tolmach and his wife, Helen, contract with some of the Central Coast's best growers to buy grapes by the acre, an arrangement that encourages quality, not quantity. Tolmach makes up to 20 wines each vintage, many in tiny lots, and is particularly skilled with Syrah.

○ **The Ojai Vineyard Bien Nacido Vineyard Chardonnay / 2008 / Santa Maria Valley / $$** Winemaker Adam Tolmach ferments this wine in old French oak, which keeps it impressively fresh.

● **The Ojai Vineyard Syrah / 2008 / Santa Barbara County / $$** From the Bien Nacido Vineyards, this is savory and dense.

PAPAPIETRO PERRY WINERY

Part-time amateur winemakers and full-time newspapermen Ben Papapietro and Bruce Perry eventually retired and started this smallish winery in 1998. The duo are obsessed with Pinot, which the winery makes in tiny lots in a rich, fruity style. Grapes come from prime vineyards, chiefly in the Russian River Valley.

● **Papapietro Perry Peters Vineyard Pinot Noir / 2007 / Russian River Valley / $$$** Dark and powerful, this displays notes of ripe black cherry edged with anise.

● **Papapietro Perry Timbercrest Farms Zinfandel / 2007 / Dry Creek Valley / $$$** This full-throttle Zin offers tremendously ripe kirsch and dried-berry flavors.

PATZ & HALL

Donald Patz and James Hall became friends while working at Napa's Flora Springs winery in the '80s. They hatched a plan to create this *négociant*-style brand with Heather Patz and Anne Moses. Thanks in part to an all-star collection of vineyard sources, the four partners have built Patz & Hall into one of the country's most sought-after names for Chardonnay and Pinot Noir.

○ **Patz & Hall Hyde Vineyard Chardonnay / 2008 / Carneros / $$$** Supple and balanced, with seamlessly integrated ripe fruit and toasty oak.

● **Patz & Hall Chenoweth Ranch Pinot Noir / 2008 / Russian River Valley / $$$** A silky, cherry-scented red from a famous site in the cool Green Valley subregion.

PAUL HOBBS WINERY

Paul Hobbs's winemaking magic is in high demand at wineries in California, South America and as far away as Armenia. Yet the genial Hobbs maintains a keen focus on his own estate, where he crafts many single-vineyard wines including Cabernets from Napa and Burgundian varietals from Sonoma.

○ **Paul Hobbs Chardonnay** / 2009 / Russian River Valley / $$$
This generously textured wine explodes with spice and peach.

● **Paul Hobbs Cabernet Sauvignon** / 2008 / Napa Valley / $$$$
A streamlined Cabernet with concentrated black currant and intriguing earth flavors.

PINE RIDGE VINEYARDS

Founded in 1978 in Napa's Stags Leap District, Pine Ridge is best known for elegant Cabernet-based reds from prized estate vineyards. The winery also has carved out a surprising niche with a tasty Chenin Blanc–Viognier blend, made with grapes from Lodi and the under-the-radar Clarksburg district.

○ **Pine Ridge Chenin Blanc–Viognier** / 2009 / California / $
An unusual, light-bodied blend with perfect harmony in its tangy lemon-lime and green apple flavors.

● **ForeFront by Pine Ridge Vineyards Pinot Noir** / 2009 / Santa Barbara, San Luis Obispo and Monterey counties / $$
Sourced from coastal vineyards, this brims with spicy red berry and blackberry notes.

QUIVIRA VINEYARDS & WINERY

Complex Zinfandel and biodynamic farming are the specialties of this eco-friendly estate in Dry Creek Valley. Under Pete and Terri Kight, who bought it in 2006 and upgraded quality, Quivira also has been focusing on Rhône grapes. Current winemaker Hugh Chappelle (formerly of Lynmar Estate) joined in 2010.

● **Quivira Vineyards and Winery Wine Creek Ranch Petite Sirah** / 2008 / Dry Creek Valley / $$ Textbook Petite Sirah, with a brooding mix of black fruit and potent tannins.

● **Quivira Vineyards and Winery Zinfandel** / 2008 / Dry Creek Valley / $$ A juicy, robust wine with wild berry and plum flavors that firm up in the finish.

QUPÉ

A Rhône fanatic, Bob Lindquist is one of the country's most renowned interpreters of Syrah as well as of Rhône whites Roussanne and Marsanne. Based in Santa Barbara's famed Bien Nacido Vineyards, Lindquist makes Qupé's refined wines with grapes from some of the most prized Central Coast sites.

○ **Qupé Marsanne** / 2009 / Santa Ynez Valley / $$
Made with Marsanne that was fermented and aged in neutral oak and a bit of Roussanne aged in French oak for a year, this white shows a thick texture, zesty citrus and minerals.

● **Qupé Syrah** / 2009 / Central Coast / $
A restrained, elegant Syrah with lovely notes of peppercorn, herbs and pomegranate.

RAMEY WINE CELLARS

David Ramey earned fame as winemaker for boutique producers such as Chalk Hill, Matanzas Creek and Rudd. For the past 16 years he has made wine under his own name in the Sonoma town of Healdsburg. His single-vineyard Chardonnays are cult favorites; his Cabernet and Syrahs are made with equal finesse.

○ **Ramey Hyde Vineyard Chardonnay** / 2008 / Carneros / $$$
This orange-infused white is energetic and bright, thanks to the signature acidity of grapes from the Hyde Vineyards.

● **Ramey Cabernet Sauvignon** / 2008 / Napa Valley / $$$
Its effusive blackberry flavors meld with powerful tannins.

RAVENSWOOD

When Joel Peterson started making Zinfandel in the 1970s, most Americans knew it only as a sweet pink wine (a.k.a. White Zinfandel or blush). Ravenswood's powerhouse versions helped turn a generation of wine drinkers on to Zinfandel. Ravenswood now makes 750,000 cases annually, including boutique cuvées and site-specific wines from historic vineyards such as Old Hill.

● **Ravenswood Old Vine Zinfandel** / 2007 / Sonoma County / $
Petite Sirah and Carignane add weight to this exuberant Zin.

● **Ravenswood Vintners Blend Zinfandel** / 2008 / California / $
There are nice vanilla tones in this flavorful, berry-driven red, thanks to a year of oak aging.

RAYMOND VINEYARDS

Founded in 1970 by one of California's pioneering wine families, this midsize Napa estate has offered solid, reasonably priced wines for years. In 2009, Boisset Family Estates purchased the winery, bringing famous French consultant Philippe Melka and winemaker Stephanie Putnam on board—which means newly invigorated and ambitious wines are no doubt on the way.

○ **Raymond Reserve Chardonnay / 2009 / Napa Valley / $$**
Green pear and banana flavors have a lively hint of lemon.

● **R Collection by Raymond Lot No. 7 Field Blend / 2009 / California / $** A sturdy, spicy kitchen-sink blend that includes Cabernet, Zinfandel, Petite Sirah and Syrah.

RIDGE VINEYARDS

One of the most celebrated names in American wine, Ridge Vineyards makes a legendary Cabernet blend, called Monte Bello, from the Santa Cruz Mountains. Winemaker Paul Draper, who joined Ridge less than a decade after it was founded in 1962, credits superb vineyards and a minimalist approach for the wines' success. Don't overlook Ridge's accessibly priced old-vine Zins.

○ **Ridge Estate Chardonnay / 2009 / Santa Cruz Mountains / $$$**
This reliably wonderful Chardonnay is effusive and complex.

● **Ridge Estate Cabernet Sauvignon / 2008 / Santa Cruz Mountains / $$$** A baby sibling to Ridge's famous Monte Bello Cab, this is made with grapes from the same vineyard.

ROBERT BIALE VINEYARDS

Pietro Biale started growing grapes in Napa Valley back in the 1930s, but it was son Aldo and grandson Bob who began bottling wines under the family name 60 years later. The winery specializes in hearty, dense single-vineyard Zinfandels and Petite Sirahs from some of Napa's oldest vineyards.

● **Robert Biale Vineyards Black Chicken Zinfandel / 2009 / Oak Knoll District of Napa Valley / $$$** Named for the Biale family's code word for bootleg wine, this is soft, ripe and spicy.

● **Robert Biale Vineyards Stagecoach Vineyards Zinfandel / 2008 / Napa Valley / $$$** Juicy blackberry fruit is held in check by Stagecoach's trademark firm tannins.

ROBERT CRAIG WINERY

Robert Craig built his eponymous winery and one of his estate vineyards at the end of a winding, rugged road nearly 2,300 feet up Napa Valley's Howell Mountain. It's a perch that suits Craig well, given his passion for mountain-grown grapes. Craig makes a quartet of always excellent, firmly structured Cabernets, along with small amounts of Chardonnay, Zinfandel and a Cab blend.

○ **Robert Craig Durell Vineyard Chardonnay** / 2009 / **Sonoma Valley** / $$$ This racy, layered Chardonnay comes from one of Sonoma's most famous vineyards.

● **Robert Craig Cabernet Sauvignon** / 2008 / **Howell Mountain** / $$$$ Tight tannins will enable this dense, herb- and blackberry-flavored wine to age well.

ROBERT MONDAVI WINERY

After a series of shake-ups in the mid-2000s, Robert Mondavi's industry-transforming winery found stable footing under current owner Constellation Wines. The winery's talented winemaker, Genevieve Janssens, continues the brand's tradition of greatness with high-end cuvées such as the Reserve Cabernet.

○ **Robert Mondavi Winery Napa Valley Fumé Blanc** / 2008 / **Napa Valley** / $$ Juicy passion fruit and guava flavors are matched by brisk grapefruit notes.

● **Robert Mondavi Winery Reserve Cabernet Sauvignon** / 2007 / **Napa Valley** / $$$$ The 2007 Reserve shows layers of velvet-textured black currant and earth woven with chewy tannins.

ROCHIOLI VINEYARDS & WINERY

The Rochioli family had been farming for decades when they began making wine under this Sonoma label in the early '80s. Joe Jr. and Tom Rochioli run the show now. It can take years to get on the mailing list for their Burgundy-inspired single-vineyard wines; thankfully, their other offerings are easier to find.

○ **Rochioli Sauvignon Blanc** / 2009 / **Russian River Valley** / $$$ Exotic and sleek, with grapefruit, cardamom and nice acidity.

● **Rochioli Pinot Noir** / 2008 / **Russian River Valley** / $$$ Sourced from several estate vineyards, this Pinot offers weightless density and a hint of spice.

RODNEY STRONG VINEYARDS

Rodney Strong helped develop Sonoma's fine-wine niche when he retired from a Broadway dancing career and established his winery in 1959. Owned since 1989 by the Klein family, the brand has been on the upswing recently, thanks to a switch to sustainable farming and an assist from star consultant David Ramey.

○ **Rodney Strong Estate Vineyards Chardonnay / 2009 / Chalk Hill / $$** Rodney Strong was the first to plant Chardonnay in Sonoma's Chalk Hill district; this version is bright and citrusy.

● **Rodney Strong Estate Vineyards Pinot Noir / 2009 / Russian River Valley / $$** There's a charming floral undertone to this Pinot's minty berry and spice flavors.

ROMBAUER VINEYARDS

Rombauer's decadent Chardonnay became one of the best-known examples of the buttery, oaky style that defined California Chardonnay in the 1990s. Today this family-run estate—founded in St. Helena in 1982 by Koerner and Joan Rombauer—enjoys a loyal following. The wines, including the Napa Valley Merlot and Cabernet, are consistently well made.

○ **Rombauer Vineyards Chardonnay / 2009 / Carneros / $$$** Lavishly oaked, with sweet pear, vanilla and citrus flavors.

● **Rombauer Vineyards Cabernet Sauvignon / 2008 / Napa Valley / $$$** Savory herbs and dense black fruit are layered with generous, coffee-tinged oak.

ROSENBLUM CELLARS

Kent Rosenblum established this cutting-edge winery in 1978. He excelled at sourcing fruit from stellar old-vine Zinfandel plots and built Rosenblum Cellars into a Zin powerhouse. He sold the winery to Diageo in 2008, but thanks to his protégé John Kane, who has stayed on, the single-vineyard Zins continue to impress; regional blends showcase the grape's stylistic range.

● **Rosenblum Cellars Zinfandel / 2008 / Contra Costa County / $$** An up-front burst of plush dried berry, black plum and toasty oak coats the palate in this inviting red.

● **Rosenblum Cellars Zinfandel / 2008 / Paso Robles / $$** With lush, spicy berry flavors, this is a classic Paso Robles Zin.

SAINTSBURY

Soon after it was created by David Graves and Dick Ward in 1981, Saintsbury helped prove that Carneros, with its warm afternoons and cool breezes, was ideal territory for Pinot Noir and Chardonnay. Recent vintages have shown new finesse under winemaker Jerome Chery, an alum of cult producer Littorai.

- ● **Saintsbury Pinot Noir** / 2008 / **Carneros** / **$$**
  Cherry flavors start supple and end on a firm, cedary note.
- ● **Saintsbury Stanly Ranch Pinot Noir** / 2008 / **Carneros** / **$$$**
  This hearty, full-bodied Pinot comes from a large vineyard just south of downtown Napa.

SANFORD WINERY & VINEYARDS

In the early 1970s, Richard Sanford and Michael Benedict planted the first Pinot Noir vines in the Santa Rita Hills, a then low-profile valley in Santa Barbara County. The vineyard became a celebrated Pinot Noir source, and Sanford's brand a cult favorite. Sanford is now majority-owned by the Terlato family, which has maintained the winery's focus on small-lot Pinot Noir and Chardonnay.

- ○ **Sanford Chardonnay** / 2009 / **Santa Barbara County** / **$$**
  This delivers a soft, rich mouthful of smoky yellow apple.
- ● **Sanford Sanford & Benedict Vineyard Pinot Noir** / 2008 / **Sta. Rita Hills** / **$$$$** A ripe yet balanced Pinot made with grapes from Santa Rita Hills' first vineyard.

SEGHESIO FAMILY VINEYARDS

Winemakers in Sonoma County since the 1880s, the Seghesio clan has a deep-rooted affinity for Zinfandel. Ted Seghesio, who continues as vintner after the recent sale of the family winery to the Napa-based Crimson Wine Group, is a Zin master. The Seghesio portfolio also includes examples of estate-grown Italian varieties such as Aglianico, Barbera and Arneis.

- ● **Seghesio Family Vineyards Sonoma Zinfandel** / 2009 / **Sonoma County** / **$$** Sourcing from 20 vineyard blocks gives layered depth to this wine's ripe berry and plum profile.
- ● **Seghesio Family Vineyards Home Ranch Zinfandel** / 2009 / **Alexander Valley** / **$$$** A well-structured Zin bursting with berry, mineral and herb flavors that linger on the palate.

SHAFER VINEYARDS

Shafer's bold, beautifully made wines enjoy almost universal acclaim. Chalk that up to the estate's prime vineyard locations (which include 79 acres in Napa's Stags Leap District) and the steady hand of intensely focused winemaker Elias Fernandez. The Hillside Select Cabernet is an ageworthy classic, and the One Point Five is a delicious (relative) value.

- **Shafer Hillside Select / 2006 / Stags Leap District / $$$$**
  A dense Cab with muscular layers of cassis and cherry liqueur.
- **Shafer One Point Five / 2008 / Stags Leap District / $$$$**
  There's an impressive depth to the black currant, cedar and violet tones of this intense and well-structured Cabernet.

SILVER OAK CELLARS/TWOMEY CELLARS

Silver Oak makes just two wines, both Cabs—one from Napa, the other from Sonoma's Alexander Valley. Aged in American oak, they share a fruity style that drew a national following to the brand in the 1980s and '90s. The company later started Twomey Cellars, specializing in Pinot Noir, Merlot and Sauvignon Blanc.

- **Twomey Pinot Noir / 2009 / Russian River Valley / $$$**
  A fresh and bright Pinot, thanks to a cool vintage, with a pleasant herbal edge and bright cherry flavors.
- **Silver Oak Cabernet Sauvignon / 2007 / Alexander Valley / $$$$** Distinctive and ripe, with waves of black currant and coconut-tinged oak.

SONOMA-CUTRER

Sonoma-Cutrer makes a bit of Pinot Noir, but Chardonnay is the star at this estate, where several excellent estate vineyards regularly yield superlative grapes. In 2010, winemaker Terry Adams passed the torch to Mick Schroeter, who became the third talent to head the winery since it was founded in 1981.

- ○ **Sonoma-Cutrer Les Pierres / 2007 / Sonoma Coast / $$$**
  Entirely fermented in barrel, this Chardonnay wraps its flavors of lemon and grapefruit in a rich, creamy texture.
- ○ **Sonoma-Cutrer Russian River Ranches / 2009 / Sonoma Coast / $$$** Chardonnay's classic invigorating citrus tones are woven with ripe pear flavors in this well-balanced white.

SOUVERAIN

Winemaker Ed Killian has been with Souverain for 20 years, providing the Alexander Valley winery with impressive continuity. Much of Souverain's fruit comes from a 120-year-old estate vineyard at the valley's northern end. Its Winemaker's Reserve wines are terrific bargains given their quality; the partially oak-fermented Sauvignon Blanc offers freshness and complexity.

● Souverain Cabernet Sauvignon / 2007 / Alexander Valley / $$
A good value, this is brawnier than typical Alexander Valley Cabs, with loads of black fruit, cedary oak and tannins.

SPOTTSWOODE ESTATE VINEYARD & WINERY

This charity-minded Napa Valley winery, owned by Mary Novak, donates 1 percent of its profit to environmental nonprofits. But there's another reason to buy its wines: Winemaker Jennifer Williams, with consultation from Rosemary Cakebread, produces superb Cabernet (from organic grapes) and a deliciously fresh Sauvignon Blanc, among other wines.

○ Spottswoode Sauvignon Blanc / 2009 / Napa Valley and Sonoma Mountain / $$$ Partial barrel fermentation imparts lushness to vibrant flavors of melon and lemon curd.
● Spottswoode Cabernet Sauvignon / 2008 / St. Helena / $$$$
Gorgeously polished, with currant and sandalwood notes.

STAG'S LEAP WINE CELLARS

Warren Winiarski's legendary Napa estate vaulted to stardom when its Cabernet triumphed over marquee Bordeaux names at a famous Paris tasting in 1976. Winiarski sold the winery to Chateau Ste. Michelle and Tuscan vintner Piero Antinori in 2007, but skilled winemaker Nicki Pruss has stayed on. The Sauvignon Blanc is made in a distinctly Bordelais style, and the estate's Cabernets and Chardonnay are always great.

○ Stag's Leap Wine Cellars Sauvignon Blanc / 2009 / Napa Valley / $$ Aging in French oak adds some body and heft to this tropical, citrusy white.
○ Stag's Leap Wine Cellars Karia Chardonnay / 2009 / Napa Valley / $$$ A juicy, apple-driven Chardonnay made mostly with grapes from southern Napa Valley.

ST. CLEMENT VINEYARDS

Up-and-coming winemaker Danielle Cyrot took the helm at St. Clement Vineyards in 2005, fresh from a position at Napa's Stags' Leap Winery. She inherited a Cabernet-dominated portfolio that relies on strong relationships with top growers for most of its Napa fruit. Four single-vineyard Cabs top the portfolio, but don't overlook the Sauvignon Blanc.

○ **St. Clement Vineyards Sauvignon Blanc** / 2009 / Napa Valley / $$ A tropical-scented white with a citrusy finish.
● **St. Clement Vineyards Merlot** / 2008 / Napa Valley / $$ This delicious Merlot displays an abundance of the variety's classic, supple black-fruit flavors.
● **St. Clement Vineyards Oroppas** / 2007 / Napa Valley / $$$ Made with grapes from both hillside and valley-floor vineyards, this intense Bordeaux-style blend has firm tannins.

STERLING VINEYARDS

Offering panoramic views of Napa Valley, Sterling is a stunning winery to visit. New winemaking facilities have reinvigorated Sterling's reserve wines, particularly the SVR Bordeaux-style blend, a structured red made for the long haul. For great value look to the Vintner's Collection and the Napa Appellation tier.

○ **Sterling Vineyards Sauvignon Blanc** / 2009 / Napa County / $ Succulent melon and tangy lime flavors define this straight-forward, refreshing white.

ST. FRANCIS WINERY & VINEYARDS

Full-bodied wines have been the St. Francis signature since it was founded in 1979 by San Francisco businessmen Joe Martin and Lloyd Canton. Longtime winemaker Tom Mackey supplements 600 acres of estate vineyards with grapes purchased from prime Sonoma sites. The Wild Oak label is a step up from the entry-level bottlings, and at the top are single-vineyard reds.

○ **St. Francis Chardonnay** / 2009 / Sonoma County / $$ Medium-bodied, with yellow apple, lemon and vanilla notes.
● **St. Francis "Old Vines" Zinfandel** / 2008 / Sonoma County / $$ Vines at least 50 years old impart good intensity to this plummy, spice-edged Zinfandel.

ST. SUPÉRY VINEYARDS & WINERY

Owned by the Skallis, a winemaking family in southern France, St. Supéry is famous for its excellent Sauvignon Blancs, which are among Napa's raciest. But its higher-end wines are worth exploring too, especially the Virtú and Élu red and white bottlings and the substantial Dollarhide Cabernet Sauvignon.

○ **St. Supéry Sauvignon Blanc** / 2010 / Napa Valley / $$
Guava, passion fruit and peach flavors are fragrant and crisp.

● **St. Supéry Dollarhide Cabernet Sauvignon** / 2007 / Napa Valley / $$$$ An elegant Cabernet full of intense ripe black currant wrapped in polished oak.

TABLAS CREEK VINEYARD

Launched in 1987, this joint venture between wine importer Robert Haas and the Perrin family of Châteauneuf-du-Pape is responsible for some of California's best Rhône-style wines. By importing vine cuttings from the Perrins' Château de Beaucastel vineyards and then selling them to other growers in the area, Tablas Creek also has contributed to an explosion of Rhône-style wines in the Central Coast.

> **WINE INTEL**
> Among winemakers, Tablas Creek is as famous for its vines as for its magnificent wines: Some 400 U.S. wineries grow grapes propagated from its Rhône clones.

○ **Tablas Creek Vineyard Roussanne** / 2009 / Paso Robles / $$
Offers a compelling mix of mineral, almond and melon flavors.

● **Tablas Creek Vineyard Rosé** / 2010 / Paso Robles / $$
Bursting with watermelon and berry tones, this is a super rosé.

TRINCHERO NAPA VALLEY

Bob Trinchero started the blush-wine megatrend of the 1980s by inventing White Zinfandel for his family's Sutter Home brand. The Trincheros later bought prime Napa vineyards and hired Mario Monticelli to craft wines under the Trinchero label, which gets deserved attention for well-made reds and whites.

● **Trinchero Napa Valley Chicken Ranch Vineyard Merlot** / 2008 / Rutherford / $$$ Muscular tannins provide a solid frame for this Merlot's ripe black fruit and coffee-tinged oak.

● **Trinchero Napa Valley Meritage** / 2008 / Napa Valley / $$$
Concentrated yet lively, with ample black plum and currant.

WENTE VINEYARDS

Fifth-generation winegrower Karl D. Wente is drawing new interest to his family's Livermore Valley winery, which was founded by an ancestor in 1883. Wente sources fruit from Livermore Valley and Arroyo Seco for his straightforward, affordable varietal wines as well as for more-ambitious offerings such as the Nth Degree and Small Lot tiers.

○ **Wente Vineyards Riva Ranch Chardonnay / 2009 / Arroyo Seco / $$** Grapes from the coastal Arroyo Seco region keep this tropical Chardonnay fresh.

● **Wente Vineyards Small Lot Cabernet Franc / 2008 / Livermore Valley / $$$** The addition of 25 percent Napa Cabernet in this blend provides some nice weight.

ZACA MESA WINERY & VINEYARDS

The Santa Ynez Valley owes a lot of its newfound clout to Zaca Mesa, the winery that championed the Santa Barbara subzone by producing stellar Rhône-style wines. Some of the Central Coast's most dazzling winemaking talents, including Jim Clendenen and Bob Lindquist, got their starts at this winery.

○ **Zaca Mesa Viognier / 2009 / Santa Ynez Valley / $$** A bright citrus nose is followed by apricot in this lithe white.

● **Zaca Mesa Syrah / 2008 / Santa Ynez Valley / $$** A luscious and spicy red from the estate credited with planting the first Syrah in Santa Barbara County in 1978.

● **Zaca Mesa Z Three A Red Wine / 2007 / Santa Ynez Valley / $$$** This Rhône-style blend of top estate lots is packed with ripe black cherry and cocoa flavors.

OREGON

Although Oregon is sandwiched between Washington to the north and California to the south, its wines are very different from those of its neighbors. Western Oregon's cool climate is especially suited to growing Pinot Noir, as well as Pinot Gris and Chardonnay. The state's wineries are mostly small, and their total production is far less than that of Washington, New York or California. While the absence of megaproducers means there are few inexpensive options, Oregon has earned a well-deserved reputation for its high-quality boutique wines.

OREGON: AN OVERVIEW

The hub of Oregon wine production is the Willamette Valley. Located in the state's northwestern corner and protected against strong Pacific winds by the Coast Ranges, the wine region experiences relatively cool temperatures and lots of rain; Pinot Noir thrives here. In the warmer regions of the Umpqua, Rogue and Applegate valleys to the south, Bordeaux and Rhône varieties tend to outperform Pinot. Northeast of the Willamette Valley, the Columbia Gorge and Valley regions run along the Washington State border, meeting the Walla Walla Valley, where Cabernet reigns and Syrah and Merlot are produced in lesser volumes.

♥ OREGON GRAPES & STYLES

Oregon has benefited from the surging demand for Pinot Noir. Although the climate in the Willamette Valley is challenging, in the best vintages—such as 2008—Oregon Pinots achieve a terrific balance between the earthy, astringent style of Burgundy and the robust, ripe styles of California. Most Oregon reds command premium prices, especially the Pinots of the Willamette Valley.

Oregon's principal white grape is Pinot Gris, which tends to produce generous yet refreshing wines. Chardonnay shows great promise in Oregon; dry Rieslings have achieved some success in certain areas, particularly in the Willamette Valley.

Producers/ Oregon

ADELSHEIM VINEYARD

Adelsheim makes some of the Willamette Valley's most respected Pinot Noirs. David Adelsheim founded the winery in 1972 with his wife, Ginny; he passed winemaking duties to Dave Page 11 years ago, though the focus on high-quality, estate-grown wines remains constant. Whites are silky, vibrant and more affordable.

○ **Adelsheim Ribbon Springs Vineyard Auxerrois** / 2009 / Ribbon Ridge / $$ An effusive, citrusy take on an Alsace grape.
● **Adelsheim Pinot Noir** / 2009 / Willamette Valley / $$$ Taut and light-bodied, with pronounced tangy cherry flavors.

ARGYLE WINERY

Vintner Rollin Soles is as skilled at crafting seductive, deeply flavored still wines as he is at making elegant sparkling wines. Soles founded Argyle (with Australian winemaker Brian Croser) in the Dundee Hills in 1987. Pinot Noir and Chardonnay are his specialties; the Nuthouse Pinot Noir is among Oregon's finest.

○ **Argyle Nuthouse Chardonnay** / 2008 / Willamette Valley / $$$
Concentrated tart pear and lush apple notes are heightened by this wine's zippy acidity.

● **Argyle Reserve Pinot Noir** / 2008 / Willamette Valley / $$$
An Indian summer got grapes for this plush red beautifully ripe.

A TO Z WINEWORKS

A to Z Wineworks' founders, Bill and Deb Hatcher and Cheryl Francis and Sam Tannahill, turned their brand into the state's biggest wine producer just a few years after they launched it in 2002. They are expert blenders, working with more than 60 vineyards to achieve their delicious, seamlessly balanced wines with the help of winemaker Michael Davies.

○ **A to Z Pinot Gris** / 2009 / Oregon / $
A great value, with bright apple and lime on the palate.

○ **A to Z Riesling** / 2009 / Oregon / $$
This offers a hint of sweetness amid vibrant peach flavors.

CHEHALEM

From the unoaked Chardonnay to the graceful Pinot Noirs and wildly aromatic Pinot Gris, Chehalem wines reflect vintner Harry Peterson-Nedry's obsession with purity and freshness. Peterson-Nedry's midsize, carbon-neutral winery, now 22 years old, lies in the Chehalem Mountains AVA, with additional vineyards in Ribbon Ridge and the Dundee Hills.

○ **Chehalem INOX** / 2009 / Willamette Valley / $$
This unoaked Chardonnay, which brims with lemon, lime and green pear, is an excellent value.

○ **Chehalem Reserve Dry Riesling** / 2009 / Willamette Valley / $$
Appealingly lean, with bright grapefruit and apple flavors.

● **Chehalem Reserve Pinot Noir** / 2008 / Ribbon Ridge / $$$
Notes of cedar and spice punctuate velvety cherry flavors.

DOMAINE DROUHIN OREGON

Established in 1987, this U.S. outpost of Burgundy's Maison Joseph Drouhin winery (see p. 42) sticks to a Burgundian model. Véronique Drouhin-Boss, the fourth-generation vintner who oversees the family's cellars in France and Oregon, makes wines only from estate-grown Pinot Noir and Chardonnay.

WINE INTEL
Domaine Drouhin's wines are fabulous but pricey. For a taste of the winery's style, look for the two value-priced bottlings Drouhin-Boss makes for the Cloudline label.

● **Domaine Drouhin Oregon Pinot Noir** / 2009 / **Willamette Valley** / $$$ Graceful ripe berry and cedar flavors are beautifully balanced in this Pinot.
● **Domaine Drouhin Oregon Laurène Pinot Noir** / 2008 / **Dundee Hills** / $$$$ This flagship bottling culls from the best barrels.

DOMAINE SERENE

This Willamette winery consistently turns out some of the most remarkable Pinot Noirs in the U.S., including the bold, rich Evenstad Reserve, named for owners Ken and Grace Evenstad. Three Chardonnays and a Walla Walla Syrah round out the portfolio.

○ **Domaine Serene Côte Sud Vineyard Chardonnay** / 2008 / **Willamette Valley** / $$$ Grapes from the Côte Sud vineyard's sunny, south-facing slopes ripen more reliably, yielding this zesty, peach-driven white with toasty, vanilla oak notes.
● **Domaine Serene Evenstad Reserve Pinot Noir** / 2007 / **Willamette Valley** / $$$ A seamless, supple mix of cherry, strawberry and cedary oak undertones.

EYRIE VINEYARDS

When David Lett planted Pinot Noir vines in the rainy Willamette Valley in 1965, most wine experts thought he was crazy. His Eyrie Vineyards proved them wrong, and the winery—now run by son Jason—continues to make the sleek Pinots and vivid whites that earned it a reputation as one of Oregon's best.

○ **Eyrie Vineyards Original Vines Reserve Chardonnay** / 2009 / **Dundee Hills** / $$$ Old vines yield this especially vibrant pear- and peach-flavored Chardonnay.
● **Eyrie Vineyards Original Vines Reserve Pinot Noir** / 2009 / **Dundee Hills** / $$$$ Lovely, with silky plum and berry flavors.

KING ESTATE WINERY

The estate founded by the King family in 1991 is known for two things: terrific Pinot Gris and its vast organic ranch, located southwest of Eugene. The winery's top wines are the estate-grown offerings made under the Domaine label. The Acrobat tier offers super value; the Signature wines are a step up.

○ **Acrobat Pinot Gris / 2009 / Oregon / $**
A great value; full of satiny quince, nut and apple flavors.

○ **King Estate Domaine Pinot Gris / 2009 / Oregon / $$**
This white's citrus and apple notes have a creamy texture thanks to eight months of aging on lees.

● **King Estate Signature Pinot Noir / 2009 / Oregon / $$**
Half the grapes for this beautiful, light-bodied red are from King Estate's certified organic vineyard.

PENNER-ASH WINE CELLARS

Lynn Penner-Ash's talent with Pinot Noir marked her as a rising star during her stint as winemaker at Oregon's Rex Hill. In 2001 she quit to build her own small winery in the Yamhill-Carlton District. A Pinot Noir devotee, Penner-Ash also makes tiny lots of Syrah, Viognier and Riesling.

● **Penner-Ash Dussin Vineyard Pinot Noir / 2009 / Willamette Valley / $$$** Five different clones of Pinot Noir help give this concentrated, spice- and herb-edged cuvée its complexity.

● **Penner-Ash Syrah / 2008 / Oregon / $$$**
Chewy and dense, with spicy chocolate and root beer flavors.

PONZI VINEYARDS

In the early 1970s, Dick Ponzi helped jump-start Oregon's wine industry when he founded Ponzi Vineyards. His winemaker daughter Luisa follows in his footsteps, making Pinot Noir, Chardonnay and Pinot Gris from some of the state's oldest vines, as well as wines with obscure grapes like Dolcetto and Arneis.

○ **Ponzi Vineyards Pinot Gris / 2009 / Willamette Valley / $$**
Stainless steel fermentation brings out lively citrus aromas.

● **Ponzi Vineyards Tavola Pinot Noir / 2009 / Willamette Valley / $$** A fresh, medium-bodied red with soft, ripe berry fruit, tingly acidity and a peppery edge.

SOKOL BLOSSER WINERY

An urban planner with a yen for rural living, Bill Blosser, along with his wife, Susan Sokol, purchased an abandoned prune orchard in the Dundee Hills to plant grapevines in the 1970s. Today Sokol Blosser's prestige rests on organically farmed Pinot Noir—made since 1998 by supertalented Ross Rosner—with the rare Single Block Pinot Noirs at the top.

○ **Sokol Blosser Pinot Gris / 2009 / Willamette Valley / $$** Fresh and medium-bodied, with intriguing notes of green fig.

● **Sokol Blosser Big Tree Block Pinot Noir / 2008 / Dundee Hills / $$$** Fragrant spice and lavender notes lead to streamlined berry flavors in this Pinot.

● **Sokol Blosser Estate Cuvée Pinot Noir / 2008 / Dundee Hills / $$$** Deliciously vibrant and expressive, with tangy red cherry, raspberry and floral flavors.

SOTER VINEYARDS

Tony Soter first gained fame as a California winemaker, helping to propel such revered labels as Spottswoode, Araujo and Etude to cult status. But this Oregon native returned to his roots when he founded Soter Vineyards in the Willamette Valley, where he makes ethereal Pinot Noirs in still and sparkling versions.

● **Soter Mineral Springs Ranch Pinot Noir / 2008 / Yamhill-Carlton District / $$$** From a vineyard overlooking the winery, this acclaimed cuvée is fragrant, rich and refined.

ST. INNOCENT WINERY

A former physician's assistant in pediatrics, vintner Mark Vlossak takes a meticulous approach to winemaking, and it pays off. Vlossak's small-lot Pinot Noirs, which come from an all-star collection of vineyards across the Willamette Valley, are among the most sought after in Oregon. Small amounts of Pinot Gris, Pinot Blanc and Chardonnay round out the portfolio.

● **St. Innocent Villages Cuvée Pinot Noir / 2009 / Willamette Valley / $$** Lithe, with strawberry, lavender and cedar accents.

● **St. Innocent Momtazi Vineyard Pinot Noir / 2008 / McMinnville / $$$** The Momtazi Vineyard's steep hillside blocks result in this structured Pinot full of concentrated fruit.

STOLLER VINEYARDS

Bill Stoller's family once ran one of Oregon's largest turkey farms; he converted some of that land to plant Pinot Noir vines. His exquisite wines are all estate-grown and vinified in the industry's first LEED Gold–certified winery. Those in the SV tier are made from older vines; JV bottlings come from younger vines.

○ **Stoller SV Estate Chardonnay / 2009 / Dundee Hills / $$**
This stylish wine shows dense citrus zest and peach flavors.

● **Stoller SV Estate Pinot Noir / 2008 / Dundee Hills / $$$**
Deeper and firmer than the JV Pinot, with an appealing meaty accent to fresh cherry fruit.

WILLAKENZIE ESTATE

Named for a sedimentary soil unique to the Willamette Valley, this boutique estate in the Chehalem Mountains is known for its tiny lots of clone- and site-specific Pinot Noirs. Thanks to talented winemaker Thibaud Mandet (whose résumé includes stints in Corsica and Texas), WillaKenzie's more affordable Pinot Gris and entry-level Pinot Noir offer plenty of drinking pleasure too.

● **WillaKenzie Estate Estate Cuvée Pinot Noir / 2009 / Willamette Valley / $$** A supremely elegant and fresh Pinot Noir with pretty berry, floral and cherry notes.

WASHINGTON STATE

Though best known for its vast output of affordable wines, Washington, the second-largest premium wine–producing state in the U.S., has become a source of complex reds that rival top California bottlings—often at half the price. The industry is growing too: In the past decade, Washington has more than tripled its number of wineries and approved six new AVAs.

WASHINGTON STATE: AN OVERVIEW

Most winemaking in Washington takes place inland, where vineyards are sheltered from the coastal weather by the Cascade Range and enjoy sunny, relatively dry summers. The state's largest wine region is the Columbia Valley, which encompasses many prominent subregions, including the Yakima Valley, Red Mountain and the Walla Walla Valley (the last of which, in southeastern Washington, straddles the border with Oregon).

🍇 WASHINGTON STATE GRAPES & STYLES

A white wine–centric state before its reds gained success, Washington produces almost as much Riesling as Chardonnay. Cool nights allow the state's vintners to make Rieslings in a range of styles—from dry to sweet—and Chardonnays that are typically lighter and more refreshing than California versions. Aromatic white varieties such as Pinot Gris, Sauvignon Blanc and Gewürztraminer do well in the state's northern climate too. The Gewürztraminer produced is ripe and floral, usually in an off-dry style.

A trio of powerhouse grapes—Cabernet Sauvignon, Merlot and Syrah—account for nearly 90 percent of Washington's red wines. Cabernets are smooth-textured and bold, and tend to be more restrained than California's dense, riper-style offerings. The state is arguably the best source in the country for Merlot; its top bottles have a distinctive, spicy complexity and seductive depth. Syrah is Washington's brightest up-and-comer, turning out wines with savory flavors and a firm structure that's missing in warm-region versions. The state also grows modest quantities of Cabernet Franc, Malbec and Pinot Noir, as well as a small but important amount of Lemberger (also called Blaufränkisch).

Producers/ Washington State

ANDREW WILL

Winemaker Chris Camarda is famous for his site-specific reds—chiefly Bordeaux-style wines—from some of Washington's greatest vineyards, like Ciel du Cheval (Red Mountain) and Champoux (Horse Heaven Hills). Their tiny quantities and high prices make them inaccessible to most. Look for Camarda's more affordable series of excellent multivineyard, single-varietal reds.

- **Andrew Will Cabernet Franc / 2009 / Columbia Valley / $$**
A beautifully made, tobacco-scented red sourced chiefly from three famous vineyards.
- **Andrew Will Ciel du Cheval Vineyard Red Wine / 2008 / Red Mountain / $$$** This black-fruited blend of Bordeaux varieties shows the muscular tannins typical of Red Mountain.

BETZ FAMILY WINERY

A legendary figure in Washington wine, Bob Betz headed up research for the state's biggest wine company, Château Ste. Michelle, for decades before starting this microwinery in 1997. Betz's six reds are among the state's best. He recently sold the winery but will continue making the wines until 2016.

- **Betz Family Winery Clos de Betz Red Wine** / 2008 / Columbia Valley / $$$ Merlot dominates this blend, which offers unsweetened-chocolate, cedar and cola flavors.
- **Betz Family Winery Père de Famille Cabernet Sauvignon** / 2008 / Columbia Valley / $$$ This Cab's concentrated cocoa, cedar and currant flavors are smoothly textured and refined.

BUTY WINERY

Superstar consultant Zelma Long is a mentor to Buty Winery's Caleb Foster and Nina Buty Foster, which helps explain how they achieved fame in so short a time. The couple founded their small Walla Walla winery in 2000, sourcing grapes from top vineyards while planting their own organic site, Rockgarden. The wines they make under the Buty and Beast labels are outstanding.

- **Buty Columbia Rediviva Phinny Hill Vineyard** / 2007 / Horse Heaven Hills / $$$ Chocolate and black cherry notes define this terrific, ageworthy Syrah-Cabernet blend.
- **Buty Merlot–Cabernet Franc** / 2009 / Columbia Valley / $$$ A tangy, cherry-driven red with impressive density.

CHATEAU STE. MICHELLE

Few wineries combine scale and quality with such success as Chateau Ste. Michelle. Head winemaker Bob Bertheau oversees the nearly two-million-case annual production, which includes some of the most reliably delicious value wines in the U.S. and top offerings such as the Eroica Rieslings and Ethos cuvées.

- ○ **Chateau Ste. Michelle & Dr. Loosen Eroica Riesling** / 2009 / Columbia Valley / $$ Light-bodied and vibrant, with bright apple, lime and orange tones.
- **Chateau Ste. Michelle Canoe Ridge Estate Merlot** / 2008 / Horse Heaven Hills / $$ This suave blend of Merlot, Cabernet and Syrah has a satiny texture and ripe, focused flavors.

COLUMBIA CREST

Winemaker Ray Einberger worked at Napa's famous Opus One winery and at Bordeaux's Château Mouton Rothschild before joining this value-oriented producer in 1993. His luxury-wine experience set high standards for Columbia Crest, which he officially passed on to protégé Juan Muñoz Oca last year.

- **Columbia Crest Grand Estates Cabernet Sauvignon** / 2008 / Columbia Valley / $ Toasty oak flavors infuse a base of coffee, cedar and chocolate in this bottling.
- **Columbia Crest H3 Cabernet Sauvignon** / 2008 / Horse Heaven Hills / $ Lavishly oaked, with caramel, chocolate and cedar flavors filled out with black fruit.

COLUMBIA WINERY

This winery marks its 50th anniversary in 2012. Named for the Columbia Valley, where it's located, the winery offers a lovely, affordable Riesling and a lineup of traditional reds in several price tiers—all crafted by winemaker Kerry Norton since 2007.

- ○ **Columbia Winery Cellarmaster's Riesling** / 2009 / Columbia Valley / $ This white's robust peach flavors are deliciously juicy and made vivid by bright acidity.
- ○ **Columbia Winery Pinot Gris** / 2009 / Columbia Valley / $ Silky yet crisp, with almond, apple and herb notes.

DUNHAM CELLARS

Walla Walla native Eric Dunham was moonlighting from his day job when, in 1995, he started making his own wine on the side. He transitioned quickly to the role of successful proprietor, thanks to a string of impressive reds. Today he makes outstanding Cabernet, Syrah and Merlot, along with some value-priced whites and multivineyard blends.

> **WINE INTEL**
> Its label doesn't say so, but the Columbia Valley Cabernet blend Pursued by Bear is a joint creation of Washington-born actor Kyle MacLachlan and Eric Dunham.

- **Dunham Cellars Trutina** / 2007 / Columbia Valley / $$ A spicy blend of Cabernet, Syrah, Merlot and Cabernet Franc.
- **Dunham Cellars XIII Cabernet Sauvignon** / 2007 / Columbia Valley / $$$ Fragrant black cherry notes and smooth tannins are evidence of 2007's warm growing season and cool, dry fall.

THE HOGUE CELLARS

Started in 1979 with fewer than six acres of Riesling vines planted on the Hogue family's Columbia Valley farm, Hogue Cellars had become one of the state's largest producers by the time brothers Mike and Gary Hogue sold it in 2001 to wine giant Constellation. The brand specializes in affordable, aromatic whites (with Riesling still the star) plus well-made Cabernet, Merlot and Syrah.

○ **Hogue Riesling** / 2009 / Columbia Valley / $
Citrus and peach flavors mark this lovely off-dry bargain.
● **Genesis Syrah** / 2008 / Columbia Valley / $$
The cool 2008 vintage gave this spicy, fragrant Syrah its particularly firm structure.

JANUIK WINERY/NOVELTY HILL

These brands share a winery and a winemaker, Mike Januik, best known for being head winemaker at Chateau Ste. Michelle for most of the 1990s. Novelty Hill grapes come chiefly from its owners' estate vineyard in Columbia Valley; for his brand, Januik selects fruit from some of the state's most vaunted vineyards.

○ **Novelty Hill Stillwater Creek Vineyard Chardonnay** / 2009 / Columbia Valley / $$ Elegant peach, apple and vanilla flavors are matched by refreshing acidity.
● **Januik Champoux Vineyard Cabernet Sauvignon** / 2008 / Horse Heaven Hills / $$$ Polished and powerful, this red reveals layers of supple dark chocolate, oak and mocha.

K VINTNERS/CHARLES SMITH WINES

Rock band manager–turned–vintner Charles Smith (FOOD & WINE's Winemaker of the Year in 2009) earned instant fame with his Syrah-based K reds. But these small-lot wines are hard to find and expensive, so fans have been jubilant over Smith's introduction of affordable new labels like the House Wine series and other value offerings, such as the Velvet Devil Merlot.

● **The Boy** / 2008 / Walla Walla Valley / $$$
This hearty Grenache shows robust spicy and cherry flavors.
● **The Creator** / 2008 / Washington State / $$$
A powerful blend of Cabernet and Syrah, with ripe tannins, generous spice and black fruit.

L'ECOLE NO. 41

Marty and Megan Clubb did what lots of wine-loving urbanites dream about: In 1989, they left corporate jobs in San Francisco to take over a tiny winery started by Megan's parents in rural Washington. The Clubbs focused L'Ecole No. 41 on Bordeaux varietals, later expanding to Syrah and Chardonnay. Their elegant wines helped set Walla Walla's reputation as a premier wine zone.

● **L'Ecole Nº 41 Merlot** / 2008 / Columbia Valley / $$
This chocolaty, herb-accented blend is crafted with fruit from several Columbia Valley vineyards.

● **L'Ecole Nº 41 Cabernet Sauvignon** / 2008 / Walla Walla Valley / $$$ Firm tannins nicely frame this Cabernet's pretty herb and mocha notes.

LONG SHADOWS VINTNERS

After a 20-year career as CEO of a giant Washington wine company, Allen Shoup founded Long Shadows, a label devoted to luxury wines from top Washington vineyards, in partnership with winemaking stars. Among those are Tuscany's Folonari family, Napa's Philippe Melka and Australia's John Duval. All wines are produced at Shoup's state-of-the-art Walla Walla facility.

● **Feather** / 2007 / Columbia Valley / $$$
Winemaker Randy Dunn goes for freshness and balance in this big, classically structured Cabernet.

● **Sequel Syrah** / 2007 / Columbia Valley / $$$
Australian John Duval blends grapes from a diverse selection of Columbia Valley vineyards for this dense, richly layered red.

PEPPER BRIDGE WINERY/AMAVI CELLARS

Owned by the Goff and McKibben families and Swiss-born winemaker Jean-François Pellet, these boutique sister wineries in Walla Walla make superb reds from stellar vineyards. Pepper Bridge focuses on ageworthy Merlots, elegant Cabernets and blends; Amavi specializes in Cabernet and Syrah.

● **Amavi Cellars Syrah** / 2008 / Walla Walla Valley / $$
Big but graceful, with a spicy, savory side to its cherry flavors.

● **Pepper Bridge Merlot** / 2008 / Walla Walla Valley / $$$
A serious, ageworthy Merlot with spicy, fresh plum flavors.

SEVEN HILLS WINERY

For a winemaker, getting permission to buy grapes from the Seven Hills Vineyard in Walla Walla is like being admitted into an exclusive club. Casey McClellan had an advantage: His family planted the vineyard in the 1980s. It's a key source for their well-regarded Seven Hills Winery. McClellan's Cabernet and Merlot are reliably good; varietal wines from less-common Bordeaux grapes, such as Malbec and Petit Verdot, are compelling.

○ **Seven Hills Riesling / 2009 / Columbia Valley / $**
An outstanding value worth stocking by the case for its refreshing, sweet-and-sour lime-and-peach profile.
○ **Seven Hills Talcott Vineyard Viognier / 2009 / Columbia Valley / $$** Fleshy but not flabby, this Viognier showcases ripe, soft peach and vanilla notes.

WOODWARD CANYON

Though its fame has grown in the years since Rick Small founded this boutique Walla Walla winery in 1981, Woodward Canyon's output is still modest (about 15,000 cases). The winery's approach is old-school, opting for tiny-lot fermentations and traditionally styled, balanced wines. Woodward Canyon's Cabernets and three whites are among the state's most sought-after wines.

○ **Woodward Canyon Chardonnay / 2009 / Washington State / $$$** An exuberant, creamy mix of coconut, vanilla and poached-pear flavors.
● **Nelms Road Cabernet Sauvignon / 2008 / Washington State / $$** Impressive depth and balance make this plum- and cherry-inflected red a good value.
● **Woodward Canyon Artist Series #17 Cabernet Sauvignon / 2008 / Washington State / $$$** Beautifully integrated coconut and toasted-oak notes linger on the palate in this supple red.

OTHER U.S. STATES

A handful of non–West Coast producers in the U.S. have been able to overcome the challenges of harsh climates, poor soils, a highly competitive wine market and distribution difficulties to achieve great success. Today every state can claim at least one winery, and some of America's fastest-growing wine regions are in the least likely of locations.

OTHER U.S. STATES: AN OVERVIEW

Climate is the biggest challenge facing vintners in most states. Because cold winters and hot, humid summers spell trouble for the traditional European *Vitis vinifera* grape varieties (such as Chardonnay, Cabernet Sauvignon, Sauvignon Blanc), winemakers in many states often choose to work with the hardier native American or French-American hybrid grapes.

New York's Finger Lakes and Long Island are well-established vinifera regions, but new wineries focused on European grapes are proliferating in Virginia, Maryland and the Southwest, especially Arizona and Texas. New Mexico's high-elevation vineyards produce very fine European-style sparkling wines (see p. 267) as well as appealing reds. In mid-Atlantic and Midwestern states, winemakers are using hybrid grapes that resemble European varieties in flavor more closely than native grapes do.

❧ OTHER U.S. STATES GRAPES & STYLES

When it comes to white varieties, Riesling and Gewürztraminer thrive in parts of the Northeast—especially New York's Finger Lakes region. Chardonnay and Sauvignon Blanc benefit from the slightly longer growing season on Long Island, which also produces some good-quality sparkling wines. Hybrid white grapes such as Vidal Blanc are used to make delicious dessert wines in New York, Virginia and Texas. Despite a relatively warm, humid growing season, Virginia winemakers produce terrific Chardonnay and Viognier. Idaho is also becoming a source of well-crafted vinifera-based white wines.

Red wine producers are doing well in many pockets throughout the country. In New York, Long Island vintners work with Cabernet Sauvignon, Merlot and Cabernet Franc, while winemakers in the cool-climate Finger Lakes region farther north focus on Cabernet Franc and Pinot Noir, which can excel in good vintages (such as 2007). In Virginia, local grape varieties like Norton grow alongside increasing amounts of vinifera varieties, such as Cabernet Sauvignon, Cabernet Franc, Merlot and (surprisingly) Tannat, a powerful red grape native to the Madiran region of southwestern France. In Texas and Arizona, Merlot, Cabernet Sauvignon and Syrah vines do well, and producers are also creating some interesting red wines with Grenache, Mourvèdre, Tempranillo and Sangiovese. Finicky Pinot Noir thrives in New Mexico's high-elevation vineyards.

Producers/ Other U.S. States

ARIZONA
CADUCEUS CELLARS

Mayard James Keenan, the lead singer of hard-rock band Tool, founded Arizona's respected Caduceus Cellars in 2004. Together with winemaker Eric Glomski, Keenan works with a diverse mix of grapes at his vineyards near Sedona, in the state's center.

- Merkin Vineyards Shinola / 2009 / Arizona / $$
  Under the winery's Merkin label, this blend of Cabernet, Merlot and Sangiovese has intriguing mineral and meaty undertones.
- Caduceus Sancha / 2008 / Cochise County / $$$
  This ripe red is mostly Tempranillo with a splash of Grenache.

MISSOURI
STONE HILL WINERY

Founded in 1847, Stone Hill had become the second-largest winery in the U.S. by the time Prohibition shut it down. Current owners Jim and Betty Held revitalized the run-down Missouri estate and today champion the indigenous Norton grape, as well as French-American hybrids such as Chardonel and Vignoles.

- Stone Hill Winery Vignoles / 2010 / Missouri / $
  The hybrid Vignoles grape yields fragrant, sweetish whites with citrus and tropical fruit flavors, as in this appealing example.
- Stone Hill Winery Norton / 2008 / Hermann / $$
  A great introduction to this native variety, with firm black fruit and chunky tannins.

NEW YORK
CHANNING DAUGHTERS WINERY

Tennis courts are more common than vineyards in Bridgehampton, Long Island, where Walter Channing planted some of the region's first Chardonnay vines in a former potato farm in 1982. Today his boutique winery, with the skilled Christopher Tracy as winemaker, is one of Long Island's benchmark producers.

○ **Mosaico** / 2008 / The Hamptons, Long Island / $$
A fragrant, lithe blend of five white grape varieties.
○ **Scuttlehole Chardonnay** / 2009 / Long Island / $$
Made without oak in a fruity style, with pear and apple notes.

HERMANN J. WIEMER VINEYARD

This winery in New York's Finger Lakes region produces some of the nation's finest Rieslings—exhilarating bottlings that rival the best from overseas. In 2007, founder Hermann Wiemer turned the estate over to his gifted protégé, Fred Merwarth, who continues making wines exclusively from three estate vineyards.

○ **Hermann J. Wiemer Dry Riesling** / 2009 / Seneca Lake /
$$ Each estate vineyard contributes to this lively, apple- and lime-driven bottling.
○ **Hermann J. Wiemer Semi-Dry Riesling** / 2009 / Seneca Lake /
$$ Apple and grapefruit notes have a hint of sweetness.

TEXAS
FLAT CREEK ESTATE

When Rick and Madelyn Naber bought their Texas Hill Country estate in 1998, the plan was to enjoy an early retirement growing peaches and riding Harleys. But the soil was better suited to grapes, so they planted everything from Syrah to Sangiovese. Today their wines are recognized as being among Texas's best.

○ **Flat Creek Estate Pinot Grigio** / 2009 / American / $$
An appealing mix of green almond and sweet apple flavors.
● **Flat Creek Estate Syrah** / 2008 / American / $$
Light and juicy, with vanilla-edged chocolate and berry notes.

VIRGINIA
KESWICK VINEYARDS

This Virginia winery was created in 2000 by entrepreneur Al Schornberg on a historic plantation near Charlottesville. South African winemaker Stephen Barnard crafts bright, silky Viogniers, among others; all show how terrific Virginia wines can be.

○ **Keswick Vineyards Estate Reserve Viognier** / 2009 /
Monticello / $$ Neutral French oak adds weight to this wine's fragrant peach, pear and apricot notes.

Australia

Wine Region

Australian wine is at an interesting crossroads. A single powerhouse brand, Yellowtail, sells more than 40 percent of the Australian wine in the U.S. Yet Australia's wines are vastly more diverse than this statistic suggests: Complex reds and whites are produced from coast to coast, from the Yarra Valley's elegant Pinot Noirs to Western Australia's ageworthy Cabernet blends. And dry, intense Australian Rieslings are a national treasure.

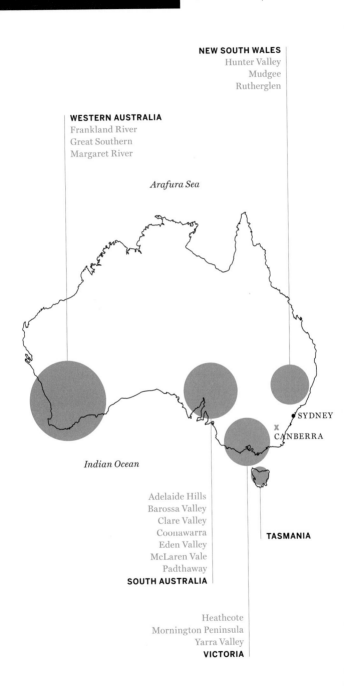

NEW SOUTH WALES
Hunter Valley
Mudgee
Rutherglen

WESTERN AUSTRALIA
Frankland River
Great Southern
Margaret River

Arafura Sea

SYDNEY
x
CANBERRA

Indian Ocean

Adelaide Hills
Barossa Valley
Clare Valley
Coonawarra
Eden Valley
McLaren Vale
Padthaway
SOUTH AUSTRALIA

TASMANIA

Heathcote
Mornington Peninsula
Yarra Valley
VICTORIA

Australia

USTRALIA IS THE world's fourth-largest exporter of wine, with more than 2,000 wineries across 64 designated growing regions in six states. South Australia is home to the country's most acclaimed regions, among them the Shiraz-centric Barossa Valley and McLaren Vale; the cooler Clare and Eden valleys, where Riesling thrives; and Coonawarra, synonymous with Cabernet Sauvignon. Pinot Noir excels in Victoria's Yarra Valley. Hunter Valley in New South Wales is known for its Shiraz, Sémillon, Cabernet and Chardonnay. Western Australia makes some of the country's best Chardonnays.

❖ AUSTRALIAN GRAPES & STYLES

Chardonnay is Australia's most important white. Most Australian Chardonnays are multiregion blends made in a full-bodied, often lightly sweet style and bearing the South Australia or South Eastern Australia designation. (The latter is a zone about five times the size of California.) But other than these industrial bottlings, Australian Chardonnays are generally fresher and less sweet these days. That's particularly true of wines from cooler regions, such as South Australia's Adelaide Hills, Victoria's Mornington Peninsula and Tasmania. The Margaret River region in Western Australia makes very minerally, complex versions.

Riesling is Australia's second most important high-quality white grape. The Clare Valley produces mainly austere, dry Rieslings with citrus and mineral flavors. Good Sauvignon Blanc can also be found, though the Sémillon grape tends to eclipse it in Australia, yielding mostly dry white wines with intriguing honey-lemon characteristics. The widely grown Portuguese grape Verdelho produces a few noteworthy wines marked by lovely citrus, herb and nut flavors. Gewürztraminer, Viognier and Pinot Gris are all increasing in popularity.

Australia's leading red grape and signature wine is Shiraz. Remarkably different from French Syrah (they are from the same grape variety), Shiraz has more-explosive berry flavors as well as spice and eucalyptus notes. Grown throughout the country, Shiraz is at its best in the Barossa Valley and McLaren Vale, in South Australia; the Hunter Valley, in New South Wales; and several Victoria regions. Shiraz is often aged in American oak (rather than French barrels), which complements its jammy, ripe fruit flavors—and adds to its affordability.

Cabernet Sauvignon thrives here as well. Australian Cabernets run from simple and light to complex and full-bodied; the finest are capable of extensive aging. Warmer areas tend to bring out berry and chocolate flavors, whereas cooler-climate places such as the Margaret River region produce more-refined versions. Tiny Coonawarra, with its unique "terra rossa" soil, yields some of the country's greatest Cabernets. Winemakers often blend Shiraz with Cabernet for everyday wines as well as for iconic ones such as Penfolds Grange.

Australia's less heralded reds are Grenache and Mourvèdre, both originally from France's Rhône Valley. Grenache displays many of the same fruit-forward characteristics as Shiraz but with a lighter body, while Mourvèdre shows a smokier, spicier personality. Many vintners combine the two with Shiraz in blends labeled *GSM* (Grenache, Shiraz, Mourvèdre). Planted in several wine regions throughout Australia, Pinot Noir has succeeded mainly on the island of Tasmania and in Victoria's Yarra Valley and Mornington Peninsula.

AUSTRALIAN WINE LABELS

Most Australian labels specify producer, region, vintage and grape. Blends tend to be named with the dominant grape listed first; sometimes only the initials are given, as in *GSM*.

Producers/ Australia

ANGOVE FAMILY WINEMAKERS

An immigrant from Cornwall, England, Dr. William Angove established this winery in 1886 as a complement to his medical practice outside Adelaide and prescribed wine to patients as a tonic. Today Angove is one of Australia's biggest family-owned wineries, offering well-made wines from across South Australia.

○ **Angove Family Winemakers Vineyard Select Sauvignon Blanc / 2009 / Adelaide Hills / $$** The fruit for this tangy, cool-climate white comes from the southern reaches of the Adelaide Hills.

● **Angove Family Winemakers Vineyard Select Shiraz / 2008 / McLaren Vale / $$** This red serves up bold vanilla and cedar flavors rounded out with ripe dark-fruit and earth tones.

BAROSSA VALLEY ESTATE

Though best known for its iconic, powerful E&E Black Pepper Shiraz, this 80-plus-member cooperative also makes an array of reasonably priced wines. Offerings include Shiraz from some of the region's oldest vines, as well as Chardonnay, Riesling and Tempranillo. The E Minor wines are terrific values.

○ **Barossa Valley Estate E Minor Chardonnay / 2008 / Barossa Valley / $** Stuart Bourne makes this Chardonnay, which shows nice balance between its oak influence and lemony acidity.

● **Barossa Valley Estate E&E Black Pepper Shiraz / 2005 / Barossa Valley / $$$$** Beautifully ripe and supple, with dense black cherry, cola and dark chocolate flavors.

BROKENWOOD WINES

Founded in 1970 by three lawyer friends, including now well-known Australian wine writer James Halliday, this Hunter Valley estate has become one of the country's most reputable table wine producers. Iain Riggs has been winemaker since 1982, and many of his refined wines, including the famous Graveyard Shiraz, are small-production cuvées from single vineyards.

○ **Brokenwood ILR Reserve Semillon** / 2005 / Hunter Valley / $$$ Despite its considerable age, this is focused and fresh, with green almond and bracing citrus flavors.

● **Brokenwood Cricket Pitch Cabernet Sauvignon–Merlot– Shiraz** / 2009 / South Eastern Australia / $$ This streamlined blend shows concentrated herb and red berry flavors.

● **Brokenwood Graveyard Vineyard Shiraz** / 2006 / Hunter Valley / $$$$ Decant this formidable Shiraz to give its earthy blackberry and chocolate flavors time to unwind.

CAPE MENTELLE

Brothers David, Mark and Giles Hohnen founded Cape Mentelle in the then undiscovered Margaret River region on Australia's southwest coast in 1970; their red blends soon garnered inter-national acclaim. Now owned by French luxury-goods group LVMH, the winery also offers a racy Chardonnay and an always tasty Sauvignon Blanc–Sémillon, plus Shiraz and Zinfandel.

○ **Cape Mentelle Sauvignon Blanc–Semillon** / 2010 / Margaret River / $ A grassy, crisp white with lime and lanolin notes.

○ **Cape Mentelle Chardonnay** / 2007 / Margaret River / $$ Refreshing, with lemon-lime and pear flavors and vanilla nuances, this illustrates the winery's rich yet elegant style.

● **Cape Mentelle Cabernet Sauvignon** / 2004 / Margaret River / $$ This great example of a brawny Cabernet from a relatively cooler climate has a minty black currant profile.

CIMICKY WINES

Charles Cimicky, the son of a Czech immigrant, uses no chemi-cal fertilizers and for years has been reducing his reliance on irrigation. Barossa's naturally lean soils and scarcity of water result in small, intensely concentrated grapes. Cimicky and his wife, Jennie, focus mostly on estate-grown reds, making limited amounts of complex, multilayered Shiraz, Grenache and blends.

● **Charles Cimicky Reserve Shiraz** / 2006 / Barossa Valley / $$$ Dense blueberry and dark chocolate flavors are layered with hints of peppermint and generous vanilla oak.

● **Charles Cimicky The Autograph Shiraz** / 2006 / Barossa Valley / $$$ The black licorice and dark-fruit flavors in this red have a firmly tannic structure.

CLARENDON HILLS

Winemaker Roman Bratasiuk established Clarendon Hills in McLaren Vale in 1990, and the property since has become one of the most sought-after names in single-vineyard, old-vine Australian reds. Its top wines—particularly the flagship Astralis Shiraz—are as known for their high cost as they are for their hedonistic flavors (though prices have come down recently).

- Clarendon Hills Clarendon Grenache / 2007 / Clarendon / $$$ A heavyweight, marked by big tannins and a wallop of kirsch and ripe raspberries.
- Clarendon Hills Hickinbotham Cabernet Sauvignon / 2007 / Clarendon / $$$ Old vines, hand-harvesting and wild yeast fermentation result in this powerful, dark, tannic red.
- Clarendon Hills Piggott Range Syrah / 2007 / Clarendon / $$$$ This burly single-vineyard red adds exotic sandalwood spice accents to dark fruit.

D'ARENBERG

Chester Osborn—current head of this family-owned winery founded in 1912—helped originate the trend toward oddly named Australian wines with offerings such as the Hermit Crab and the Laughing Magpie. But don't be deceived by the whimsical monikers: The d'Arenberg lineup includes ambitious cuvées that rank among Australia's finest, like Dead Arm Shiraz.

- d'Arenberg The Stump Jump Grenache-Shiraz-Mourvèdre / 2009 / McLaren Vale / $ Named for a 19th-century plow invented in South Australia, this fresh wine is berry-driven.
- d'Arenberg The Coppermine Road Cabernet Sauvignon / 2007 / McLaren Vale / $$$$ Mint and black currant notes mingle in this muscular, concentrated Cabernet.

ELDERTON WINES

Neil and Lorraine Ashmead released their first vintage in 1982, from one of the world's largest plots of ancient vines. Their 72-acre estate vineyard, where some blocks are 116 years old, yields one of Barossa's top wines, Command Shiraz. Winemaker Richard Langford supplements organically farmed estate grapes with some purchased fruit and opts for a more restrained style than many Barossa counterparts.

● **Elderton Cabernet Sauvignon** / 2007 / Barossa / $$
Time spent in American and French oak barrels contributed
nice hints of cedar and chocolate to this Cabernet.
● **Elderton Ode to Lorraine Cabernet Sauvignon–Shiraz–Merlot** /
2006 / Barossa / $$$ A blackberry-infused, three-variety
blend made with the best fruit from the estate vineyard.

FRANKLAND ESTATE

Western Australia's Frankland Estate is in the Frankland River
subregion, where cool temperatures and gravelly soils produce
superb Riesling—which is what this esteemed winery is now
known for. Judi Cullam, who founded Frankland with husband
Barrie Smith on his family's former sheep farm, has a knack for
crafting vivid whites and complex reds. The Isolation Ridge
wines are made with grapes from an organic estate vineyard.

○ **Rocky Gully Dry Riesling** / 2008 / Frankland River / $
Frankland's entry-level Riesling is a steal, loaded with petrol,
green apple and tangy lime tones.
○ **Frankland Estate Isolation Ridge Vineyard Dry Riesling** / 2009 /
Frankland River / $$ This is one of Australia's most famous
Rieslings, full of intense mineral, lemon and apple notes.
● **Frankland Estate Rocky Gully Shiraz-Viognier** / 2008 /
Western Australia / $ A touch of the white grape Viognier
adds a floral note to this fresh, blackberry-inflected red.

GRANT BURGE WINES

Grant Burge founded his namesake winery in 1988 after revital-
izing and then selling the historic Krondorf winery. Today he's
one of the Barossa Valley's largest private vineyard holders, and
the repurchased Krondorf winery now serves as his main facility
for making white wine. Grant Burge offerings range from every-
day bottlings made with fruit sourced from regions across South
Australia to a trio of high-end estate reds.

○ **Grant Burge Benchmark Chardonnay** / 2008 / South
Australia / $ This stainless steel–fermented Chardonnay offers
fresh lemon and green pear flavors.
● **The Holy Trinity Grenache-Shiraz-Mourvèdre** / 2006 /
Barossa / $$$ A peppermint-edged Rhône-style blend with
exuberant wild berry and cherry flavors.

GROSSET WINES

Jeffrey Grosset apprenticed under legendary Australian winemaker John Vickery before starting his own Clare Valley estate in 1981. Since then he's become famous for his masterful Rieslings—dry, steely wines that helped convince the world to take Australian Rieslings seriously. Top bottles include the Polish Hill and Watervale wines, though Grosset's non-Riesling offerings should not be overlooked.

○ **Grosset Piccadilly Chardonnay / 2005 / Adelaide Hills / $$**
Barrel fermentation adds cedar and vanilla to peach flavors.

○ **Grosset Polish Hill Riesling / 2010 / Clare Valley / $$$**
The 30th vintage of this benchmark Riesling has classic crisp green apple, lime and mineral flavors.

HARDYS

English immigrant Thomas Hardy planted a few acres of Grenache and Cabernet Sauvignon on a riverbank south of Adelaide in 1854, kick-starting one of the best-known labels in Australia. Hardys nearly single-handedly established the South Australia wine region. Family-owned until 1992, Hardys today is one of the world's biggest wine brands and a source of affordable bottlings. The top red, a Shiraz named for matriarch Eileen Hardy, lends sheen to the portfolio.

● **Hardys Nottage Hill Pinot Noir / 2009 / South Eastern Australia / $** Juicy watermelon and raspberry flavors are up front in this tangy, light-bodied Pinot.

● **Hardys Nottage Hill Shiraz / 2008 / South Eastern Australia / $** This easy-drinking, value-priced Shiraz features a soft touch of oak nicely woven with red-fruit flavors.

HENRY'S DRIVE VIGNERONS

Up-and-coming Henry's Drive is making some of Australia's best value wines from estate vineyards in Padthaway and McLaren Vale. Founders Kim and Mark Longbottom named it after Padthaway's 19th-century mail-coach driver. The Trial of John Montford Cabernet Sauvignon and the Reserve Shiraz are deliciously complex; the Morse Code wines are great values.

○ **Morse Code Chardonnay** / 2010 / Padthaway / $
From a vineyard with limestone and loamy soils, this features lots of quince, green pear and lemon flavors at a terrific price.

● **Morse Code Shiraz** / 2009 / Padthaway / $
A nicely affordable Shiraz that delivers a juicy, generous mouthful of black licorice, spice and ripe blackberry.

● **Henry's Drive Vignerons The Trial of John Montford Cabernet Sauvignon** / 2006 / Padthaway / $$ In this outstanding red, plush black currant flavors complement savory herb tones.

JIM BARRY WINES

With his wife, Nancy, Jim Barry helped pioneer modern Clare Valley winemaking in the 1960s and '70s, planting vineyards that have become some of the region's best-known sites. Among these is the Armagh Vineyard, the source of a monumentally dense Shiraz that's arguably the Clare Valley's most famous red. A handful of stellar Rieslings, the acclaimed McRae Wood Shiraz and three Cabernets are highlights in the stunning lineup.

○ **Jim Barry The Lodge Hill Dry Riesling** / 2010 / Clare Valley / $$ Barry purchased this vineyard in 1977, confident it would yield excellent Rieslings like this aromatic, tropical example.

● **The Cover Drive Cabernet Sauvignon** / 2009 / Coonawarra / $$
Grapes for this dark, fruity, herb-edged red come from the winery's newest vineyard, an old cricket ground in Coonawarra, where cooler temperatures make for ideal Cabernet.

JOHN DUVAL WINES

John Duval's elegant wines defy the stereotype of supersized Aussie reds. As Penfolds's chief winemaker from 1986 to 2002, Duval was renowned for his blending expertise. At his own, much smaller winery, he makes wines from some of the best Barossa vineyards: the Eligo and Entity Shirazes plus a Rhône-inspired red blend and a brand-new white under the Plexus label.

○ **John Duval Wines Plexus Marsanne-Roussanne-Viognier** / 2010 / Barossa Valley / $$ Duval ages about half of this Rhône-style blend in new and old French oak for six months.

● **John Duval Wines Plexus Shiraz-Grenache-Mourvèdre** / 2008 / Barossa Valley / $$$ This beautifully balanced red blend highlights dark fruit and expertly integrated oak.

KAESLER

Estate-made wines from old, dry-farmed vines are the focus of this boutique Barossa winery. The vineyards were established in 1893 by the Kaesler family. Winemaker Reid Bosward and wife Bindy, along with a Swiss family as backers, bought it in 2001 and have been turning out beautiful wines ever since.

● **Kaesler Stonehorse Shiraz** / 2008 / **Barossa Valley** / $$
A gutsy red with ripe dark-fruit and gravelly earth tones.

● **Kaesler The Bogan** / 2007 / **Barossa Valley** / $$$
Mostly from an old-vine site planted in 1899, this dense Shiraz is marked by black licorice and dark chocolate flavors.

KILIKANOON

This Clare Valley–based winery built its formidable reputation on its sleek, steely Rieslings and vibrant, polished reds. Most acclaimed are Kilikanoon's Mort's Block Riesling and a quartet of powerhouse Shirazes, from the Clare Valley (Oracle), Barossa Valley (Green's Vineyard and R Reserve) and McLaren Vale (M Reserve). Look also for the affordable Killerman's Run label.

○ **Kilikanoon Mort's Reserve Watervale Riesling** / 2009 / **Clare Valley** / $$$ Vibrant, mineral-laden lime and green apple flavors have a pleasant hint of petrol.

● **Kilikanoon Green's Vineyard Shiraz** / 2006 / **Barossa Valley** / $$$$ This rare Shiraz deftly balances its decadent chocolate, black pepper and dark-fruit notes.

LEEUWIN ESTATE

Few names in Australian wine are as prestigious as Leeuwin Estate. This tiny winery helped develop the Margaret River region in the mid-1970s and gained fame for its refined Chardonnays. Leeuwin's Art Series Chardonnay remains the flagship, but the more affordable Siblings cuvées are also worth seeking out.

○ **Leeuwin Estate Siblings Sauvignon Blanc–Semillon** / 2010 / **Margaret River** / $$ Dominated by Sauvignon Blanc, this juicy blend shows bright flavors of grapefruit, lime and herbs.

● **Leeuwin Estate Art Series Cabernet Sauvignon** / 2004 / **Margaret River** / $$$ A fragrant, stylish Cabernet with currant and savory herb and cedar flavors.

LINDEMAN'S

Melbourne-based Treasury Wine Estates owns this megawinery, known for value wines from across Australia. Winemaker Wayne Falkenberg has been at Lindeman's for over 34 years, providing continuity to a company that has grown in tandem with the Australian wine industry. Lindeman's wines range from inexpensive to quite pricey; the Bin line delivers good value.

○ Lindeman's Bin 90 Moscato / 2010 / South Eastern Australia / $ A light-bodied, slightly sweet white brimming with fragrant lime zest and orange blossom tones.

● Lindeman's Bin 40 Merlot / 2009 / South Eastern Australia / $ This shows surprisingly robust tannins for a value-priced red.

PENFOLDS

In the early 1950s, Penfolds created a red blend that eventually became Australia's most famous wine: the iconic Shiraz-based Penfolds Grange. Today this historic Barossa Valley producer (established in 1844) makes an array of wines across multiple price levels, employing a team of winemakers led by Peter Gago.

● Penfolds Bin 128 Shiraz / 2008 / Coonawarra / $$ Lively dark-fruit flavors have herb and cedar highlights.

● Penfolds RWT Shiraz / 2006 / Barossa Valley / $$$$ Aged for 14 months in 70 percent new French oak, this is a superb, ageworthy red with layers of ripe, concentrated fruit.

PENLEY ESTATE

Longtime Coonawarra winemaker Kym Tolley—a descendant of Penfolds's founder—started his own winery in 1988 after working at Penfolds for 15 years. While Australian reds have a reputation for going overboard with sweet fruit flavors, Tolley's all-estate-grown wines show a restrained hand; his top Cabernet and Shiraz wines are among the region's greatest.

● Penley Estate Hyland Shiraz / 2008 / Coonawarra / $$ A supple, spicy mix of blackberry and cherry fruit that is extraordinarily balanced and complex.

● Penley Estate Reserve Cabernet Sauvignon / 2006 / Coonawarra / $$$ This herb-infused, small-lot red is defined by a beautiful layering of firm tannins and black currant flavors.

PETALUMA

Brian Croser founded Petaluma with the goal of sourcing every grape from its best *terroir*. The winery buys Chardonnay grapes from the cool-climate Adelaide Hills region (where Petaluma is based), Riesling from the Clare Valley and Cabernet and Merlot from Coonawarra. Croser is no longer involved, but winemaker Andrew Hardy stays true to the house style of elegant wines.

○ **Petaluma Piccadilly Valley Chardonnay / 2005 / Adelaide Hills / $$** The mild 2005 vintage yielded this especially refreshing Chardonnay with bright, vibrant fruit.

● **Petaluma Shiraz / 2005 / Adelaide Hills / $$**
Adelaide Hills' cooler climate comes through in this wine's peppermint notes, which add nice lift to blackberry flavors.

PETER LEHMANN WINES

Fifth-generation Barossan Peter Lehmann started his winery as a way to save Barossa Valley grape growers facing bankruptcy during a massive grape glut in the late 1970s. Owned since 2003 by Swiss entrepreneur Donald Hess, Peter Lehmann Wines is one of the region's largest producers, and although it makes a range of wines, old-vine Barossa Shiraz remains responsible for the winery's top cuvées, such as the Stonewell Shiraz.

○ **Peter Lehmann Wines Layers / 2010 / Adelaide / $$**
A silky five-variety blend with yellow apple and lychee flavors.

● **Peter Lehmann of the Barossa Eight Songs Shiraz / 2005 / Barossa Valley / $$$** A velvety, rich and plummy Shiraz made from select parcels of old vines.

PEWSEY VALE VINEYARD

Pewsey Vale wines come from one of South Australia's oldest vineyard sites, a plot 1,600 feet above the Barossa Valley floor that was first planted in 1847. Riesling thrives in this cool region, and that's what Pewsey Vale co-founder Geoffrey Parsons wisely planted in 1961. The white wine–focused portfolio includes the famous Contours Riesling, released after five years of aging.

○ **Pewsey Vale Riesling / 2010 / Eden Valley / $$**
Individual blocks of grapes were picked separately at maximum ripeness for this racy, mineral-rich white.

PLANTAGENET

Plantagenet was established near Mount Baker in the vast Great Southern region in 1974. Its specialties, crafted today by wine-maker John Durham, are spicy Shiraz, crisp Riesling and vivid Cabernet Sauvignon, all of which get their signature vibrancy from the coolish climate. Wines fall under three labels (in ascending price order): Hazard Hill, Omrah and Plantagenet.

○ **Plantagenet Riesling** / 2009 / **Great Southern** / $$
Abundant minerals, low alcohol and tart lime flavors make this Riesling incredibly food-friendly.

● **Plantagenet Omrah Shiraz** / 2007 / **Western Australia** / $$
Firm and tangy, with loads of black fruit and vanilla accents.

ROSEMOUNT ESTATE

Rosemount's ubiquitous Diamond Label is the brand's calling card, encompassing a dozen bottlings designed for easy drinking at affordable prices. Step up a few dollars to the Show Reserve tier to find wines with more oomph; they're made in the same fruit-forward style, and the best examples offer real value. The Flagship tier includes three region-specific cuvées.

● **Rosemount Show Reserve GSM** / 2006 / **McLaren Vale** / $$
A fine, supple Rhône-style blend with ripe blueberry, spice and lively black cherry notes.

● **Rosemount Balmoral Syrah** / 2004 / **McLaren Vale** / $$$
Hitting its stride now (2004 is the current release), this Syrah shows bright flavors of spicy black fruit and lively tannins.

TORBRECK VINTNERS

Talented winemaker David Powell of Torbreck is known for fabulous (and fabulously expensive) Barossa Valley reds such as the RunRig Shiraz. His Grenache and Shiraz grapes are mostly from old vines, an obsession Powell picked up while working at Barossa's famous Rockland estate.

● **Torbreck Cuvée Juveniles** / 2009 / **Barossa Valley** / $$
Named for a hip Parisian wine bar, this raspberry-driven, Grenache-dominated blend is silky and has terrific depth.

● **Torbreck The Struie** / 2006 / **Barossa** / $$$
Plush black fruit and Asian spices mark this stylish Shiraz.

TWO HANDS

The "two hands" at this high-end *négociant* are owners Michael Twelftree and Richard Mintz, who acquire top-quality grapes throughout Australia. Winemaker Matt Wenk crafts showy wines, chiefly Shiraz. The Picture Series wines are the most affordable; the Single Vineyard and Garden Series tiers are more expensive; and the top cuvées are named after Greek gods.

- **Two Hands Bella's Garden Shiraz / 2008 / Barossa Valley / $$$**
  Its lushly textured black cherry and cedar flavors finish tight.
- **Two Hands Max's Garden Shiraz / 2007 / Heathcote / $$$**
  At nearly 15 percent alcohol, this powerful wine shows spicy mint and bittersweet chocolate flavors framed by big tannins.

VASSE FELIX

Vasse Felix was the first winery in the coastal Margaret River region, and it remains one of the best. Perth cardiologist Tom Cullity planted the original vines in 1967. Twenty years later Cullity sold it to the Holmes à Court family, and under their stewardship Vasse Felix has thrived, crafting noteworthy Chardonnay and Cabernet Sauvignon.

- ○ **Vasse Felix Chardonnay / 2009 / Margaret River / $$**
  A tart, bracing Chardonnay with ample lime and cream flavors woven with refreshing notes of sea salt.
- **Vasse Felix Cabernet Sauvignon / 2007 / Margaret River / $$**
  This red delivers ripe black currant flavors framed by oak.

WOLF BLASS

Although Wolf Blass is more famous for red wines (its Black Label Cabernet-Shiraz has won Australia's prestigious Jimmy Watson Trophy four times), this megawinery also produces stellar Rieslings and Chardonnays. The Yellow and Gold labels are value-oriented; Gray, Black and Platinum tiers are pricier.

- **Wolf Blass Gold Label Cabernet Sauvignon / 2006 / Coonawarra / $$** Aged in French and American oak for 15 months, this showcases balanced herb and currant flavors.
- **Wolf Blass Platinum Label Shiraz / 2004 / Barossa / $$$$**
  A bit of age on this Shiraz has helped integrate beautiful, velvety flavors of cocoa, black cherry and spice.

WOOP WOOP WINES

Woop Woop is Australian slang for "out in the middle of nowhere"—which is apt, as winemaker Ben Riggs travels thousands of miles between remote vineyards across southeastern Australia to source fruit for Woop Woop's six wines. His efforts pay off in juicy, fruit-driven whites and reds that offer unusually high quality at relatively low prices.

○ **Woop Woop Chardonnay** / 2009 / **South Eastern Australia** / **$**
Yellow apple and lemon zest flavors make for easy drinking.

● **Woop Woop Shiraz** / 2009 / **South Eastern Australia** / **$**
Grapes from Wrattonbully and Langhorne Creek contribute to this fleshy Shiraz marked by chocolate and black cherry.

YALUMBA

At 163, Yalumba is Australia's oldest family-owned winery, but this Barossa-based producer is no stodgy operation. Led by dynamic scion Robert Hill Smith, Yalumba is constantly innovating. Its portfolio of more than 50 wines includes Tempranillo and Vermentino, yet Shiraz and Cabernet remain the focus. Its benchmark Octavius Shiraz is one of the country's finest wines.

○ **Yalumba The Y Series Viognier** / 2010 / **South Australia** / **$**
Lemon, lychee and apricot flavors shine in this exotic white.

● **Yalumba Patchwork Shiraz** / 2008 / **Barossa** / **$$**
This focused, polished Shiraz spent a relatively brief six months in new and old French and American oak.

YANGARRA ESTATE VINEYARD

Every grape Yangarra crushes comes from a single 250-acre estate vineyard south of Adelaide. Yangarra, founded in 2001 and now owned by the Kendall-Jackson wine company, has developed a reputation for terrific Grenache, which hails from a prized parcel of gnarly 60-plus-year-old vines. Winemaker Peter Fraser has a deft hand with Shiraz and Chardonnay too.

● **Yangarra Estate Vineyard Old Vine Grenache** / 2008 / **McLaren Vale** / **$$** Delicious ripe raspberry flavors are accented by a touch of peppermint.

● **Yangarra Estate Vineyard Shiraz** / 2008 / **McLaren Vale** / **$$**
Zippy acidity lifts toasty oak, chocolate and black-fruit flavors.

New Zealand

Wine Region

New Zealand Sauvignon Blanc is one of the world's great wine-success stories. Vineyard plantings have tripled in the past decade, and the popularity of the country's signature peppery style continues to increase. But red wine production here is on the rise too, driven by world-class Pinot Noirs from Central Otago and Martinborough and outstanding Syrahs from up-and-coming regions like the North Island's Gimblett Gravels.

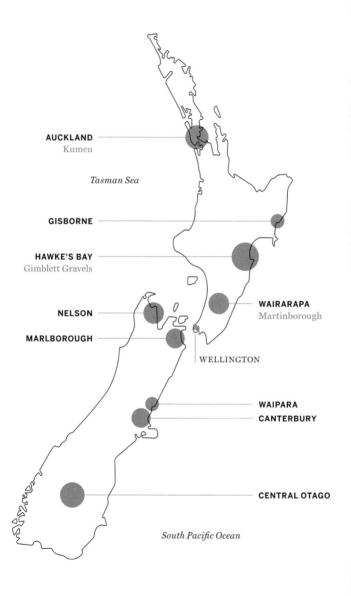

AUCKLAND
Kumeu

Tasman Sea

GISBORNE

HAWKE'S BAY
Gimblett Gravels

NELSON

MARLBOROUGH

WELLINGTON

WAIRARAPA
Martinborough

WAIPARA
CANTERBURY

CENTRAL OTAGO

South Pacific Ocean

New Zealand

THE FIRST MODERN commercial grapevines weren't planted in New Zealand until the 1970s. Today the country's winegrowing areas extend from the warm, northern reaches of subtropical Northland to southerly Central Otago. Climate on New Zealand's two main islands varies as much as the *terroir*: Conditions range from humid, rainy and temperate on the North Island to nearly continental in the South Island's Central Otago, where hot, dry summers follow cold winters.

❧ NEW ZEALAND GRAPES & STYLES

Few countries are as identified with a single grape as New Zealand is with Sauvignon Blanc. While the traditional style here is zingy and unoaked, with mouthwatering grass, lime and grapefruit flavors, warmer vintages and a move toward more tropically fruity wines have resulted in a wider array of styles.

More than two-thirds of New Zealand's Sauvignon Blanc comes from the South Island's Marlborough region. North Island Sauvignon Blancs tend to be riper and fruitier than those from Marlborough. Chardonnay runs from crisp and lean to ripe and melony; a trend toward less oak aging has improved the wines. Wairarapa and its subregion Martinborough—areas that originally established New Zealand's reputation as a great Pinot Noir producer—turn out noteworthy Chardonnays. Aromatic whites such as Riesling, Gewürztraminer and Pinot Gris are becoming increasingly fashionable, with the last now ranked as the country's fourth most planted grape. Gisborne, on the North Island, and the South Island's Waipara region have emerged as specialists in these varieties.

Vibrant acidity is a hallmark of New Zealand Pinot Noir, the most popular red. Bottlings from cooler regions such as Marlborough offer bright red-fruit flavors, whereas the Pinot Noirs from Central Otago are lusher, richer and more voluptuous.

Merlot and Cabernet Sauvignon are found mainly on the North Island, especially its warm Hawke's Bay subregion. Some of the best Cabernet grapes go into Bordeaux-style blends, which can be excellent. Syrah is the up-and-coming red. The finest examples come from the Gimblett Gravels subzone and show the grape's hallmark floral, spice and black-fruit notes.

NEW ZEALAND WINE LABELS

Labels generally list region, grape, vintage and, in some cases, vineyard name. The term *reserve* may be used to designate higher-quality wines but has no legal meaning.

Producers/ New Zealand

ATA RANGI

In 1980, pioneering vintner Clive Paton purchased and planted the Ata Rangi (Maori for "new beginning") property in Martinborough, and today the estate produces some of New Zealand's greatest Pinot Noirs. Winemaker Helen Masters, now at the helm, gets most of her fruit from estate vines; the entry-level cuvées come from a mix of purchased and estate grapes.

○ **Ata Rangi Sauvignon Blanc / 2010 / Martinborough / $$**
Fresh and bright, with equal parts lime, herbs and minerals.

● **Ata Rangi Pinot Noir / 2009 / Martinborough / $$$**
Green tea and black pepper notes accentuate the red berry flavors that are the hallmark of Martinborough Pinot Noir.

BABICH WINES

Founded by Croatian immigrant Josip Babich in 1916, Babich Wines is one of New Zealand's largest family-owned wine companies, and it's still located on the site of the family's Auckland homestead. Babich produces several tiers of mostly value-driven bottlings crafted by vintner Adam Hazeldine. Look for its Marlborough Sauvignon Blancs and Hawke's Bay Chardonnays.

○ **Babich Unoaked Chardonnay** / 2009 / Hawke's Bay / $
Creamy and broad, with expressive peach and lemon notes.

● **Babich Pinot Noir** / 2008 / Marlborough / $$
A blend of grapes from various parcels throughout Marlborough produces an alluring mix of wild berry and herb flavors.

● **Babich Winemakers' Reserve Pinot Noir** / 2008 / Marlborough / $$ This stellar reserve bottling offers supple, spice-edged strawberry fruit and a mineral-rich finish.

BRANCOTT ESTATE

With vast vineyard holdings on both islands, Brancott has a broad geographical reach that helps make it one of New Zealand's most successful producers. Ivan Yukich founded Brancott in 1934, and his son Frank planted the South Island's first commercial Sauvignon Blanc, in Marlborough, in 1973. Sauvignon Blanc remains Brancott's signature wine, though its lineup includes a cross section of popular varietals.

○ **Brancott Estate Marlborough Sauvignon Blanc** / 2010 / Marlborough / $ Zippy citrus zest, grass and herb flavors mark this as textbook New Zealand Sauvignon Blanc.

● **Brancott South Island Pinot Noir** / 2008 / South Island / $
Wild strawberry and raspberry flavors take on herb accents in this silky red crafted in an elegant, medium-bodied style.

CLOUDY BAY

This Marlborough winery earned world recognition for New Zealand with its iconic citrus- and green bell pepper–inflected Sauvignon Blanc. Arguably the country's best-known wine brand, Cloudy Bay has toned down its herbaceous style in recent years. At the helm today (founding winemaker Kevin Judd left in 2009), Nick Blampied-Lane and Tim Heath turn out vibrant Sauvignon Blancs plus great Chardonnay and Pinot Noir.

○ **Cloudy Bay Sauvignon Blanc** / 2010 / **Marlborough** / $$
A lively, savory white that's tailor-made for raw oysters.

● **Cloudy Bay Pinot Noir** / 2007 / **Marlborough** / $$$
This Pinot spent 12 months in French oak (new and used), yet
its tart cherry and red currant flavors remain vividly fresh.

CRAGGY RANGE

New Zealand's climate favors whites, but Craggy Range founder
Terry Peabody is a big believer in the country's ability to produce
world-class reds. Acclaimed winemaker Steve Smith cherry-
picks fruit from warmer vineyards all over New Zealand and
then crafts mostly single-vineyard bottlings. The resulting wines
are all truly outstanding, though Peabody confesses that Craggy
Range's Martinborough Sauvignon Blanc is his favorite.

○ **Craggy Range Te Muna Road Vineyard Sauvignon Blanc** /
2009 / **Martinborough** / $$ Limestone soils give this sleek, lime-
inflected white its deep mineral notes.

● **Craggy Range Gimblett Gravels Vineyard Sophia** / 2004 /
Hawke's Bay / $$$ This polished, black currant–infused red
shows the region's potential with Merlot-based blends.

● **Craggy Range Te Muna Road Vineyard Pinot Noir** / 2009 /
Martinborough / $$$ Solid tannins and green tea nuances
balance this red's supple berry flavors.

FELTON ROAD

The most famous winery in Central Otago, Fel-
ton Road helped establish New Zealand's repu-
tation for extraordinary Pinot Noir in the
1990s with its coveted Block 3 cuvée. Skilled
vintner Blair Walter uses fruit from organic
and/or biodynamic estate vineyards for Felton
Road's graceful wines, which also include
small-lot Chardonnays and Rieslings.

WINE INTEL
Goats, free-range
chickens and
wildflower fields
are part of Felton
Road's integrated
farming; it's one
of few wineries in
New Zealand to
farm completely
biodynamically.

○ **Felton Road Riesling** / 2009 / **Central Otago** / $$
A slight hint of sweetness makes this crisp apple- and lime-
accented Riesling a terrific choice for spicy foods.

● **Felton Road Pinot Noir** / 2009 / **Central Otago** / $$$
A benchmark bottling that overflows with juicy, concentrated
berry flavors and mineral notes.

GROVE MILL

Marlborough's Grove Mill winery buys carbon offsets for every case of wine it ships and was the world's first producer to achieve carbon-neutral certification. Another reason to buy its wines: Grove Mill's Marlborough Pinot Noir and Sauvignon Blanc are reliably delicious. Winemaker Dave Pearce's fragrant Rieslings and crisp Pinot Gris are also worth seeking out.

○ **Grove Mill Sauvignon Blanc** / 2009 / Marlborough / $
A racy mix of herb, lime and vegetable flavors.

● **Grove Mill Pinot Noir** / 2008 / Marlborough / $$
The winery's entry-level Pinot Noir displays chocolate-coated plum and berry flavors with well-integrated oak nuances.

KIM CRAWFORD WINES

A pioneer of New Zealand's unoaked Chardonnay and a skilled producer of delicious Sauvignon Blanc, the Kim Crawford brand began in 1996 as the virtual label of its eponymous winemaker: Despite instant success, Kim Crawford owned no vines or winery for years. Though Crawford is no longer involved, the brand maintains his trademark ripe, bright and pure style.

○ **Kim Crawford Sauvignon Blanc** / 2010 / Marlborough / $$
A wonderful balance of brash lime, herb and tropical flavors.

○ **Kim Crawford Unoaked Chardonnay** / 2009 / Marlborough / $$
Aging in stainless steel keeps this Chardonnay's crisp pear and citrus flavors zippy and fresh.

KUMEU RIVER

The three Brajkovich brothers—Milan, Paul and winemaker Michael (who's also New Zealand's first Master of Wine)—run revered Chardonnay specialist Kumeu River. Fruit picked by hand, fermentation with wild yeasts and aging in French oak are some of the Burgundy-inspired techniques Michael uses to create this Auckland winery's famously elegant, silky whites.

○ **Kumeu River Estate Chardonnay** / 2007 / Kumeu / $$$
Tart citrus and mineral flavors exhibit a lemon-curd richness.

○ **Kumeu River Maté's Vineyard Chardonnay** / 2007 / Kumeu / $$$ Fermenting with native yeasts adds complexity to this vivid, mineral-laden Chardonnay.

MATUA VALLEY

This large producer makes a great many, mostly mid-priced wines. But its focus on quality comes across most clearly in its Estate Series offerings and in its two Ararimu wines (a Chardonnay and a Cabernet-Merlot blend). Its basic Sauvignon Blanc and Chardonnay are terrific values.

○ **Matua Valley Paretai Sauvignon Blanc / 2010 / Marlborough / $$** Fresh herbs, grass and zesty lime lead to a mineral finish that lingers.

● **Matua Valley Pinot Noir / 2009 / Marlborough / $** Supple and lively, with bright red berry and spice flavors.

MT. DIFFICULTY WINES

Though planted in 1992, Mt. Difficulty's vineyards are among Central Otago's oldest. Masterminded by the affable Matt Dicey, who comes from a family of South African vintners, the terrific lineup includes the flagship Pinot Noir–focused Mt. Difficulty label plus the more affordable Roaring Meg bottlings.

○ **Mt. Difficulty Roaring Meg Pinot Gris / 2010 / Central Otago / $** Cool fermentation preserves the freshness of this sultry, peach-laden white offset with a touch of sweetness.

● **Mt. Difficulty Pinot Noir / 2009 / Central Otago / $$$** The slightly grainy tannins in this crisp, cherry-inflected Pinot will mellow with a little age.

NAUTILUS ESTATE

Owned by Australia's Hill Smith family, who also own that country's venerable Yalumba winery, Nautilus makes a fabulous Wairau Valley Pinot Noir. For its noteworthy Sauvignon Blancs, winemaker Clive Jones blends riper fruit from sites throughout Marlborough in order to capture a complex range of flavors, from green nuances to lusher fruit notes.

○ **Nautilus Sauvignon Blanc / 2010 / Marlborough / $$** Crisp notes of lime are nicely woven throughout this Sauvignon Blanc's pretty oyster-shell mineral flavors.

● **Nautilus Pinot Noir / 2009 / Marlborough / $$** A blend made from vineyard sites around Marlborough, this has mineral notes and a firm, peppery red-fruit profile.

PALLISER ESTATE

Founded in 1984, Palliser was one of the first wineries in Martinborough. Although Pinot Noir has been a focus for the winery from the start, winemaker Allan Johnson also produces outstanding Sauvignon Blancs, along with some beautiful Rieslings. For good value, check out Palliser's second label, Pencarrow.

○ **Palliser Estate Sauvignon Blanc** / 2010 / Martinborough / $$
A crisp and juicy mix of lime, mineral and tropical flavors.

● **Palliser Estate Pinot Noir** / 2008 / Martinborough / $$
This well-made Pinot Noir features Martinborough's signature stony minerality along with spicy red fruit.

PEGASUS BAY

Neurologist Ivan Donaldson moonlighted as a *garagiste* winemaker for decades until 1985, when he and his wife, Christine, founded Pegasus Bay, in the South Island's Waipara Valley. Their boutique winery quickly became one of Waipara's flagship estates. Today their son, Matthew, makes Pegasus Bay's wines, which include seductive Pinot Noirs and elegant Rieslings.

○ **Pegasus Bay Bel Canto Dry Riesling** / 2009 / Waipara / $$$
Older vines impart a wonderful intensity to rich, fresh flavors of lemon-curd and stone fruit.

● **Pegasus Bay Pinot Noir** / 2008 / Waipara / $$$
An outstanding example of New Zealand Pinot, with fragrant crushed-violet and raspberry notes and silky finesse.

PEREGRINE WINES

This Central Otago producer focuses on Burgundian varietals (Pinot Noir, Chardonnay) plus Riesling and Pinot Gris. In 2003, Peregrine constructed a beautiful new winery on the Kawarau River; its gracefully winged roof, which alludes to the winery's namesake bird, has become an iconic Central Otago image.

○ **Peregrine Pinot Gris** / 2008 / Central Otago / $$
This quince- and apple-flavored wine spent three months aging on its lees, which contributed to its luscious texture.

● **Peregrine Pinot Noir** / 2008 / Central Otago / $$$
There's a lovely purity to the spice, stone and ripe strawberry notes in this savory, supple Pinot.

SPY VALLEY WINES

Named for the mysterious U.S. spy station located near this Marlborough estate, Spy Valley relies primarily on its single (albeit enormous) 360-acre vineyard. Owners Bryan and Jan Johnson, with winemaker Paul Bourgeois, have earned Spy Valley a reputation for bright, rich whites (such as its Chardonnay, Gewürztraminer and Pinot Gris) and reasonable prices.

○ **Spy Valley Sauvignon Blanc** / 2010 / Marlborough / $$
A lush combination of peach, lime and grass flavors that gets its creamy texture from aging on lees.

● **Spy Valley Pinot Noir** / 2009 / Marlborough / $$
This delicious blend of grapes from two Marlborough sites showcases bright cherry, tea and stone flavors.

VILLA MARIA ESTATE

This large, quality-oriented company—founded and still owned by the Fistonich family—encompasses four wineries on New Zealand's North and South islands. Its wines are made under four labels: Vidal, Esk Valley, Thornbury and Villa Maria (the best-known brand). The Villa Maria offerings range from reliable, everyday wines to often outstanding Estate Line cuvées.

○ **Villa Maria Private Bin Dry Riesling** / 2010 / Marlborough / $
Pleasantly accessible, with bold peach, apple and lime tones.

● **Villa Maria Cellar Selection Pinot Noir** / 2009 / Marlborough / $$ From vineyards in the Wairau and Awatere valleys, this displays lively berry, savory herb and cedar notes.

WAIRAU RIVER WINES

Phil and Christine Rose faced skepticism from their neighbors when they planted vineyards along Marlborough's Wairau River in 1978. Now run by their five children, the winery continues to turn out impressive estate-made Sauvignon Blanc and Pinot Noir. It's also one of New Zealand's few carbon-neutral wineries.

○ **Wairau River Sauvignon Blanc** / 2010 / Marlborough / $$
The tropical fruit flavors in this silky-textured wine are uplifted by bright acidity before a long, voluptuous finish.

● **Wairau River Pinot Noir** / 2008 / Marlborough / $$
Cherry-scented and full of juicy, supple red-fruit notes.

Argentina / Wine Region

Argentine Malbec, dark-fruited, spicy and almost always a bargain, has seduced American wine drinkers—it's now the fastest-growing red wine in the U.S. But there's more to Argentina than Malbec. Lively, aromatic Torrontés is a white wine that's well worth investigating, and the cool-climate Patagonian desert has become one of the world's newest sources of outstanding Pinot Noir.

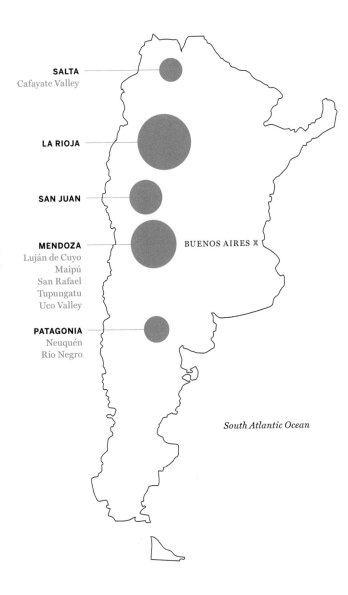

SALTA
Cafayate Valley

LA RIOJA

SAN JUAN

MENDOZA
Luján de Cuyo
Maipú
San Rafael
Tupungatu
Uco Valley

BUENOS AIRES **X**

PATAGONIA
Neuquén
Río Negro

South Atlantic Ocean

Argentina

ARGENTINA'S ARID CLIMATE and blazing sunshine mean that its best wine regions cling to the foothills of the Andes, where there are cooler temperatures and ample irrigation. More than 80 percent of the country's wine comes from the vast central region of Mendoza. Of its five major growing areas, Maipú and Luján de Cuyo are the oldest and best known, while the newer, higher-altitude Uco Valley yields structured reds and whites. North of Mendoza, remote Salta province encompasses some of the highest-altitude vineyards in the world, and the region's Cafayate Valley is a source of terrific, refreshing white wines. La Rioja and San Juan are traditional wine regions that have been moving from bulk production to high-quality winemaking. The most recent buzz, though, is about glacier-studded Patagonia, where the world's most southerly vineyards have begun producing truly impressive wines from Malbec and, surprisingly, Pinot Noir.

♥ ARGENTINE GRAPES & STYLES

Though Argentina makes some lovely whites, reds are its specialty. Few countries turn out as many reliably delicious red wines at such low prices. Malbec is Argentina's main red grape. While it yields tough, tannic wines in its native France, Malbec becomes alluringly supple in Argentina, producing peppery black-fruit flavors. Cabernet Sauvignon, which accounts for some of the country's oldest vines, also makes powerful wines here. Bonarda, another red grape, is being taken more seriously today, with complex examples joining pleasant, cherry-flavored bottlings. Argentine Syrah is often blended with Malbec and other grapes, but on its own it can produce great wines full of fruit and spice. Pinot Noir from Patagonia has been generating a lot of excitement, thanks to the polished wines it creates.

Argentina's most distinctive white grape is Torrontés, which offers exuberantly floral aromas. Chardonnay is widely produced and ranges in style from lightly oaked and light-bodied to full-bodied and creamy. Sauvignon Blanc is the other white wine of real significance in Argentina. Pinot Gris (Pinot Grigio), Riesling, Sémillon and Viognier play minor roles.

ARGENTINE WINE LABELS

Most Argentine wine labels identify grape variety, the region where the grapes were grown, the producer's name and the vintage. Producers often use *reserva* or *reserve* on higher-quality wines, though these terms have no legal meaning.

Producers/ Argentina

ACHAVAL-FERRER

Italian winemaker Roberto Cipresso and his four partners in Achaval-Ferrer are obsessed with two things: gnarly old vines and Malbec. Their winery turns out three single-vineyard Malbecs from ancient vineyards in Luján de Cuyo that are among Argentina's most sought-after wines. Cipresso also crafts two more-accessibly priced bottlings: Quimera, a polished blend made from three sites, and the basic Mendoza Malbec.

- **Achaval-Ferrer Malbec / 2009 / Mendoza / $$**
  A classy, violet-scented red with layers of plum and minerals.
- **Achaval-Ferrer Finca Mirador / 2008 / Mendoza / $$$$**
  The tannins in this powerful Malbec demand aging or steak.

BODEGA CATENA ZAPATA

Nicolás Catena transformed the bulk-focused wine property he inherited into one of Argentina's most successful fine-wine pioneers. Today his children help manage what has become one of Argentina's iconic estates. Its Uco Valley and Mendoza wines include the Classic, Alta and Zapata tiers, plus the well-made, entry-level Alamos line.

○ **Alamos Chardonnay** / 2009 / Mendoza / $
Oak aging adds a vanilla note to tangy citrus and pear flavors.

● **Catena Malbec** / 2008 / Mendoza / $$
This bright, berry-rich red is from a high-altitude vineyard.

● **Catena Alta Cabernet Sauvignon** / 2007 / Mendoza / $$$
Polished black currant flavors are framed by big tannins.

BODEGA COLOMÉ

Swiss-born wine entrepreneur Donald Hess and winemaker Thibaut Delmotte are pushing the boundaries of high-altitude winemaking in the Salta region. Hess's Colomé winery and biodynamically farmed vineyards lie at elevations up to 10,000 feet; the resulting wines display terrific freshness and purity.

○ **Colomé Torrontés** / 2010 / Calchaquí Valleys / $
Lively and fragrant, with orange blossom and lime notes.

● **Colomé Estate Malbec** / 2008 / Calchaquí Valleys / $$
A bit of Tannat gives this lush, big red its beefy structure.

BODEGA LUIGI BOSCA

The Arizu family, which owns Luigi Bosca, has been one of Luján de Cuyo's most prominent wine dynasties for over a century. The winery, run by great-grandsons of founder Leoncio Arizu, with help from their father, has grown to encompass several labels and a boutique side project, Viña Alicia. Despite the Arizus' history, their wines are modern and fruit-forward.

● **Luigi Bosca de Sangre** / 2008 / Luján de Cuyo and Maipú / $$
A cherry-infused, Cabernet-based blend from three vineyards.

● **Luigi Bosca Reserva Malbec** / 2008 / Luján de Cuyo / $$
Loaded with rich berry notes and complex layers of minerals.

BODEGA NAVARRO CORREAS

In Argentina, Navarro Correas is best known for sparkling wines and a sleek visitors center, a short ride from the city of Mendoza. But in the U.S., this large producer has been earning a reputation for its still wines—thanks to a quality boost that started over a decade ago when drinks giant Diageo purchased the winery. Colección Privada is the entry-level label, followed by the reserve Alegoría tier and high-end Structura Ultra blend.

- Navarro Correas Colección Privada Malbec / 2008 / Mendoza / $ Smooth and lush, with plum and coffee flavors.
- Bodega Navarro Correas Alegoría Gran Reserva Malbec / 2008 / Mendoza / $$ The winery's top Malbec has dense, ripe berry flavors with a touch of sweet vanilla.

BODEGA NORTON

Bodega Norton is responsible for some of Argentina's best value wines, all made with estate fruit from its vast Mendoza acreage. Founded by an Englishman in 1895 and owned since 1989 by the Langes-Swarovski family (of Austria's Swarovski crystal company), Norton has added more-ambitious bottlings to its lineup in recent years; its Privada red remains the portfolio star.

- Bodega Norton Privada / 2007 / Mendoza / $$
  Cabernet bolsters Malbec and Merlot in this firm, spicy blend.
- Bodega Norton Reserva Malbec / 2007 / Mendoza / $$
  Muscular tannins support rich berry, herb and vanilla flavors.

BODEGA Y CAVAS DE WEINERT

Started by Brazilian businessman Bernardo Weinert in 1975, Weinert was part of Argentina's first generation of modern, quality-minded producers. For the past 15 years, Swiss wine-maker Hubert Weber has crafted its traditionally styled wines, which include the top Cavas de Weinert cuvée as well as the mid-priced Carrascal blends. Weinert's recent venture into cool-climate winemaking in Patagonia holds promise.

- Weinert Cabernet Sauvignon / 2004 / Mendoza / $$
  This rustic Cabernet shows minty notes and firm tannins.
- Weinert Carrascal / 2006 / Mendoza / $$
  A savory, old-school blend of Malbec, Merlot and Cabernet.

CLOS DE LOS SIETE

When French superstar winemaker Michel Rolland first visited Argentina to offer consulting advice, he was so impressed by the country's potential that he founded his own winery, with a handful of French investors as partners. Today Clos de los Siete encompasses four distinct wineries spread across 2,100 acres in the Uco Valley. Each partner contributes wine for a single Malbec-based blend, called simply Clos de los Siete.

● **Clos de los Siete / 2009 / Mendoza / $$**
This mostly Malbec blend features rich, velvety flavors reminiscent of warm cherry pie.

DOÑA PAULA

Doña Paula's reputation for affordable, high-quality wines is well deserved. The winery uses only estate fruit, much of which comes from older vineyards, including nearly 200 acres planted in the 1970s in Luján de Cuyo. The Selección de Bodega Estate series consists of a Chardonnay and a Malbec (the latter made with grapes from a high-altitude property in Tupungato). All Doña Paula wines, including the bargain Los Cardos line, over-deliver for the price.

○ **Doña Paula Estate Torrontés / 2010 / Cafayate Valley / $**
An intense jasmine nose is followed by compelling white peach and succulent tropical flavors.

● **Doña Paula Estate Malbec / 2010 / Mendoza / $**
Made with grapes from Luján de Cuyo and Uco Valley, this Malbec offers waves of plum, red currant, tobacco and smoke.

● **Doña Paula Los Cardos Cabernet Sauvignon / 2009 / Mendoza / $** Vineyards 3,300 feet above sea level yield this amazing value-priced wine full of exuberant blackberry.

RUTINI WINES

Like many of Argentina's oldest wineries, Rutini was founded by immigrants from Italy's Le Marche region—in this case Don Felipe Rutini, who planted Cabernet Sauvignon vines in Mendoza's Maipú in 1885. Now part-owned by respected vintner Nicolás Catena, the largish producer owns vineyards in five Mendoza subregions. Its wines include the entry-level Trumpeter line and the Felipe Rutini label.

○ **Trumpeter Torrontés** / 2010 / Mendoza / $
Aromatic lime zest is up front in this vibrant white.

○ **Rutini Chardonnay** / 2009 / Mendoza / $$
Creamy citrus and peach flavors are woven with a hint of oak.

● **Trumpeter Malbec** / 2009 / Mendoza / $
A juicy, highly drinkable Malbec packed with freshly ground coffee and bold red-fruit notes.

TERRAZAS DE LOS ANDES

Terrazas gets its name from the steep terraces where chief wine-maker Hervé Birnie-Scott and his skilled team cultivate their vines (3,500 feet above sea level for Malbec; 3,900 feet for Chardonnay). It is owned by French luxury-goods company LVMH, and its wines range from the straightforward Terrazas bottlings to the more refined, estate-grown *reserva* and single-vineyard (Afincado) cuvées.

○ **Terrazas de los Andes Reserva Torrontés Unoaked** / 2010 / Mendoza / $$ Expressive orange blossom flavors are balanced with lychee and peach notes.

● **Terrazas de los Andes Reserva Malbec** / 2008 / Mendoza / $
The depth and concentration in this jammy red comes from grapes sourced from higher-elevation vineyards.

VALENTÍN BIANCHI

Lots of quality-focused wineries handpick their grapes and sort them twice to select only pristine fruit. But very few take that kind of care for wines that sell for less than $10 a bottle, as Casa Bianchi does for Valentín Bianchi and its second label, Elsa Bianchi. Needless to say, its top-tier wines receive even more attention, which is why this family-owned estate—now run by the third generation—is one of Mendoza's best.

○ **Elsa Bianchi Torrontés** / 2010 / Mendoza / $
Orange blossom and minerals mark this delicious white from one of the coolest areas in Mendoza's San Rafael subregion.

○ **Valentín Bianchi Sauvignon Blanc** / 2010 / Mendoza / $
This first-vintage wine is full of mineral and lime flavors.

● **Elsa Bianchi Malbec** / 2010 / Mendoza / $
Made with grapes from the Doña Elsa vineyard, this juicy, dark berry–flavored Malbec is another great value.

Chile
Wine Region

The image of Chile as a source
for value wine is becoming outdated.
There's no question that excellent,
affordable Chilean wines can still be
found, but that's only a part of what
the country offers. Top Cabernet-
based reds challenge premier
California wines. Sauvignon Blancs
from cool-climate regions are among
the world's best. And recent ventures
into other grape varieties—Syrah,
Pinot Noir—are a testament to the
ambitions of Chile's top winemakers.

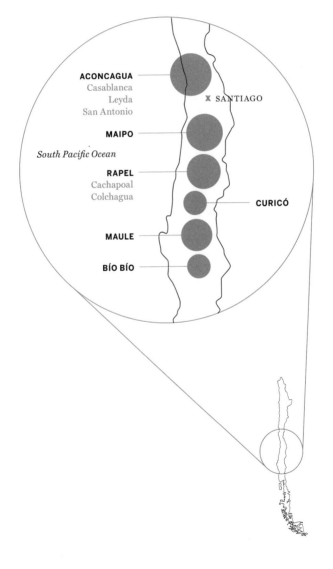

ACONCAGUA
Casablanca
Leyda
San Antonio

✗ SANTIAGO

MAIPO

South Pacific Ocean

RAPEL
Cachapoal
Colchagua

CURICÓ

MAULE

BÍO BÍO

Chile

WEDGED BETWEEN THE Andes and the Pacific, Chile is a skinny slip of a country, nearly 3,000 miles long and less than 300 miles across at its widest point. Since the beginning of Chile's wine renaissance in the early 1990s, the sunny Central Valley has fueled the industry's growth. Solid, value-oriented wines—chiefly reds—have driven economic success, while quality Cabernet Sauvignon from the Maipo Alto district has earned prestige. More recently, Chilean winemakers have ventured into cool-climate winemaking. Young areas such as Casablanca, Limarí, Bío Bío, Elquí and San Antonio (and its Leyda district) are producing exciting wines. Chile is also seeing growth in the number of independent vintners at work here.

CHILEAN GRAPES & STYLES

Three-quarters of Chile's table wine production is red. Cabernet Sauvignon, Merlot and Carmenère (a French variety for years mistaken for Merlot) dominate, with some Syrah as well. Cabernet thrives in Maipo and in the Rapel Valley's Colchagua zone, and Carmenère does well in the Cachapoal zone. Look for cool-climate Pinot Noir from Bío Bío and Syrah from Elqui. The best Sauvignon Blanc and Chardonnay come from Casablanca, Limarí and San Antonio valleys and the Leyda district.

CHILEAN WINE LABELS

Chilean labels list variety and often a proprietary name for blends. Producers increasingly are using single-vineyard designations and adding the term *reserva* to top-quality wines.

Producers/ Chile

CASA SILVA

Today many Chilean wineries can boast a French connection, but Colchagua's Casa Silva was among the first to be able to do so. Bordeaux native Emile Bouchon brought Casa Silva's first vines over from France more than a century ago; those plantings continue to provide grapes for this large-volume, family-owned winery, now in its fifth generation. The value-priced Carmenère and Sauvignon Blanc are particularly tasty.

○ **Casa Silva Reserva Sauvignon Blanc / 2010 / Colchagua Valley / $** Snappy and bright, with grass, lime and herbs.

● **Casa Silva Los Lingues Gran Reserva Carmenère / 2006 / Colchagua Valley / $$** A firm, plummy Carmenère from one of the first vineyards planted in Colchagua's Andes foothills.

CONCHA Y TORO

The largest producer in Chile, Concha y Toro makes wine from every major grape in every major region of the country. Of its dizzying lineup—there are 11 subbrands—the mid-priced Marqués de Casa Concha line offers great value. Look to the more pricey Terrunyo tier for world-class Sauvignon Blanc as well as Carmenère. Two flagship reds, the Don Melchor Cabernet Sauvignon and Carmin de Peumo Carmenère, top the portfolio.

○ **Concha y Toro Terrunyo Sauvignon Blanc / 2008 / Casablanca Valley / $$** From a vineyard located near the Pacific, this delicious Sauvignon Blanc is flinty and fresh.

● **Concha y Toro Don Melchor Cabernet Sauvignon / 2007 / Puente Alto / $$$$** Heady stuff, with lovely balanced tones of earth, cassis and black cherry liqueur.

COUSIÑO-MACUL

Cousiño-Macul helped create Chile's reputation as a source of quality value wines. Founded in 1856, it's now run by a sixth-generation owner, Arturo Cousiño, and still produces affordable, quality wines—though its top cuvées, the Lota and Finis Terrae Cabernet blends, compete with the country's best.

○ **Cousiño-Macul Sauvignon Gris / 2009 / Maipo Valley / $**
Lemon-lime flavors reveal a pleasant trace of sweetness.

● **Cousiño-Macul Finis Terrae Cabernet Sauvignon–Merlot / 2008 / Maipo Valley / $$** A supple blend of Cabernet, Merlot and 10 percent Syrah with lush cherry flavors.

LAPOSTOLLE

Alexandra Marnier-Lapostolle (as in Grand Marnier, the French liqueur) cofounded this Colchagua estate and imported a French wine-making team that includes superstar consultant Michel Rolland and winemaker Jacques Begarie. Lapostolle's bold, rich wines include a terrific, bargain-priced Sauvignon Blanc, the mid-priced Cuvée Alexandre tier and the iconic Bordeaux-style blend Clos Apalta.

> **WINE INTEL**
> Opened in 2006, Lapostolle Residence offers four private hillside casitas; the $500–$600 per person room rates include meals, bike rentals and private tours of the winery.

○ **Lapostolle Casa Sauvignon Blanc / 2010 / Rapel Valley / $**
This crisp, invigorating wine includes 7 percent Sémillon.

● **Lapostolle Cuvée Alexandre Las Kuras Vineyard Syrah / 2007 / Cachapoal Valley / $$** Plush, deliciously ripe flavors of chocolaty black cherries are layered with exotic spice notes.

MATETIC VINEYARDS

Founded in 1999 in the San Antonio Valley, the Matetic family's winery is best known for wines made under the Corralillo and EQ labels, with Syrah its signature variety (all are made with organic grapes). The region's cool climate and granite-based soils result in racy wines made by rising star Paula Cárdenas.

● **Matetic Vineyards Corralillo Syrah / 2009 / San Antonio Valley / $$** This balanced red is wonderfully ripe and fresh.

● **Matetic Vineyards EQ Syrah / 2009 / San Antonio Valley / $$$** A cool-climate Syrah with peppery notes and gripping tannins.

MONTES

Visionary winemaker Aurelio Montes cultivates heat-loving Bordeaux red varieties in the Colchagua Valley and Pinot Noir and white grapes in cooler, coastal regions like Casablanca and Leyda. Montes has three tiers: Classic Series, Limited Selection and Montes Alpha. The portfolio star is a Carmenère called Purple Angel, one of Chile's best renditions of the variety.

○ **Montes Limited Selection Sauvignon Blanc** / 2010 / Leyda Valley / $ Packed with zesty grass, citrus and tropical notes.

● **Montes Limited Selection Apalta Vineyard Cabernet Sauvignon–Carmenère** / 2009 / Colchagua Valley / $ Tastes like a wine twice its price, with great concentration and polish.

SANTA EMA

Founded by an Italian immigrant from Piedmont, Santa Ema began as a grape-growing business, then morphed into a winery in the 1950s. Today this family-owned producer turns out a wide array of reliably delicious wines, with the reserve bottlings ideal for everyday drinking and the Amplus series (including an unusual Carignane) well worth the step up in price.

○ **Santa Ema Amplus Chardonnay** / 2008 / Leyda Valley / $$ Ten months' aging in French oak adds a creamy vanilla note to this white's pure, fresh pear flavors.

● **Santa Ema Barrel Select 60/40** / 2008 / Maipo Valley / $ This Cabernet-Merlot blend reveals layers of earth and fruit.

SANTA RITA

Australian winemaking guru Brian Croser consults for this Maipo Valley mainstay, one of Chile's most recognizable names thanks to its large production and 130-plus-year history. Forays into newer growing regions such as Limarí and Leyda are paying off with crisp whites and structured, elegant reds.

○ **Santa Rita Reserva Sauvignon Blanc** / 2010 / Casablanca Valley / $ Consistently an amazing value, this Sauvignon Blanc is loaded with fragrant lime, herb and tropical flavors.

● **Santa Rita Casa Real Cabernet Sauvignon** / 2007 / Maipo Valley / $$$$ Made in exceptional vintages, this rich, full-bodied red offers a mix of black currant, earth and cedar.

VERAMONTE

Veramonte was a Casablanca Valley trailblazer back in the early 1990s; its crisp Sauvignon Blancs helped put both the winery and the cool region on the map. Founded by the Huneeus family (Chilean natives who also own Napa's Quintessa winery), Veramonte specializes in cool-climate Chardonnay, Sauvignon Blanc and Pinot Noir, plus reds from the warmer Colchagua Valley.

○ **Veramonte Reserva Sauvignon Blanc / 2010 / Casablanca Valley / $** Bold tropical aromas are followed by lime flavors.

● **Ritual Pinot Noir / 2009 / Casablanca Valley / $$**
This showcases vivid, oak-inflected berry and thyme flavors.

VIÑA CASA MARIN

María Luz Marin helped pioneer cool-climate winemaking in Chile when she founded Casa Marin less than three miles from the Pacific Ocean in the San Antonio region in 2000. Her racy Sauvignon Blancs, aromatic Rieslings and elegant Pinot Noirs are much sought after; Marín also makes lower-profile wines from estate-grown grapes such as Syrah and Sauvignon Gris.

○ **Casa Marin Casona Vineyard Gewürztraminer / 2009 / San Antonio Valley / $$$** Pretty rose and pink grapefruit flavors finish on a tangy note in this expertly balanced white.

● **Casa Marin Lo Abarca Hills Pinot Noir / 2009 / San Antonio Valley / $$$** This spicy, balanced Pinot shows layers of fruit.

VIÑA ERRÁZURIZ

Eduardo Chadwick, a descendant of Errázuriz's founder, has transformed this historic Aconcagua winery into one of Chile's most cutting-edge producers. Its offerings include the powerful La Cumbre Shiraz, numerous wild-fermented cuvées and cool-climate whites from new coastal vineyards. Chadwick's top cuvées are the Viñedo Chadwick Cabernet Sauvignon and Seña, a Bordeaux blend from a biodynamically farmed vineyard.

○ **Errázuriz Estate Reserva Chardonnay / 2010 / Casablanca Valley / $** A lively, luscious pear- and lemon-driven white.

● **Errázuriz Single Vineyard Cabernet Sauvignon / 2007 / Aconcagua Valley / $$** A silky, ultra-smooth texture and multiple layers of rich, dense cherry make this a great value.

VIÑA LOS VASCOS

Bordeaux's Rothschild family has owned this Colchagua estate since 1988. As one might expect from a company that owns Pauillac's fabled Château Lafite (plus five other Bordeaux wineries), its five red wines are all Cabernet-based, including Le Dix, a suavely structured luxury cuvée. Yet the winery's most consistent value may be its Casablanca Sauvignon Blanc.

○ **Los Vascos Sauvignon Blanc / 2010 / Casablanca Valley / $**
Zippy and refreshing, with savory lime and grass flavors.

● **Le Dix de Los Vascos / 2008 / Colchagua Valley / $$$**
A dense, concentrated blend with rich black currant flavors.

VIÑA SANTA CAROLINA

Quality has soared at the 136-year-old Santa Carolina winery ever since Andrés Caballero, an alumnus of Australia's Rosemount Estate, took over as winemaker several years ago. Today many of its affordably priced wines are exceptional, especially those under the Reserva de Familia label.

○ **Santa Carolina Reserva Chardonnay / 2010 / Casablanca Valley / $** The Casablanca Valley's cooler climate imparts a nice vibrancy to ripe apricot and peach flavors.

● **Santa Carolina Reserva de Familia Cabernet Sauvignon / 2008 / Maipo Valley / $$** A classy, seductive mix of succulent blackberry, subtle oak and smooth tannins.

VIU MANENT

Viu Manent was the first Chilean winery to bottle Malbec on its own. Longtime *négociants* who made jug wines, the Viu family switched to premium wine in 1966 when Miguel Viu-Manent purchased a vineyard in Colchagua. Good bets in the wide portfolio include the San Carlos and La Capilla Estate wines and most of the Carmenères. Viu Manent's best cuvée, Viu 1, is made from ancient vines only in outstanding years.

○ **Viu Manent Secreto Sauvignon Blanc / 2010 / Casablanca Valley / $** Marked by vivacious passion fruit and grapefruit.

● **Viu Manent El Incidente Carmenère / 2007 / Colchagua Valley / $$$** This full-bodied, muscular Carmenère shows ripe, dark-fruit flavors and a lingering earthiness.

South Africa

Wine Region

Though South Africa's winemaking history stretches back more than 350 years, only in the past two decades have the country's wines truly come of age. South Africa now boasts delicious Chenin Blancs, ageworthy Cabernets and graceful Syrahs—as well as a new generation of ambitious young winemakers pushing boundaries in less-heralded regions such as Elgin and Swartland.

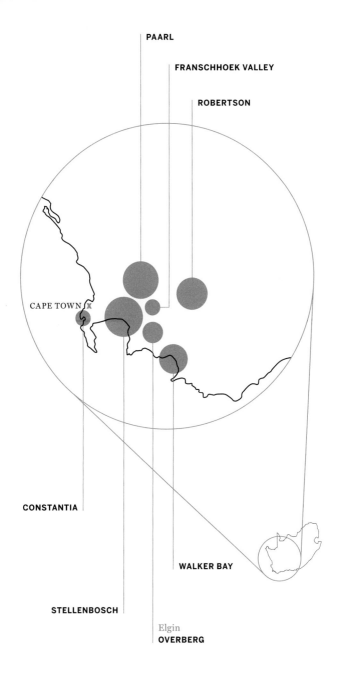

PAARL

FRANSCHHOEK VALLEY

ROBERTSON

CAPE TOWN

CONSTANTIA

WALKER BAY

STELLENBOSCH

Elgin
OVERBERG

South Africa

COOLED BY ATLANTIC winds and Antarctic currents, South Africa's best wine districts are clustered around the country's southwestern tip. The Stellenbosch and Paarl zones turn out most of the top red wines. Marked by craggy mountains and a diverse mix of soils, their terrain is ideal for growing a range of grapes. Sauvignon Blanc, Chardonnay and Pinot Noir production is focused in the cooler district of Constantia, a suburb south of Cape Town, and in areas to the southeast: Walker Bay, Overberg and especially the latter's subzone, Elgin.

SOUTH AFRICAN GRAPES & STYLES

More than 40 percent of South African vineyards have been replanted in recent years as vintners have switched from high-yielding, workhorse grapes to premium varieties such as Cabernet Sauvignon and Shiraz (Syrah). Chenin Blanc, South Africa's most important white variety, appears in styles from bright and zippy to lush. Sometimes referred to locally as Steen, it creates wines with more citrus and tropical flavors than traditional Chenin Blancs from France. The country's other key white grapes, Sauvignon Blanc and Chardonnay, generally yield medium-bodied wines with pronounced mineral flavors; Sauvignon Blancs also display herbal and exotic fruit flavors.

But refined red wines make South Africa's most convincing case for greatness. Cabernet Sauvignon is now the country's dominant red grape, and plantings of Shiraz have more than doubled in the past decade. These reds tend to split into two camps, with some vintners aiming for ripe, plush styles akin to California's and Australia's and others making earthier, herb-inflected versions that evoke comparisons with French bottlings. Once South Africa's preeminent red grape, Pinotage—a local crossing of Pinot Noir and Cinsaut—now ranks behind French grapes in popularity. Pinotage's distinctively pungent, funky flavors have limited its appeal abroad, though a few winemakers have been able to harness the fruitier side of the grape. With an increase in plantings in cool-climate regions, Pinot Noir production is on the rise, though not much is exported yet to the U.S.

SOUTH AFRICAN WINE LABELS

Labels used by South African winemakers are straightforward, listing the winery name, variety, region and vintage. Blends may be given proprietary names, and the varieties that went into them usually appear on the back label.

Producers/ South Africa

BACKSBERG ESTATE CELLARS

In the past decade, third-generation vintner Michael Back has retooled his family's Paarl estate, ripping out so-so vineyards and scaling back all non-wine-related farm operations. In addition to moving to biodynamic farming, Backsberg also became the country's first carbon-neutral wine estate. The efforts have been good for the wines, which include a crisp Chenin Blanc, the luscious Pumphouse Shiraz and a line of kosher bottlings.

○ **Backsberg Kosher Chardonnay** / 2010 / Paarl / $
A refreshing unoaked white full of apricot and lemon flavors.

● **Backsberg Pumphouse Shiraz** / 2007 / Paarl / $$
Serve this concentrated, black licorice–inflected Shiraz with a juicy steak to tame its formidable tannins.

BOEKENHOUTSKLOOF

Marc Kent makes some of South Africa's best Syrahs, including a culty flagship cuvée, the Chocolate Block, which has dark, savory flavors that evoke comparisons with northern Rhône wines. Kent and seven partners founded Boekenhoutskloof in 1994 near Paarl. The winery offers many good everyday wines too, including Wolftrap red and Porcupine Ridge bottlings.

○ **Boekenhoutskloof Semillon** / 2008 / Franschhoek / $$
Oak aging adds toasty nuances to this luscious, lemony white.

● **The Wolftrap** / 2009 / Western Cape / $
Pronounced blackberry, dark plum and spice notes define this affordable and tasty Syrah-Mourvèdre blend.

● **The Chocolate Block** / 2008 / Western Cape / $$$
A spicy Syrah-based red with cola, chocolate and cherry notes.

BUITENVERWACHTING

Buitenverwachting is one of the grand old names in Constantia, with a history dating to 1796 and a range of worthwhile wines. Its flagship red, a well-regarded Bordeaux-style blend called Christine, is unavailable in the U.S., but winemakers Hermann Kirschbaum and Brad Paton also have a sure hand with characterful whites, which can be found in many American shops.

○ **Buitenverwachting Sauvignon Blanc** / 2010 / Constantia / $
A firm backbone of acidity and brisk grass and mineral flavors reflect the coolness of the 2010 vintage.

○ **Buitenverwachting Chardonnay** / 2009 / Constantia / $$
Thanks to 10 months in barrel, this shows sweet vanilla notes.

FAIRVIEW/GOATS DO ROAM

Charles Back's innovative Fairview estate was the first in South Africa to plant Viognier and is still the only one making Petite Sirah. Back and winemaker Anthony de Jager experiment with other grapes uncommon in the region, such as Tannat and Tempranillo. But their passion is Rhône varietals, which make up the basis of Back's value label, the Goats do Roam, a cheeky homage to France's Côtes-du-Rhône district.

WINE INTEL
In 2003 when the French tried to sue Charles Back over the name Goats do Roam, he brought gifts of wine and cheese—along with protest signs and goat dung—to the French consulate in Cape Town.

○ Goats do Roam White / 2010 / Western Cape / $
Citrus and nectarine flavors come together in this Rhône-style blend of Viognier, Roussanne and Grenache Blanc.

● Goats do Roam Rosé / 2010 / Western Cape / $
A savory undertone balances the hint of sweetness in this fruit-driven rosé made with mostly Shiraz and Grenache.

● Fairview Shiraz / 2008 / Coastal Region / $
Shiraz is Fairview's specialty; this intense, blackberry-infused example provides an affordable introduction.

GLEN CARLOU

Now part of Swiss entrepreneur–art collector Donald Hess's Hess Family Estates company, Glen Carlou is in Paarl's Simonsberg district, where warmer temperatures create a perfect environment for red grapes such as Cabernet Sauvignon and Syrah. Bold red wines are Glen Carlou's signature. Its richly styled Chardonnays are another strong suit, thanks to traditional techniques like lees-stirring, which gives these whites a creamy texture and nutty notes.

○ Glen Carlou Chardonnay / 2009 / Paarl / $$
Glen Carlou's entry-level Chardonnay is wonderfully vibrant, loaded with up-front vanilla, pear and citrus flavors.

● Glen Carlou Grand Classique / 2008 / Paarl / $$
This dark berry–driven Bordeaux-style blend offers lots more flavor for just a few more dollars than the winery's basic reds.

INDABA

Indaba's five highly drinkable wines are known for offering pleasure far beyond their modest prices. Bruwer Raats (who owns a well-regarded label, Raats Family Wines, himself) consulted with Indaba for two years before coming on board full time as winemaker in 2010. Long-term contracts on specific prime vineyards and sites (including parcels of old-vine Chenin Blanc) have helped ensure Indaba's consistency.

○ Indaba Chenin Blanc / 2010 / Western Cape / $
Lemon-lime and herb flavors mark this refreshing white.

● Indaba Merlot / 2010 / Western Cape / $
A great example of tasty, affordable Merlot, Indaba's 2010 offers equal parts savory herbs and sweet red fruit.

KEN FORRESTER VINEYARDS

Ken Forrester left his career as a restaurateur to make Chenin Blanc from old vines in Stellenbosch. In addition to using estate fruit, Forrester sources grapes for a diverse array of wines, from the value Petit tier to iconic offerings like The FMC, a luscious Chenin Blanc, and the Syrah-Grenache blend The Gypsy.

○ **Ken Forrester Chenin Blanc** / 2009 / Stellenbosch / $
There's an appealing green apple note amid citrus flavors.

● **Ken Forrester Shiraz-Grenache** / 2006 / Western Cape / $$
Syrah gives heft and body to this ripe, dark blend; Grenache fills out the berry-rich palate and adds a supple quality.

MULDERBOSCH VINEYARDS

Launched a little over two decades ago, Mulderbosch quickly gained a reputation for turning out some of South Africa's best white wines. Founding winemaker Mike Dubrovic established the winery's vibrant, citrusy style, which has continued under new owner Terroir Capital, an investment group founded by former Screaming Eagle co-owner Charles Banks.

○ **Mulderbosch Chenin Blanc** / 2009 / Western Cape / $
Bursting with intense zesty lime and green apple flavors.

● **Mulderbosch Cabernet Sauvignon Rosé** / 2010 / Coastal Region / $ With soft red currant flavors and a subtle sweetness, this is an immensely drinkable rosé.

● **Mulderbosch Faithful Hound** / 2007 / Stellenbosch / $$
This seamless Bordeaux blend offers herb and currant tones.

NEIL ELLIS WINES

Neil Ellis's winery is in Stellenbosch's Jonkershoek Valley, yet Ellis is famous for making savvy bets on vineyards across South Africa, including some in the cool Elgin zone. His balanced wines include vibrant Sauvignon Blancs, such as his Groenekloof and Vineyard Selection Jonkershoek Valley, and spicy, *terroir*-driven reds. Also look for his value-oriented Sincerely label.

● **The Left Bank** / 2009 / Western Cape / $
A mostly Cabernet-and-Shiraz blend full of spice and berries.

● **Neil Ellis Pinotage** / 2008 / Stellenbosch / $$
A lush, earthy Pinotage with ripe plum and berry flavors.

PAUL CLUVER WINES

In the 26 years since neurosurgeon–turned–grape grower Paul Cluver planted the first vines on his family's farm in Elgin, this emerging cool-climate coastal zone has become one of the country's most exciting wine districts, and Paul Cluver Wines one of its leading estates. Son-in-law Andries Burger, the winemaker since 1997, turns out stylish whites and refined Pinot Noirs.

○ **Paul Cluver Gewürztraminer / 2010 / Elgin / $**
Superaromatic, this expressive wine shows a lovely purity and a hint of sweetness in its vivacious fig and floral notes.

● **Paul Cluver Pinot Noir / 2009 / Elgin / $$**
A bracing, firm Pinot Noir made in a Burgundian style, with pretty earth, cherry and black-tea flavors.

WARWICK WINE ESTATE

Best known for its opulent Cabernet-based wines, Warwick Wine is the creation of Canadian-born winemaker Norma Ratcliffe. Her first vintages, using grapes planted on husband Stan Ratcliffe's family farm in Stellenbosch, helped pioneer South Africa's high-end, Bordeaux-inspired blends in the mid-1980s. Today the winery's eight cuvées are still sourced from the same property, and production remains small.

○ **Warwick Estate Professor Black Sauvignon Blanc / 2010 / Stellenbosch / $$** This fresh, tropical white gains complexity from grapes picked at different ripeness levels.

● **Warwick Old Bush Vines Pinotage / 2008 / Stellenbosch / $$**
Old vines and traditional pruning give this red intense wild berry notes, underscored by earth and chocolate.

● **Warwick Three Cape Ladies Cape Blend / 2007 / Stellenbosch / $$** Cabernet Sauvignon, Merlot, Pinotage and Shiraz make up this brawny, earthy blend.

Champagne & Other Sparkling Wines

Most Americans reserve sparkling wines for special occasions, cocktail parties or dessert. But that's a mistake: Few wines are as food-friendly or refreshing as Champagne and its international counterparts, such as Prosecco and cava. And with excellent examples at every price, sparkling wine is an ideal choice for everyday drinking.

THERE ARE SEVERAL ways to make sparkling wine, but the finest is the traditional method—*méthode traditionnelle*—in which vintners create carbon dioxide bubbles in a still wine by activating a second fermentation in the bottle. The pinnacle of all sparkling wine regions is Champagne, in northern France, but France's Loire Valley, northern Italy, northeastern Spain and Northern California all make exceptional examples, as do many other places with cool climates and mineral-rich soils.

CHAMPAGNE

Champagne is undeniably the greatest of the world's sparkling wines. Only wines made in the Champagne region of northern France (see map, p. 21) are entitled to be called Champagne, yet despite efforts to protect the name, it is often incorrectly used to refer to any wine with bubbles, regardless of origin.

CHAMPAGNE GRAPES & STYLES

Champagne vintners are permitted to use only three varieties: Chardonnay, Pinot Noir and Pinot Meunier. Blanc de Blancs are made from 100 percent Chardonnay; Blanc de Noirs are sparkling whites produced with red grapes Pinot Noir and/or Pinot Meunier. Rosés are created by blending a bit of red wine into white sparkling wine or by leaving the red grape skins in the pressed juice for a short time to bleed in some color.

CHAMPAGNE LABELS

Look for the word *Champagne* on the label to make sure it is the real thing. Most Champagnes are nonvintage, which means their labels don't list a year; they are blends of different vintages, a practice designed to maintain a consistent taste from year to year. Producers make vintage Champagnes only in exceptional years; these wines are typically aged longer and priced higher than their nonvintage counterparts. Most large Champagne houses create a top-tier bottling called a tête de cuvée, usually under a proprietary name such as Moët's Dom Pérignon. Sweetness levels in Champagne are categorized as follows, from driest to sweetest: brut *nature* (also known as brut *zéro, pas dosé* or *sans-dosage*), extra brut, brut, extra dry (or extra sec), sec (or dry), demi-sec and doux. Brut is the most widely produced style.

Producers/ Champagne

BOLLINGER

Founded in 1829 and still family-owned, Bollinger is known for its rich, full-bodied style, a result of fermenting some wines in barrel. Most of Bollinger's grapes come from estate vineyards—a key factor in its wines' consistent quality. Its famous vintage and *réserve* bottlings are some of the most long-lived in Champagne.

○ **Bollinger Special Cuvée** / NV / $$$$
About 80 percent of the grapes for this Pinot Noir–dominated blend are from *grand cru* and *premier cru* vineyards.

● **Bollinger Rosé** / NV / $$$$
Sleek and tangy, with concentrated cherry, toast and citrus flavors that finish long on the palate.

CHARLES HEIDSIECK

Of the three producers with the Heidsieck name, this Reims producer is the finest. *Chef de caves* Régis Camus' elegant wines gain depth from uncommonly long aging on their lees. The brut *réserve* offers tremendous complexity for the price.

○ **Charles Heidsieck Brut Réserve** / NV / $$$
There's a terrific lightness to this brut's pear and apple flavors.

○ **Charles Heidsieck Millésimé Vintage** / 2000 / $$$$
Drinking beautifully right now, this displays rare elegance and mellowed citrus and bread notes.

● **Charles Heidsieck Rosé Réserve** / NV / $$$$
The most recent addition to the winery's *réserve* range, this is a refined wine with floral, grapefruit and cherry nuances.

EGLY-OURIET

Egly-Ouriet is one of the best-known grower Champagne houses (i.e., boutique producers who use only grapes they grow on estate vineyards). Drawing from Egly-Ouriet's old-vine holdings, winemaker Francis Egly fashions small amounts of compelling wines mostly based on Pinot Noir.

○ **Egly-Ouriet Brut Premier Cru Les Vignes de Vrigny / NV / $$$**
Distinctive deep earth and green apple notes mark this 100
percent Pinot Meunier Champagne.

○ **Egly-Ouriet Blanc de Noirs Grand Cru Les Crayères / NV / $$$$**
Supple and seductively rich, with savory whole-wheat-bread
and invigorating lemon zest tones.

● **Egly-Ouriet Brut Rosé Grand Cru / NV / $$$$**
A nervy acidity courses through this beautifully balanced rosé
rounded out with citrus, cherry and toast notes.

GOSSET

Founded in the town of Aÿ in 1584, the small, top-quality house
of Gosset is one of the oldest producers in the Champagne
region. Unlike most other Champagnes, Gosset's wines do not
undergo malolactic fermentation (the secondary fermentation
process that helps to soften the wine), and as a result, they are
remarkably bright and zesty.

○ **Gosset Grand Millésime Brut / 2000 / $$$$**
Made with just slightly more Chardonnay than Pinot Noir,
this is big and savory, with peach and macadamia nuances.

● **Gosset Grand Rosé Brut / NV / $$$$**
Flavors of cherry, minerals and toast mark this fragrant,
voluptuous blend of wines from three different harvests.

HENRIOT

Now in its seventh generation of family ownership, this midsize
négociant and grower ages its wines in Roman-era chalk cellars
for exceptionally long periods. Kept at cool temperatures and
allowed extended contact with their lees, Henriot's cuvées—
from the flagship Brut Souverain to the pinnacle of the portfolio,
Cuvée des Enchanteleurs—are beautifully integrated and rich.

○ **Henriot Blanc Souverain / NV / $$$**
Made with 100 percent Chardonnay, this is balanced and toasty.

○ **Henriot Brut Souverain / NV / $$$**
A generous, creamy blend of Pinot Noir and Chardonnay that
finishes with a pleasant touch of sweetness.

● **Henriot Rosé Brut / NV / $$$$**
More than 15 vineyards produce fruit for Henriot's crisp, apple-
inflected rosé blend.

KRUG

Krug produces some of the world's most breathtakingly expensive wines (such as its Clos d'Ambonnay, introduced at $3,500). Sure, scarcity and prestige drive up the prices, but the wines can be truly thrilling, with extraordinary complexity and endless layers of flavors. Partly this results from Krug's practice of adding very high amounts of reserve (i.e., older, aged) wines; fermenting them in oak barrels adds a signature richness too.

○ **Krug Brut / 1998 / $$$$**
A beautiful, golden-hued Champagne from an outstanding year, layered with creamy almond, red berry and ginger notes.

○ **Krug Grande Cuvée Brut / NV / $$$$**
With a honey-infused, rich texture and flavors of pear, brioche and dried fruit, this epitomizes the Krug style.

LOUIS ROEDERER

Louis Roederer sources a remarkable 70 percent of its grapes from estate-owned vineyards, more by far than most major Champagne houses. That kind of quality control contributes to Roederer's remarkable consistency; another factor is winemaker Jean-Baptiste Caillon, who has been with the winery since 1989. Roederer's famous prestige cuvée, Cristal, was first created for czar Alexander II of Russia in 1876.

○ **Louis Roederer Brut Premier / NV / $$$**
Three years of lees-aging adds depth to this bottling's toast, dried-pear and apple notes.

○ **Louis Roederer Carte Blanche Extra Dry / NV / $$$**
This plush, slightly sweet blend of six vintages features roasted apple and lemon nuances and a long finish.

MOËT & CHANDON/DOM PÉRIGNON

Moët & Chandon's debonair *chef de cave*, Benoît Gouez, ably oversees Champagne's largest cellar, turning out five major cuvées sourced from a vast, scattered collection of 2,500 acres of estate vines, plus purchased fruit. The three nonvintage Impérial wines include a brut, a rosé and "Nectar," made in a sweeter style. Moët's legendary tête de cuvée, Dom Pérignon, became so successful that today it is its own brand, crafted by winemaking genius Richard Geoffroy.

○ **Moët & Chandon Impérial** / NV / $$$
  Always tasty, this widely available Champagne has satiny
  apple and pear flavors that finish with a burst of lemon.
○ **Dom Pérignon** / 2002 / $$$$
  Featuring an impressively long finish, this brims with silky fig,
  brioche, apricot and floral flavors.

PERRIER-JOUËT

Fruity, delicate, bright wines are the hallmark of this Epernay
producer, which celebrated its 200th anniversary in 2011. This
style holds true even for Fleur de Champagne, Perrier-Jouët's
best-known cuvée—instantly recognizable by its flower-strewn
enameled bottle, a design dating from the Art Nouveau period.

○ **Perrier-Jouët Grand Brut** / NV / $$$
  Made from grapes sourced from several Champagne sub-
  regions, this is lushly styled and pineapple-infused.
○ **Perrier-Jouët Fleur de Champagne Brut** / 2002 / $$$$
  A blend of Chardonnay, Pinot Noir and a bit of Pinot Meunier,
  this offers subtly sweet hints of lemon zest, caramel and toast.
● **Perrier-Jouët Blason Rosé** / NV / $$$$
  Elegant and silky, with charming berry and citrus accents.

POL ROGER

Pol Roger—now in its fifth generation of family ownership—
produces some of the most consistently high-quality wines in
Champagne. These include its impressive prestige bottling,
Cuvée Sir Winston Churchill (the English statesman was a
devoted fan of Pol Roger and a friend of the owners), and a
gorgeously balanced nonvintage wine, the Brut Réserve.

○ **Pol Roger Brut Réserve** / NV / $$$
  This regal nonvintage wine is creamy and rich, with layers of
  dried apple, toast and mango.
○ **Pol Roger Brut Blanc de Blancs** / 1999 / $$$$
  A warm vintage yielded this refined brut, whose roasted apple,
  caramel and coffee flavors show appealing signs of maturity.
● **Pol Roger Brut Rosé** / 2002 / $$$$
  The winery adds 15 percent still Pinot Noir wine from the
  same vintage to the final blend to achieve this delicate rosé,
  distinguished by warm apple, baking spice and toast notes.

TAITTINGER

A fixture in Champagne since 1734, this château was bought by the Taittinger family in 1934. Its house style is all about finesse and balancing light-bodied flavors with enough creamy lushness to keep them from tasting austere. While the Taittinger Comtes de Champagne is superb, the Prélude, produced exclusively from *grand cru* vineyards, offers more-affordable pleasure.

○ **Taittinger Brut La Française / NV / $$$**
Lean and focused, with citrus, apple and chalk flavors.

○ **Taittinger Brut Millésimé / 2004 / $$$$**
A polished, streamlined blend of equal parts Chardonnay and Pinot Noir grown in a single vineyard.

VEUVE CLICQUOT

The Clicquot Champagne house gained its full moniker from a business-savvy 19th-century matriarch who expanded the company enormously after being left a widow (a *veuve*). Today the orange label of its brut is a staple worldwide. The luxury La Grande Dame cuvées are dominated by Pinot Noir, as are all Clicquot wines, but they're crafted in a more elegant style.

○ **Veuve Clicquot Brut / NV / $$$**
Fresh and fruity, this yeasty wine offers a wealth of rich apple and peach flavors that have impressive weight.

● **Veuve Clicquot Rosé Brut / NV / $$$$**
This is firm and more mineral-laden than the brut, filled out with smoky raspberry notes and a creamy texture.

OTHER SPARKLING WINES

Champagne remains the benchmark for sparkling wines, but vintners around the world make a wide range of quality sparklers. The best are made using Champagne's *méthode traditionnelle*; less expensive versions employ other methods.

FRANCE Beyond Champagne, France abounds with sparkling wines, most made with grapes typical to each region. Seven of the country's sparkling wine appellations—the largest is the Loire—are able to use the term *Crémant* to indicate they are produced by the *méthode traditionnelle*. Other wines labeled *brut* or *Mousseux* may or may not have been made this way.

ITALY Italy's northern regions are the main source of the country's *spumante* (sparkling) wines. One of the best, very similar in taste to Champagne, comes from Lombardy's Franciacorta zone. Also noteworthy are Piedmont's flowery Moscato d'Asti and light red, berry-scented Brachetto d'Acqui. The Veneto's affordable and popular Proseccos are produced in tanks, in a process known as the Charmat method.

SPAIN Long marketed as less costly substitutes for Champagne, Spanish cavas by law must be made using the traditional method. Most come from the Catalonia region near Barcelona and are made mainly from the white Macabeo grape.

UNITED STATES The quality of American sparkling wines has been steadily improving. While the best bottlings still come from the cooler regions of Northern California—such as Carneros, Sonoma and the Anderson and Green valleys—Washington State, Oregon, New York and New Mexico are making a growing number of complex, vibrant sparklers.

Producers/ Other Sparkling Wines

FRANCE
DOMAINE DU VISSOUX / PIERRE-MARIE CHERMETTE

Beaujolais vintner Pierre-Marie Chermette is one of the region's best-known "naturalist" winemakers, eschewing common techniques such as adding sugar, yeast or sulfites to his wines. His brut, a nonvintage wine made from Chardonnay, is well worth seeking out for its citrusy intensity and affordable price tag.

○ **Pierre-Marie Chermette Vissoux Blanc de Blancs Brut / NV / Crémant de Bourgogne / \$\$** A terrific value, with savory chalky lemon notes, a creamy texture and a generous finish.

DOMAINE FRANÇOIS PINON

Former child psychologist and seventh-generation vintner François Pinon is best known for his still wines, which are among the benchmark bottlings of the Loire's renowned Vouvray subregion. It's no surprise then that his *pétillant* (sparkling) cuvées are equally compelling. Like nearly all Vouvray wines, they're made from Chenin Blanc, which Pinon farms organically.

○ **Domaine François Pinon Brut Non Dosé / NV / Vouvray / $$**
Aromatic flower, stone and pear flavors are dry and fresh.

○ **Domaine François Pinon Pétillant Brut / NV / Vouvray / $$**
This bottling's up-front mineral-edged fig and pear flavors are appealingly vivacious.

SIMONNET-FEBVRE

Simonnet-Febvre has specialized in sparkling wines since it was founded in 1840, and it's still the only winery in the Chablis region that produces Crémant de Bourgogne—Burgundy sparkling wines made using the traditional method. Based on Chardonnay and Pinot Noir, the winery's *crémants* gain lovely freshness and depth from the district's clay and limestone soils.

● **Simonnet-Febvre Brut Rosé / NV / Crémant de Bourgogne / $$**
A delicate, light-bodied, strawberry-scented rosé that's perfect for picnics or as an aperitif.

ITALY
BELLAVISTA

Bellavista turns out rich, ambitious *metodo classico* wines in a futuristic-looking facility in Lombardy's small Franciacorta subregion. Top offerings at Bellavista, which was founded in 1977 by construction magnate Vittorio Moretti and is helmed by supertalented winemaker Mattia Vezzola, can rival the best Champagnes in their structure and longevity.

○ **Bellavista Cuvée Brut / NV / Franciacorta / $$$**
With impressive Champagne-like elegance, this blend features fragrant flower blossoms and silky lemon chiffon.

○ **Bellavista Gran Cuvée Satèn Brut / NV / Franciacorta / $$$$**
Made with 100 percent Chardonnay from the Erbusco district, this offers baked apple, brioche and firm minerals.

MIONETTO

This well-known Prosecco producer has been around since the late 1800s. Close relationships with growers—and the winery's location in Valdobbiadene, home to the best Prosecco—help ensure consistent quality. The brut bottling is a perennial steal, and the Valdobbiadene shows sophistication beyond its price.

○ **Mionetto Brut** / NV / **Prosecco** / **$**
Crisp and bright, with zippy lemon and apple accents.

○ **Mionetto Brut** / NV / **Prosecco Superiore di Valdobbiadene** / **$$**
Made with grapes from a single vineyard on the border of the Cartizze region, this shows sweet pear and peach notes.

NINO FRANCO SPUMANTI

This winery began its rise to the front ranks of Prosecco producers in 1982, when Primo Franco took over the family winery in Valdobbiadene. Over the course of three decades Franco transformed its winemaking practices and made vast improvements in grape-growing. The result of his efforts: some of Italy's best Proseccos, including the flagship Primo Franco.

○ **Nino Franco Rustico** / NV / **Prosecco di Valdobbiadene** / **$$**
Accessibly priced and very appealing, this delivers a mix of stone fruit, flowers and apples.

○ **Nino Franco Grave di Stecca** / 2009 / **Prosecco** / **$$$**
This unusual single-vineyard Prosecco is exceptionally refined.

SPAIN
CODORNÍU

In 1872 Codorníu founder Josep Raventos was the first to apply Champagne techniques to Spanish grapes, making him the founder of the modern cava industry. Today Codorníu is the world's most prolific producer of traditionally made sparkling wine, having expanded to California and Argentina. But its reliably fresh cavas remain the heart of its portfolio.

○ **Anna de Codorníu Brut** / NV / **Cava** / **$**
This low-priced blend of Chardonnay and the Spanish grape Parellada is soft and apple-laden.

● **Codorníu Pinot Noir Rosé Brut** / NV / **Cava** / **$**
Strawberry and candied-cherry tones mark this rosé sparkler.

FREIXENET

Propelled by the phenomenal success of its two flagship cavas, Carta Nevada and Cordon Negro, Freixenet has become an international powerhouse, with wineries and vineyards all over the world. Created in 1861 by the marriage of the Ferrer and Sala winemaking families, Freixenet produced its first *méthode traditionnelle* sparkling wines in 1914. Still family-owned, it's a terrific source for consistently delicious and well-priced cava.

○ **Elyssia Gran Cuvée Brut** / NV / Cava / $$
A charming cava full of vanilla, citrus and apple flavors.

● **Cordon Rosado Brut** / NV / Cava / $
This lively, tangy wine is made with the Garnacha and Trepat grapes and has abundant cherry, berry and dried apple notes.

● **Elyssia Pinot Noir Brut** / NV / Cava / $$
With a modern package and taste profile, this bright rosé is loaded with frothy flavors of red cherry and strawberry.

SEGURA VIUDAS

Now owned by the Freixenet Group, cava specialist Segura Viudas maintains a distinct identity and a reputation for high quality. Its longtime winemaker Gabriel Suberviola ages the *reserva* wines in bottle for up to four years before releasing them, which imparts a toasty richness. The entry-level bottlings are wonderfully crisp, refreshing values.

○ **Segura Viudas Brut Reserva** / NV / Cava / $
This low-priced gem is packed with green apple and citrus.

○ **Segura Viudas Reserva Heredad** / NV / Cava / $$
Made from estate vineyards, this delivers a rich texture offset by crisp apple and pear flavors.

UNITED STATES
DOMAINE CARNEROS

Established in 1987, this California outpost of the Taittinger Champagne house possesses the stateliness of a French château. A full 95 percent of the fruit, all of which is certified organic, comes from estate vineyards. The lineup includes the well-known Vintage Brut Cuvée as well as prestige cuvées, most notably Le Rêve Blanc de Blancs. The winery also crafts three well-made, small-production still Pinot Noirs.

○ **Domaine Carneros Brut Cuvée / 2007 / Carneros / $$**
The green apple, lemon and mineral flavors in this vintage-dated wine are tart and refreshing.

○ **Le Rêve Blanc de Blancs / 2005 / Carneros / $$$$**
Inspired by Taittinger's famed Comtes de Champagne cuvée, this stylish wine has lemony acidity and nut nuances.

● **Domaine Carneros Cuvée de la Pompadour Brut Rosé / NV / Carneros / $$$** An exuberant mix of cherry, green apple and nut marks this slightly sweet rosé, named for Louis XV's mistress.

DOMAINE CHANDON

An extension of LVMH Group's Moët & Chandon, Chandon farms a massive 1,000 acres of vineyards in Yountville, Carneros and Mount Veeder. An extensive line of sparkling wines offers good value across the board, from the basic nonvintage Brut Classic to the prestige cuvée line Étoile. Fun curiosities include three single-appellation bruts and a sparkling red produced with Pinot Noir and Zinfandel.

○ **Chandon Brut Classic / NV / California / $$**
Meyer lemon flavors are rounded out with apple and toast nuances in this lively brut.

● **Étoile Rosé / NV / Napa and Sonoma counties / $$$**
Made with the addition of a small amount of Pinot Noir wine, this shows strawberry, cherry and baking spice flavors.

GLORIA FERRER CAVES & VINEYARDS

Spanish wine maven José Ferrer (of the Freixenet sparkling wine empire) founded this lovely estate in Sonoma in 1986, naming it after his wife, Gloria. Its success somewhat vindicates the failed attempt by José's father to locate vineyard property in New Jersey in the 1930s. The estate vineyards are heavily planted to Pinot Noir, which often takes the lead role in the finest wines, such as the Royal Cuvée.

○ **Gloria Ferrer Sonoma Brut / NV / Sonoma County / $$**
This features a nice low price and loads of mouthwatering lemon, apple and toast flavors.

○ **Gloria Ferrer Royal Cuvée / 2002 / Carneros / $$$**
Made from a blend of 16 separate base wines, this Carneros sparkler is round, supple and subtly sweet.

GRUET WINERY

As French-born Gilbert Gruet traveled through New Mexico in 1983, he realized the region might be suitable for winemaking. Gruet planted Chardonnay and Pinot Noir vines and released his first New Mexico sparklers in 1989. The accolades have been flowing in ever since, and today Gruet produces in excess of 100,000 cases of wine at astonishingly good value.

○ **Gruet Brut** / NV / New Mexico / $
Among the best value sparkling wines made anywhere, this shows a refreshing mix of citrus and green pear.

○ **Gruet Blanc de Blancs** / 2007 / New Mexico / $$
Three years of aging has softened this pear-flavored wine.

IRON HORSE VINEYARDS

Audrey and Barry Sterling had been producing still wines for several years before they began making sparkling wines in 1980. They've since attracted many influential admirers: Iron Horse sparkling wines have been served at the White House for five administrations, and chefs Charlie Palmer, Michael Mina and Bradley Ogden have chosen it for their custom cuvées.

○ **Iron Horse Vineyards Classic Vintage Brut** / 2006 / Green Valley of Russian River Valley / $$$ This suave, complex wine spent four years aging on its lees, which added richness.

○ **Iron Horse Vineyards Brut LD** / 2002 / Green Valley of Russian River Valley / $$$$ Creamy and poised, with a supple, streamlined texture and delicious intensity.

J VINEYARDS & WINERY

Created in 1986 by Judy Jordan, daughter of the founder of Sonoma's Jordan Vineyard, J has been dedicated almost from the start to producing Russian River sparkling wine by the *méthode champenoise*. J Vineyard's ultra-rich and elegant Late-Disgorged series benefits from extra aging on lees.

○ **J Cuvée 20 Brut** / NV / Russian River Valley / $$
A lithe, vibrant mix of yeasty apple and peach flavors.

● **J Brut Rosé** / NV / Russian River Valley / $$
This expressive wine is made with just slightly more Pinot than Chardonnay and bursts with red berry and apple.

MUMM NAPA

Vintner Ludovic Dervin brings a Champagne pedigree to Mumm's Napa winery, thanks to his experience at G.H. Mumm and Charles Heidsieck. Yet Mumm has a California touch too, making innovative sparklers like its Blanc de Blancs with Pinot Gris in the blend and the slightly sweet Cuvée M with some Muscat in it. The DVX Cuvée is a showstopper in great vintages.

○ **Mumm Napa Cuvée M / NV / Napa Valley / $$**
White peach and apricot notes underscore Cuvée M's tangy Granny Smith apple flavors.

○ **Mumm Napa DVX / 2002 / Napa Valley / $$$**
A bit of barrel fermentation adds rich toast and nut notes to lush yellow apple flavors in this vintage of the winery's outstanding signature cuvée.

ROEDERER ESTATE

Louis Roederer's outpost in California's Anderson Valley sticks closely to Champagne tradition. All vineyards are estate-owned, and the cuvées benefit from the addition of reserve wines, aged in French oak casks. The two nonvintage bruts and the vintage white and rosé L'Ermitage wines could rival true Champagne.

○ **Roederer Estate Brut / NV / Anderson Valley / $$**
This offers refined, toasty green apple and pineapple tones.

● **Roederer Estate Brut Rosé / NV / Anderson Valley / $$**
A blend of 60 percent Pinot and 40 percent Chardonnay, this is juicy and fragrant, with nut, apple and strawberry flavors.

SCHRAMSBERG VINEYARDS

Jack and Jamie Davies purchased Napa's dilapidated 218-acre Schramsberg estate in 1965, an era when making traditional sparkling wine seemed a lofty goal. Today Hugh Davies maintains his parents' legacy, aging the wines, including the J. Schram and Schramsberg Reserve, in hillside caves dug in the 1870s.

○ **Schramsberg Blanc de Blancs / 2007 / North Coast / $$$**
There's a nutty edge to the intense lemon and pear flavors in this terrific Blanc de Blancs.

● **Schramsberg Brut Rosé / 2007 / North Coast / $$$**
Lively apple and lemon are woven with bright cherry notes.

Fortified & Dessert Wines

Though few people drink them in the U.S., fortified wines are finally beginning to see some buzz. Mixologists are promoting port in cocktails, and sherry seems to be the latest enthusiasm for young, adventurous sommeliers. Unfortunately, traditional dessert wines haven't yet lucked out in that way—a shame, given their alluring flavors and impressive complexity.

FORTIFIED WINES

The practice of fortifying wines involves adding a neutral spirit, such as brandy, before bottling. Traditional fortified wines include sherry, port, Madeira and Marsala, although variations abound. These wines have a higher alcohol content—usually 16 to 20 percent—than most unfortified wines. A fortified wine's style depends largely on when the spirit is added. Adding it during fermentation, as in most port and Madeira, yields wines with a lot of natural grape sugar. When brandy is added after fermentation, the result can be drier, such as a fino sherry.

FORTIFIED WINES

SHERRY

Made in southern Spain's Jerez region, sherry gains its complex flavors from both the area's chalky soils and a peculiar yeast that appears on the wine's surface while it ages at the bodega (winery). Sherry styles range from utterly dry to incredibly sweet.

SHERRY GRAPES & STYLES

Most sherries are blends from different years. The dominant grape is Palomino, though sweeter styles often contain Pedro Ximénez or Moscatel. Winemakers employ a fractional blending system called solera, which combines wines from different vintages in such a way that all sherries bottled contain a portion of the oldest wine in that specific solera. Sherry comes in two basic varieties, fino and oloroso, both of which have subcategories.

FINO Flor, a yeast that protects wine from oxygen, gives fino sherry its unusual flavors. Other dry sherries in the fino category are manzanilla, with chamomile notes and a salty tang, and nutty, minerally amontillado. Pale cream sherry is a sweetened fino.

OLOROSO This sherry does not develop flor, and the presence of oxygen during aging creates a nutty, smoky, earthy flavor and a darker hue. Most olorosos are sweet; some are sweetened further by adding Pedro Ximénez, which creates cream sherry. (Rich, viscous and raisiny sweet, Pedro Ximénez, or PX, is made in many sherry houses, though technically it's not a true sherry.)

Producers/ Sherry

GONZÁLEZ BYASS

Established in 1855 by a sherry producer, Manuel María González, and his English agent, Robert Blake Byass, this firm is still family-owned. In recent years the company has expanded to include wineries in Rioja and Somontano, but its focus remains on sherry from Jerez, including the flagship Tío Pepe (the world's best-selling fino sherry) and eponymous González Byass brands.

○ **Tío Pepe Palomino Fino / NV / $$**
A fabulous aperitif, thanks to its crisp, refreshing apple and straw tones and a hint of saltiness.

○ **González Byass Amontillado Del Duque Muy Viejo / NV / $$$**
(375 ml) A dry sherry from a 30-year-old solera, this brims with smoke, toasted almond and spice.

LUSTAU

Emilio Lustau was founded in 1896 as an *almacenista*, a sherry wholesaler selling to larger companies. Today, however, it's Lustau that does the buying. Its stunning portfolio includes more than 40 wines, encompassing every style from cream sherry to the limited 30-year-old VORS (very old rare sherry) bottlings.

○ **Lustau Dry Amontillado Los Arcos / NV / $$**
A perfect food wine, with lightly smoky citrus and nut flavors.

○ **Lustau Palo Cortado Península / NV / $$**
Palos cortados are brighter and fresher than amontillados. Dry and elegant, Lustau's shows terrific balance and silky, dried-apricot and orange flavors.

SANDEMAN

A fortified-wine powerhouse, Sandeman produces port, Madeira and sherry as part of Sogrape Vinhos of Portugal. The brand's signature black-cloaked *don* image adorns a complete range of basic sherries, but look especially for the stellar amontillados. Wines in the 20-year-old series are very rich and complex.

○ **Sandeman Don Fino / NV / $**
Zesty, dry citrus flavors mark this generously styled fino.
○ **Sandeman Character Medium Dry Amontillado / NV / $$**
With bright apricot flavors and a touch of sweetness, this
amontillado is reminiscent of jam on toast.

FORTIFIED WINES

PORT

Portugal's second-largest city, Oporto, gave its name to the coun-
try's emblematic wine. Made in the Douro Valley and fortified
with brandy to arrest fermentation, port is typically a dark, sweet
wine with a high alcohol content.

PORT GRAPES & STYLES

The grapes most often used to make port are Touriga Nacional,
Touriga Franca and Tinta Roriz (Tempranillo). Port comes in
two main styles, ruby and tawny, as well as the occasional white.

RUBY The most common style of port, ruby is a blend of young
wines. Ruby reserve ports are more complex, often bearing pro-
prietary names like Graham's Six Grapes. Late Bottled Vintage
(LBV) ports are single-vintage rubies that have been aged four
to six years in barrel and are drinkable upon release, unlike most
vintage ports. Made in the finest years and aged in oak for two
to three years, vintage ports require decades of bottle aging to
reach their potential. Single-quinta vintage ports are made with
grapes from one vineyard, usually in nondeclared vintages.

TAWNY This port, in theory, has been aged in wood longer than
a ruby and thus taken on a tawny hue. In reality, most inexpen-
sive tawny ports are the same age as most rubies; they are just
made with lighter wines. Aged tawny port, however, is made from
blends of the highest-quality ports. Tawny port labels indicate
the average age of the blend's components (10, 20 or 30 years,
for example). Tawnies are ready to drink upon release and ex-
hibit delicate nutty aromas and dried-fruit flavors.

WHITE The best port for summer drinking, served (often with
tonic) over a glass of ice, white port has bright, citrusy flavors.
Recently Croft introduced a new style of rosé—or pink—port.

Producers/ Port

DOW'S

Symington Family Estates became Dow's sole owner in 1961, but this house has been in the port trade for over two centuries. Identified with a drier style, Dow's displays its expertise with wines such as the vintage 2003. Dow's also pioneered the use of automated grape-treading machines.

- **Dow's 10 Year Old Tawny / NV / $$$**
  This soft, mellow tawny is redolent of almonds and caramel.
- **Dow's Vintage / 2007 / $$$$**
  It's hard to go wrong with 2007 vintage ports, and Dow's—complex and graceful, with spicy currant flavors—is superb.

FONSECA GUIMARAENS

This famous producer is in the hands of supertalented wine-maker David Guimaraens, a descendant of the founding family. Soon after taking over, Guimaraens made flawless wines in the heralded 1994 vintage. The popular, lushly styled Fonseca Bin No. 27 represents a bargain buy from this prestigious house.

- **Fonseca Bin No. 27 Finest Reserve / NV / $$**
  A widely available, chocolaty, raspberry-infused ruby port.
- **Fonseca Late Bottled Vintage / 2005 / $$**
  Made in a round, smoky and rich style, this unfiltered port displays a luscious core of black cherries.
- **Fonseca 20 Year Old Tawny / NV / $$$**
  Aging has brought out butterscotch tones, a silky texture and warm spice notes in this complex tawny.

NIEPOORT

Dirk Niepoort leads this family winery (see p. 127), lending a sense of humor (as in a 10-year-old tawny called Drink Me) to port's stodgy image. But don't doubt the firm's seriousness: Its aged tawnies vie with the best, and the second-label Secundum is excellent (and ready to drink sooner than true vintage port).

- **Niepoort Late Bottled Vintage / 2005 / $$**
  Sourced from Cima Corgo, the Douro's most prestigious
  subregion, this elegant, ageworthy bottling is intensely fruity.
- **Niepoort 10 Year Old Tawny / NV / $$**
  Master blender José Nogueira layers wines of many ages to
  achieve a flavorful, toffee-edged offering with citrus notes.

QUINTA DO NOVAL

Almost two decades ago, AXA Millésimes—owner of several
Bordeaux châteaus, including Château Pichon-Longueville-
Baron—purchased Noval, marking an important turnaround
for the then ailing port house. Today the entire range shines:
The LBV is offered in both filtered and unfiltered versions, and
Noval's vintage port is trumped only by its costly Nacional, made
with grapes from a single plot of ungrafted vines.

- **Quinta do Noval Black / NV / $$**
  This supple, accessible, blackberry-flavored ruby reserve
  requires no aging or decanting.
- **Quinta do Noval Silval / 2007 / $$$**
  A baby brother to Noval's vintage ports, this velvety, complex
  bottling comes at a more affordable price.

RAMOS PINTO

Adriano Ramos Pinto founded this winery in 1880, focusing on
exports to Brazil. A century later, the original family was instrumental in winnowing the Douro's many grape varieties into the
select five for port production. Now owned by the French Roederer Group, Ramos Pinto (see p. 129) holds close to 900 acres of
prime Douro vineyards, which allows the winery to be highly
selective with its sourcing, given the modest size of production.

- **Ramos Pinto Collector / NV / $$**
  A good value for a reserve ruby, this tasty port is packed with
  soft, spicy blackberry and date layers.
- **Ramos Pinto Quinta de Ervamoira 10 Year Tawny / NV / $$$**
  A plush single-vineyard (quinta) offering, with expressive
  sweet red plum and caramel notes.
- **Ramos Pinto Quinta do Bom Retiro 20 Year Tawny / NV / $$$$**
  From one of the oldest vineyards in the Douro, this delivers
  silky layers of nuts, red fruit and toffee.

TAYLOR'S

With David Guimaraens in charge of wine-making, Taylor's frequently joins sister winery Fonseca (both are owned by the Fladgate Partnership) at the top of the heap in great vintage years. In lesser vintages, Taylor's Quinta de Vargellas is hardly a concession prize, with much of the brooding power and concentration you'd expect of a vintage port.

WINE INTEL
Luxury-seeking travelers should check out The Yeatman in Oporto. Opened in 2010 by Taylor's owners, the hotel features a wine-centric spa and a decanter-shaped pool.

- **Taylor Fladgate First Estate Reserve / NV / $$**
  Supple, balanced mocha and sweet plum flavors make this a wonderful introduction to ruby port.
- **Taylor Fladgate Late Bottled Vintage / 2005 / $$**
  Taylor's LBVs are known for their powerful, darkly fruity flavors, and this stellar vintage is no exception.
- **Taylor Fladgate 20 Year Old / NV / $$$**
  Beautifully woven with tiers of smooth, spicy dried-cherry and rich crème brûlée flavors.

W. & J. GRAHAM'S

The Symingtons are the second Scottish family to helm this house, following the original Grahams. The Quinta dos Malvedos property, the estate's shining star, merits its own bottling in years when its wines are not needed to make a vintage port. It also contributes to the much-loved Six Grapes, a reserve ruby.

- **W. & J. Graham's Six Grapes Reserve / NV / $$**
  More youthful than many reserve ruby ports, this shows vibrant black fruit, smoke and spice.
- **W. & J. Graham's Vintage / 2007 / $$$$**
  From a top producer in a fabulous vintage, this ambitious, multifaceted port is well worth the splurge.

DESSERT WINES

As the name implies, dessert wines are typically enjoyed with or in place of dessert. Sauternes from France's Bordeaux region has long been considered the pinnacle of sweet wines. Producers in Australia make high-quality examples (locally referred to as "stickies"), as do vintners in California and Canada. Ample sweet fruit and zippy acidity characterize the best of these wines.

DESSERT WINES GRAPES & STYLES

Red dessert wines do exist, but whites are far more common. The finest white dessert wines display intense flower, spice and honey flavors, with high levels of acidity, which keeps them refreshing despite a high sugar content. All dessert wines are made by concentrating the grapes' sugars and flavors in various ways.

LATE HARVEST This dessert wine is made from grapes harvested very late in the season, when they have high sugar levels. The best-known come from Germany (marked *Auslese* or *Beerenauslese*, indicating progressively greater sweetness) and Alsace (where they're called Vendanges Tardives). California, Australia, South Africa, Chile and Greece's isle of Samos make good versions too.

PASSITO An Italian specialty, *passito* wines are made from grapes that have been dried before pressing. Tuscan vintners use Trebbiano to make the local version, *vin santo*, while Sicilian vintners use the Zibibbo grape for their delicious *passito* wines.

BOTRYTIS Botrytized wines owe their unique flavors to *Botrytis cinerea*, a mold ("noble rot") that concentrates the wine's sugars and adds smoke and truffle notes. The finest are Bordeaux's Sauternes, made of Sémillon, Sauvignon Blanc and Muscadelle. Superb examples come from the Barsac subregion, while nearby Loupiac and Cadillac yield less costly versions. Loire Valley vintners make terrific sweet wines with Chenin Blanc. In Alsace, the best grapes go into sweet Sélection de Grains Nobles wines. German and Austrian vintners use mainly Riesling to craft sublime botrytized wines, labeled *Beerenauslese* (BA) or *Trockenbeerenauslese* (TBA), depending on sugar levels (see p. 134). California, Australia and South Africa also make botrytized wines.

ICE WINE/EISWEIN This wine is made by pressing frozen-on-the-vine grapes, a process that yields small amounts of sweet, concentrated juice. The finest ice wines are made from Riesling in Germany and Austria; good examples also come from Canada.

VIN DOUX NATUREL Fortified with brandy during fermentation, these wines are made mainly in southern France. The two most noteworthy examples are Muscat de Beaumes-de-Venise from the Rhône and Muscat de Rivesaltes from Roussillon.

TOKAJI This highly distinctive wine is infused with a mash of botrytis-affected grapes (*aszú*). Produced primarily in Hungary, Tokaji is graded by the amount of crushed grapes added to the base, on a scale measured by *puttonyos*—the more *puttonyos*, the more intense the wine. All Tokaji tend to exhibit delicious ripe apricot, orange and almond flavors and high acidity.

Producers/ Dessert Wines

CHAMBERS ROSEWOOD

Located in the Australian state of Victoria since 1858, this lauded Aussie winery produces dry, sweet and fortified wines under the leadership of sixth-generation vintner Stephen Chambers. Although Chambers Rosewood is most famous for its rich, concentrated Grand and Rare cuvées, its basic Rutherglen bottlings are two of Australia's best dessert-wine values.

○ **Chambers Rosewood Vineyards Muscadelle / NV / Rutherglen / $$** (375 ml) Leaving Muscadelle grapes to dry on the vine yields a sweet, peachy wine; oak aging adds spice.

○ **Chambers Rosewood Vineyards Muscat / NV / Rutherglen / $$** (375 ml) Stephen Chambers blends fortified wines that have been aged between six and ten years for this opulent bottling.

CHÂTEAU COUTET

This is the oldest and largest estate in Bordeaux's Barsac subregion; Thomas Jefferson praised its Sauternes in 1787. The château's rich style is evident in the superbly crafted estate bottling, but even more decadent is the Cuvée Madame, made in exceptional vintages from Sémillon vines averaging 40 years of age.

○ **Château Coutet / 2007 / Barsac / $$$$**
This offers tremendous finesse, with delicate floral notes and a fine acidity offsetting honeyed orange and peach flavors.

○ **Château Coutet / 2008 / Barsac / $$$$**
Though it's slightly richer than the 2007, this is still fresh and balanced, with a broad swath of rich, satiny apricot.

INNISKILLIN

Founded in Niagara-on-the-Lake, Ontario, in 1975 by Karl Kaiser and Donald Ziraldo, Inniskillin made its first Icewine in 1984. Since then, its fresh and unctuous offerings have put Canadian ice wines on the map. Today the Niagara winery has been joined by Inniskillin Okanagan in British Columbia.

○ **Inniskillin Riesling Icewine** / 2007 / **Niagara Peninsula** / **$$$$** (375 ml) One of Canada's benchmark wines, this offers super-sweet apple and citrus flavors cut with racy acidity.

● **Inniskillin Cabernet Franc Icewine** / 2007 / **Niagara Peninsula** / **$$$$** (375 ml) A vivid cranberry hue, this features candied-berry and plum flavors; it's ideal with fruit desserts.

KRACHER

This famed Austrian estate produces both dry and sweet wines, but it is Kracher's dessert wines, pioneered by the late Alois Kracher, that inspire the greatest reverence. While the Auslese, Beerenauslese and ice wines are all marvelous, the innovative Trockenbeerenauslese bottlings are legendary.

○ **Kracher Auslese** / 2009 / **Burgenland** / **$$** (375 ml) This juicy, harmonious blend of Welschriesling and Chardonnay offers honeyed citrus and mineral notes.

○ **Kracher Cuvée Beerenauslese** / 2008 / **Burgenland** / **$$** (375 ml) Creamy, lusciously sweet apricot and orange flavors get their intensity from the noble rot, botrytis.

ROYAL TOKAJI

Founded in 1990 with wine writer Hugh Johnson as a partner, this Hungarian winery has been instrumental in the revival of Tokaji dessert wines. Károly Áts is responsible for crafting the wines, including the very rare and costly Royal Tokaji Essencia.

○ **Royal Tokaji Mád Cuvée** / 2008 / **Tokaj** / **$$** (375 ml) Named for the town in which the winery is based, this caramel- and peach-accented bottling offers superb value.

○ **Royal Tokaji Essencia** / 2000 / **Tokaj** / **$$$$** (375 ml) The pinnacle of modern Hungarian sweet wines, this legendary cuvée, with less than 3 percent alcohol and up to 85 percent sugar, sells for more than $500—if you can find it.

Pairing / Wine & Food

These days the old adage "White wine with fish and red with meat" seems to have been replaced with "Drink whatever you like with whatever you want." Both approaches have advantages, but neither is a hard and fast rule, and the truth is that there is no single "perfect" wine match for any given dish. Ideally, you want to bring together dishes and wines that highlight each other's best qualities rather than obscure them. To help you make delicious matches at home and in restaurants, the following pages provide six easy-to-follow general rules for matching and a primer on pairing by grape variety, including specific bottle recommendations from the guide.

GENERAL RULES FOR MATCHING

BE BODY-CONSCIOUS Delicately flavored food goes best with a light and delicate wine; heavy, full-flavored dishes call for heftier wines. The subtle flavors of sole meunière are going to get lost if paired with a big, oaky Chardonnay, and a light Beaujolais will seem like water if served with braised short ribs.

BALANCE EXTREMES If a dish is rich and creamy, you need a tart, high-acid wine to cut through the fat and to cleanse your palate. A bit of sweetness in wine balances salty or spicy foods. If you can't wait to drink those young and astringent Bordeaux, Barolos or California Cabernet Sauvignons, the protein and fat of a rich cut of meat will help moderate their tannins.

PAIR LIKES Peppery meat dishes work well with spicy red wines like those from the Rhône Valley. Play fruit sauces off rich and fruity wines. Pair grassy, herbal whites with green vegetables.

LOOK TO THE LOCALS Wines from a particular region often match well with foods from the same place.

MIX & MATCH The "red with meat, white with fish" rule is a good fallback when you're unsure what to pair with a dish, but it's a rule made to be broken. Try a light, acidic red such as a Burgundy with a rich fish like salmon, or pair a rich Chardonnay with grilled chicken.

BRIDGE THE GAP If your table has ordered steak, salmon and sea scallops, and you have to pick the wine, choose one that offers a bit of something for each dish. Full-bodied rosés such as those from Bandol or Tavel or lighter-bodied reds like non-Riserva Chianti Classico or a light-style Oregon Pinot Noir have the subtlety not to overwhelm delicate dishes and the substance to stand up to a hearty steak.

Pairing  by Grape

Of the thousands of different grape varieties in the world, only about 20 are regularly represented on wine shelves in the United States. Each variety has its own particular characteristics that yield different styles of wine and result in a greater affinity with certain foods than others. Here is a guide to the most common grape varieties, with suggestions for dishes that pair especially well with each and a selection of wines that express each grape's distinctive qualities.

CABERNET FRANC

Cabernet Franc adds spicy pepper and bright red cherry flavors to Bordeaux red wines, but it stars in France's Loire Valley, where it makes light, spicy reds. California, Washington State and Long Island also make good examples.

BEST PAIRINGS Cabernet Franc tends to be somewhat lighter and more herbal than Cabernet Sauvignon, so pair it with dishes like herb-rubbed roast chicken (or any light meat dishes involving a lot of herbs), roast pork loin or veal chops. Earthier, more structured Old World versions of Cabernet Franc—for instance, those hailing from the Chinon region of the Loire Valley—are an ideal match for roast duck or other game birds.

- Andrew Will / 2009 / Columbia Valley / $$ / p. 201
- Bernard Baudry Le Clos Guillot / 2008 / Chinon / $$ / p. 48
- Le Macchiole Paleo / 2007 / Tuscany / $$$$ / p. 90

CABERNET SAUVIGNON

Cabernet Sauvignon is revered around the world for its bold, rich flavors and its ability to improve with age. Bolstered by substantial tannins, its signature black currant and blackberry flavors can gain notes of green bell pepper in cooler climates. The most renowned examples of Cabernet Sauvignon come from Bordeaux, where it is blended with Merlot, Cabernet Franc and Petit Verdot, as well as from California's Napa Valley, Chile's Upper Maipo Valley and Tuscany.

BEST PAIRINGS Cabernets from California, Australia and South America, with their rich fruit and substantial tannins, pair best with meat—well-marbled steaks, braised short ribs, hearty roasts. European Cabernets and Bordeaux blends tend to have higher acidity and less overtly ripe flavors; lamb, or game of any kind, is a great match for them.

- Betz Family Winery Père de Famille / 2008 / Columbia Valley / $$$ / p. 202
- Château Brane-Cantenac / 2008 / Margaux / $$$ / p. 30
- Louis M. Martini Lot No. 1 / 2007 / Napa Valley / $$$$ / p. 181
- Santa Carolina Reserva de Familia / 2008 / Maipo Valley / $$ / p. 251
- Souverain / 2007 / Alexander Valley / $$ / p. 191

CHARDONNAY

Chardonnay styles vary wildly, from crisp, unoaked versions to the powerful, mineral-laden whites from France's Burgundy. Chardonnay's mild apple, citrus and pear flavors take well to oak aging, which gives the wine notes of toast and caramel. Warmer-climate regions such as California and Australia produce lusher, sweeter, fruit-driven styles.

BEST PAIRINGS Lighter, unoaked Chardonnay and Chablis pair well with most fish, shellfish and salads. Oakier versions (most California Chardonnays, for instance) are better with more substantial dishes like roast chicken with herbs, pork tenderloin or richer fish or shellfish dishes such as salmon.

- ○ Domaine Christian Moreau Père & Fils / 2009 / Chablis / $$ / p. 39
- ○ Domaines Leflaive / 2009 / Mâcon-Verzé / $$$ / p. 41
- ○ Gallo Family Vineyards Two Rock Vineyard / 2008 / Sonoma Coast / $$ / p. 175
- ○ Morse Code / 2010 / Padthaway / $ / p. 219
- ○ The Ojai Vineyard Bien Nacido Vineyard / 2008 / Santa Maria Valley / $$ / p. 183

CHENIN BLANC

Full of fruit and high acidity, Chenin Blanc produces some of France's best wines, such as the Loire Valley's full-bodied, long-aging, dry whites, and dessert and sparkling wines. Chenin Blanc wines are also made in South Africa and California.

BEST PAIRINGS Dry Chenin Blanc is a good partner for white-fleshed fish, chicken or even light veal or pork dishes. Off-dry (lightly sweet) versions pair better with spicy foods such as Indian or other Asian dishes.

O **Domaine des Baumard** / 2007 / Savennières / $$ / p. 48
O **Domaine Huet Le Haut-Lieu Sec** / 2009 / Vouvray / $$ / p. 49
O **Dry Creek Vineyard Dry** / 2009 / Clarksburg / $ / p. 170
O **Mulderbosch** / 2009 / Western Cape / $ / p. 258

GEWÜRZTRAMINER

The pink-skinned Gewürztraminer grape offers exuberant aromas and flamboyant flavors ranging from honeysuckle to lychee, candied apricot, mineral and Asian spice. It is an especially important grape variety in the white wines of Alsace and Germany. New York and California are also home to some excellent Gewürztraminer-based wines.

BEST PAIRINGS Gewürztraminer almost always pairs well with Asian and Indian food. For spicier dishes, choose an off-dry example; for less spicy dishes, dry Gewürztraminer is the better match. Gewürztraminer is also a good accompaniment for stronger cheeses such as Epoisses or Muenster.

O **Domaine Zind-Humbrecht Clos Windsbuhl** / 2009 / Alsace / $$$ / p. 27
O **Paul Cluver** / 2010 / Elgin / $ / p. 259

GRENACHE/GARNACHA

The fresh, spicy cherry flavors of the Grenache grape are essential to many of the red wines of southern France, such as Châteauneuf-du-Pape and Côtes-du-Rhône. Spain's winemakers rely heavily on Grenache (Garnacha in Spanish), particularly in Catalonia's Priorat region. The variety is also important in Sardinia (where it is known as Cannonau) and shows up in wines from California and Australia.

BEST PAIRINGS Grenache, with its warm, quintessentially Mediterranean flavors, pairs well with hearty dishes like grilled sausages, lamb chops and rustic stews.

- Cantina Santadi Noras / 2008 / Cannonau di Sardegna / $$ / p. 98
- Domaine Santa Duc Les Vieilles Vignes / 2007 / Côtes-du-Rhône / $$ / p. 60
- Mas Igneus Barranc dels Closos / 2008 / Priorat / $$ / p. 118
- Yangarra Estate Vineyard Old Vine / 2008 / McLaren Vale / $$ / p. 225

MALBEC

Malbec is the signature red grape of Argentina, where it yields wines that are bursting with lush, dark-berry and rich chocolate flavors. It is no longer important in Bordeaux, its place of origin, but dominates red wine production in the French region of Cahors, where it is called Auxerrois, and shows up in the Loire Valley, California, Australia and Chile.

BEST PAIRINGS Malbec's full-bodied dark-fruit flavors and light, peppery spiciness make it a natural partner for beef, lamb, venison and other substantial meats.

- Achaval-Ferrer / 2009 / Mendoza / $$ / p. 239
- Château Lagrézette Cuvée Dame Honneur / 2003 / Cahors / $$$$ / p. 63
- Elsa Bianchi / 2010 / Mendoza / $ / p. 243
- Luigi Bosca Reserva / 2008 / Luján de Cuyo / $$ / p. 240

MARSANNE/ROUSSANNE

White grapes Marsanne and Roussanne are most at home in France's northern Rhône Valley, where they are often combined to create the great wines of Crozes-Hermitage, Hermitage and St-Joseph. Many winemakers blend them with Viognier. Good versions also come from California.

BEST PAIRINGS Full-bodied, with stone-fruit and honey flavors and moderate acidity, Marsanne-Roussanne blends pair well with lighter meats in herb-based sauces and with richer fish dishes. They are also good with roast chicken and with vegetables like parsnips, fennel and celery root.

- ○ Paul Jaboulet Aîné Domaine Mule Blanche / 2009 / Crozes-Hermitage / $$$ / p. 55
- ○ Tablas Creek Vineyard Roussanne / 2009 / Paso Robles / $$ / p. 193
- ○ Tardieu-Laurent Guy Louis / 2009 / Côtes-du-Rhône / $$ / p. 61

MERLOT

With its plum and chocolate flavors, Merlot is one of the most popular grapes in the world and is responsible for some of the greatest red wines, such as those from Bordeaux's Pomerol and from Washington State. Terrific examples are also produced in California and northeastern Italy.

BEST PAIRINGS Merlot's spicy plum flavors and full body make it a good match for everything from pork chops and roasts to pasta in meat sauce and sausages off the grill.

- Avignonesi Desiderio / 2007 / Cortona / $$$ / p. 84
- Falesco Montiano / 2007 / Lazio / $$$ / p. 94
- Pepper Bridge / 2008 / Walla Walla Valley / $$$ / p. 205
- SKN / 2008 / Napa Valley / $ / p. 170
- St. Clement Vineyards / 2008 / Napa Valley / $$ / p. 192

MUSCAT

All Muscat, both red and white, bursts with fragrant flavors such as honeysuckle, orange blossom and musk. It's widely grown, most famously in Italy as Moscato and in Spain as Moscatel, as well as in Alsace, southern France, Greece, California and Australia.

BEST PAIRINGS Most Muscat bottlings are lightly sweet; that, together with the grape's tangerine-scented fruitiness, makes it a natural partner for fresh fruit desserts.

○ Chambers Rosewood Vineyards / NV / Rutherglen / $$ / p. 282

NEBBIOLO

Nebbiolo achieves its greatest glory in Italy's Piedmont region, where the variety's cherry, tar and tobacco flavors define the elegant, long-lived reds of Barolo and Barbaresco. A small number of vintners outside of Italy work with Nebbiolo too, especially in California and Australia, but in these places the grape tends to express different characteristics.

BEST PAIRINGS This structured, aromatic red grape pairs especially well with any dish involving mushrooms, but it is also good with lamb, venison and beef (beef braised in Barolo is a classic Piedmontese dish). Older vintages go perfectly with truffles.

- La Spinetta Vigneto Garretti / 2006 / Barolo / $$$$ / p. 72
- Michele Chiarlo Tortoniano / 2006 / Barolo / $$$ / p. 73
- Poderi Luigi Einaudi Costa Grimaldi / 2006 / Barolo / $$$$ / p. 74
- Vietti Castiglione / 2006 / Barolo / $$$ / p. 75

PETITE SIRAH

Not to be confused with the Syrah grape (known as Shiraz in Australia), Petite Sirah yields wines that are lusty and dark and full of chewy tannins. A French native, originally from the Rhône Valley, the grape is believed to be a cross between the Peloursin variety and Syrah, and it grows well in California, Mexico, South America, Australia and parts of the Middle East.

BEST PAIRINGS Almost invariably full-bodied and bursting with blackberry and spice flavors, Petite Sirah is ideal with saucy barbecued meats or rich braised short ribs prepared with an array of sweet or savory spices.

● Quivira Vineyards and Winery Wine Creek Ranch / 2008 / Dry Creek Valley / $$ / p. 184

PINOT BLANC/PINOT BIANCO

Sometimes referred to as "the poor man's Chardonnay," Pinot Blanc goes by the name Pinot Bianco in Italy and Weissburgunder (white Burgundy) in Austria. Thought to be a native of France's Burgundy (though no longer common there), Pinot Blanc yields medium-bodied wines that range from crisp and zippy to creamy and rich. The best examples come from Alsace, northern Italy (Alto Adige, Collio and Friuli) and Austria.

BEST PAIRINGS Pair Pinot Blanc with delicate freshwater fish, such as trout or perch, or light meat dishes involving chicken breasts or veal scallops. Italian Pinot Biancos tend to be leaner and are best with raw shellfish or lightly dressed green salads.

○ Domaines Schlumberger Les Princes Abbés / 2008 / Alsace / $ / p. 27

○ Kellerei Terlan / 2010 / Alto Adige / $$ / p. 79

○ Trimbach / 2007 / Alsace / $ / p. 28

PINOT GRIS/PINOT GRIGIO

In Alsace and Oregon, the Pinot Gris grape yields full-bodied, nutty white wines. In Italy, where it is called Pinot Grigio, the variety makes light, brisk whites. It also has success in California's cooler regions.

BEST PAIRINGS Light and simple, Pinot Grigios make a good match for equally light fish dishes and green salads. Alsace-style Pinot Gris tends to be richer and goes better with flavorful pasta dishes or chicken in cream-based sauces; it also pairs well with modestly spiced Asian and Indian dishes.

PINOT NOIR

Known as the "heartbreak grape," Pinot Noir is difficult to grow and vinify everywhere it is cultivated. At its best, the variety yields wines that are incredibly seductive, with aromas of roses, smoke, red fruit and earth. The red wines of Burgundy are regarded as the ultimate expression of the Pinot Noir grape, but excellent examples are also produced in the Loire Valley, California, New York, Oregon, Australia and New Zealand.

BEST PAIRINGS Old World Pinot Noir (Burgundy, for example) goes best with simple, flavorful dishes such as steaks, lamb chops or wild game birds. The New World's fruitier, more straightforward versions make good matches for duck, richer fish (especially salmon) and dishes involving mushrooms and truffles.

RIESLING

Riesling can make white wines of extraordinary complexity, with high acidity and plenty of mineral flavors, in styles ranging from bone-dry to sumptuously sweet. Rieslings are made all around the world, but the best versions come from Alsace, Germany, Austria, Australia and New York. Many can age for decades.

BEST PAIRINGS Off-dry Rieslings pair very well with Asian cuisines, especially Thai and Vietnamese dishes. Dry Riesling is a good accompaniment to freshwater fish, such as trout, as well as dishes with citrus flavors.

SANGIOVESE

Sangiovese is an important grape in Italy, where it is prized for its red cherry and leather flavors and high acidity. It is most common in Tuscany, where it makes most of the red wines of Chianti and many of the exalted Super-Tuscans. The grape is also grown in California.

BEST PAIRINGS Sangiovese's bright cherry-berry flavors, firm acidity and moderate tannins are all characteristics that make it ideal for pastas with tomato-based sauces as well as pizza. Rich, starchy dishes such as risotto and full-flavored, dry-cured sausages are other good partners.

- Castello di Ama / 2007 / Chianti Classico / $$$ / p. 86
- Il Poggione / 2008 / Rosso di Montalcino / $$ / p. 89
- Monsanto Il Poggio Riserva / 2006 / Chianti Classico / $$$ / p. 86
- Selvapiana / 2009 / Chianti Rùfina / $$ / p. 88

SAUVIGNON BLANC

Sauvignon Blanc's finest expressions are the lemony, herbaceous white wines of the Sancerre and Pouilly-Fumé regions of France's Loire Valley. But many New Zealand examples, with flavors of zingy grapefruit and fresh-cut grass, are also outstanding. Winemakers in parts of California, Austria and South Africa produce excellent Sauvignon Blancs as well.

BEST PAIRINGS With its bright acidity, mixed citrus flavors and herbal notes, Sauvignon Blanc makes an ideal partner for raw shellfish, light fish dishes, salads and fresh vegetable dishes; it's also a classic partner for anything involving goat cheese.

- ○ Cakebread Cellars / 2009 / Napa Valley / $$ / p. 164
- ○ Domaine Vacheron / 2010 / Sancerre / $$$ / p. 51
- ○ Montes Limited Selection / 2010 / Leyda Valley / $ / p. 249
- ○ Palliser Estate / 2010 / Martinborough / $$ / p. 234
- ○ Santa Rita Reserva / 2010 / Casablanca Valley / $ / p. 249

SÉMILLON

The second of Bordeaux's great white wine grapes after Sauvignon Blanc, Sémillon is the primary component of the region's luxurious, sweet Sauternes wines. Winemakers in Bordeaux as well as in Australia also use the Sémillon grape either on its own or blended with Sauvignon Blanc to make some delicious, full-bodied dry wines.

BEST PAIRINGS Sémillon's lemon and honey flavors are ideal with light fish in butter-based sauces as well as with baked or roast fish; the wine is also good with light chicken dishes.

○ **Boekenhoutskloof** / 2008 / Franschhoek / $$ / p. 256
○ **Château Coutet** / 2007 / Barsac / $$$$ / p. 282

SYRAH/SHIRAZ

Typically rich, round, full-bodied and tannic, with berry, pepper and smoke aromas and flavors, wines made from the Syrah grape (called Shiraz in Australia) often show both power and finesse and can age for decades. Syrah's most renowned domains are the Hermitage and Côte-Rôtie appellations in France's Rhône Valley, but California's Central Coast, Washington State and Australia also produce impressive versions.

BEST PAIRINGS Match spicy, structured Old World Syrahs with steak, lamb or game such as venison. Fruitier New World bottlings, like most from Australia, also work well with lamb and can go with rich, cheesy dishes like eggplant Parmesan or hamburgers topped with blue cheese.

● **Beckman Vineyards Purisima Mountain Vineyard** / 2008 / Santa Ynez Valley / $$$ / p. 162
● **Delas Chante-Perdrix** / 2009 / Cornas / $$$ / p. 53
● **Lapostolle Cuvée Alexandre Las Kuras Vineyard** / 2007 / Cachapoal Valley / $$ / p. 248
● **Penley Estate Hyland** / 2008 / Coonawarra / $$ / p. 221

TEMPRANILLO

The dominant grape of Spain's Rioja, Ribera del Duero and Toro regions, Tempranillo makes delicious, cherry- and spice-filled reds that range from earthy, old-school bottlings to flashy, powerful wines brimming with lush fruit flavors.

BEST PAIRINGS Lamb in almost any form is a classic pairing for Tempranillo. Other good partners include hard sheep cheeses like Manchego and lighter roast meats like pork or veal. Tempranillo's typically cherrylike fruit also makes it nice with duck.

● **Conde de Valdemar Reserva** / 2004 / Rioja / $$ / p. 107
● **Emilio Moro** / 2007 / Ribera del Duero / $$ / p. 121
● **Marqués de Murrieta Reserva** / 2007 / Rioja / $$ / p. 108
● **R. López de Heredia Viña Tondonia Reserva** / 2001 / Rioja Alta / $$$ / p. 109
● **Sierra Cantabria Tinto** / 2009 / Rioja / $ / p. 110

VIOGNIER

The basis of many of the famed white wines of France's northern Rhône Valley, Viognier has become a favorite in California for its lush peach, citrus and floral flavors.

BEST PAIRINGS Pair low-acid, lush Viognier with fruits such as apples, pears and peaches; richer shellfish such as scallops or lobster; and white-fleshed fish with butter or cream sauces. France's Viogniers, which tend to be leaner and spicier, also make good partners for quail, rabbit, guinea hen or sweetbreads.

- ○ **Keswick Vineyards Estate Reserve** / 2009 / Monticello / $$ / p. 209
- ○ **Seven Hills Talcott Vineyard** / 2009 / Columbia Valley / $$ / p. 206
- ○ **Yalumba The Y Series** / 2010 / South Australia / $ / p. 225
- ○ **Zaca Mesa** / 2009 / Santa Ynez Valley / $$ / p. 194

ZINFANDEL

California's own red grape (by way of Croatia), Zinfandel assumes many forms, from off-dry pale rosés and simple reds to full-bodied, tannic wines with blackberry and spice flavors. Zinfandel also makes thick port-style dessert wines.

BEST PAIRINGS Zinfandel's robust, dark-berry flavors, spice notes and moderate tannins make it an ideal partner for simple, hearty meat dishes like hamburgers, sausages or lamb chops. It's also a great match for barbecue, as the wine's sweet, spicy flavors complement the sweet, spicy sauce, and for Mexican food.

- ● **Cline Ancient Vines** / 2009 / California / $ / p. 167
- ● **Robert Biale Vineyards Black Chicken** / 2009 / Oak Knoll District of Napa Valley / $$$ / p. 186
- ● **Seghesio Family Vineyards Sonoma** / 2009 / Sonoma County / $$ / p. 189

Bargain / Wine Finder

Good value for money was an important consideration in selecting the wines recommended in this guide. Following is a list of featured wines from all over the world whose quality-to-price ratio makes them exceptional values and well worth stocking up on.

$$ wines $15+ to $30 / $ wines $15 and under

WHITE

$$

Chehalem Inox, Willamette Valley, Oregon, 196

Domaine Christian Moreau Père & Fils, Chablis, France, 39

Domaine Weinbach Cuvée Théo Riesling, Alsace, France, 27

Jermann Chardonnay, Collio, Italy, 79

Laroche, Chablis, France, 40

$

Acrobat Pinot Gris, Oregon, 198

Allegrini, Soave, Italy, 77

Aveleda Follies Alvarinho-Loureiro, Minho, Portugal, 125

Bodegas Nekeas Vega Sindoa Chardonnay, Navarra, Spain, 106

Domäne Wachau Terrassen Grüner Veltliner Federspiel, Wachau, Austria, 143

Edna Valley Vineyard Paragon Chardonnay, San Luis Obispo County, California, 171

Elsa Bianchi Torrontés, Mendoza, Argentina, 243

Hogue Riesling, Columbia Valley, Washington, 204

Kenwood Vineyards Sauvignon Blanc, Sonoma County, California, 179

La Vieille Ferme, Côtes du Luberon, France, 56

Little James' Basket Press, Vin de Pays d'Oc, France, 56

Luneau-Papin Pierre de la Grange Vieilles Vignes, Muscadet de Sèvre et Maine Sur Lie, France, 50

Maculan Pino & Toi, Veneto, Italy, 80

Montes Limited Selection Sauvignon Blanc, Leyda Valley, Chile, 249

Paul Cluver Gewürztraminer, Elgin, South Africa, 259

Rocky Gully Dry Riesling, Frankland River, Australia, 217

Seven Hills Riesling, Columbia Valley, Washington, 206

Villa Matilde Rocca dei Leoni Falanghina, Campania, Italy, 101

Yalumba The Y Series Viognier, South Australia, Australia, 225

ROSÉ

$

Bieler Père et Fils Rosé, Coteaux d'Aix-en-Provence, France, 63

Château Guiot, Costières de Nîmes, France, 57

RED

$$

Ambra, Barco Reale di Carmignano, Italy, 87

Descendientes de J. Palacios Pétalos, Bierzo, Spain, 121

Domaine Santa Duc Les Vieilles Vignes, Côtes-du-Rhône, France, 60

SPARKLING

Index

of Producers

Index

of Wines

WHITE

WHITE

WHITE

- **MEDIUM (continued)**

Goats do Roam White, Western Cape, 257

Grant Burge Benchmark Chardonnay, South Australia, 217

Grosset Piccadilly Chardonnay, Adelaide Hills, 218

Grosset Polish Hill Riesling, Clare Valley, 218

Grove Mill Sauvignon Blanc, Marlborough, 232

Hanna Chardonnay, Russian River Valley, 176

Heidi Schroeck Weissburgunder, Burgenland, 146

Herdade do Esporão Esporão Reserva White, Alentejano, 126

Hess Collection Chardonnay, Napa Valley, 177

Hirsch Heiligenstein Grüner Veltliner, Kamptal, 147

Hirsch Lamm Grüner Veltliner, Kamptal, 147

Hirsch Veltliner #1, Kamptal, 147

Hofstätter Joseph Pinot Grigio, Alto Adige, 79

Hogue Riesling, Columbia Valley, 204

Honig Sauvignon Blanc, Napa Valley, 177

Indaba Chenin Blanc, Western Cape, 257

Jean-Marc Brocard En Sol Kimméridgien Chardonnay, Bourgogne, 41

Jean-Marc Brocard Sauvignon, St-Bris, 41

Jermann Chardonnay, Collio, 79

John Duval Wines Plexus Marsanne-Roussanne-Viognier, Barossa Valley, 219

Jordan Chardonnay, Russian River Valley, 178

Joseph Drouhin, Saint-Véran, 42

Joseph Phelps Vineyards Sauvignon Blanc, St. Helena, 178

Kellerei Terlan Pinot Bianco, Alto Adige, 79

Kendall-Jackson Vintner's Reserve Chardonnay, California, 179

Ken Forrester Chenin Blanc, Stellenbosch, 258

Kenwood Vineyards Sauvignon Blanc, Sonoma County, 179

Keswick Vineyards Estate Reserve Viognier, Monticello, 209

Kilikanoon Mort's Reserve Watervale Riesling, Clare Valley, 220

Kim Crawford Sauvignon Blanc, Marlborough, 232

Kim Crawford Unoaked Chardonnay, Marlborough, 232

King Estate Domaine Pinot Gris, Oregon, 198

Kumeu River Estate Chardonnay, Kumeu, 232

Kumeu River Maté's Vineyard Chardonnay, Kumeu, 232

Kunde Family Estate Chardonnay, Sonoma Valley, 180

Landmark Overlook Chardonnay, Sonoma County, 180

Lapostolle Casa Sauvignon Blanc, Rapel Valley, 248

Laroche, Petit Chablis, 40

La Scolca "White Label," Gavi di Gavi, 72

La Vieille Ferme, Côtes du Luberon, 56

Leeuwin Estate Siblings Sauvignon Blanc–Semillon, Margaret River, 220

Leitz Eins Zwei Dry 3 Riesling, Rheingau, 139

Little James' Basket Press, Vin de Pays d'Oc, 56

Livio Felluga Friulano, Colli Orientali del Friuli, 80

Loimer Grüner Veltliner, Kamptal, 144

Loios Vinho White, Alentejano, 126

Los Vascos Sauvignon Blanc, Casablanca Valley, 251

Louis Latour, Pouilly-Fuissé, 41

Lucien Crochet La Croix du Roy, Sancerre, 49

Luis Pato Maria Gomes White, Beiras, 127

Luneau-Papin L d'Or, Muscadet de Sèvre et Maine Sur Lie, 50

MacMurray Ranch Chardonnay, Sonoma Coast, 181

Marina Cvetic Trebbiano, Trebbiano d'Abruzzo, 95

Martín Códax Albariño, Rías Baixas, 112

Martínsancho Verdejo, Rueda, 120

Mas Carlot Clairette de Bellegarde, Clairette de Bellegarde, 61

WHITE

- **MEDIUM (continued)**

Sonoma-Cutrer Les Pierres, Sonoma Coast, 190

Spottswoode Sauvignon Blanc, Napa Valley and Sonoma Mountain, 191

Spy Valley Sauvignon Blanc, Marlborough, 235

Stag's Leap Wine Cellars Sauvignon Blanc, Napa Valley, 191

St. Clement Vineyards Sauvignon Blanc, Napa Valley, 192

Sterling Vineyards Sauvignon Blanc, Napa County, 192

St. Francis Chardonnay, Sonoma County, 192

Stoller SV Estate Chardonnay, Dundee Hills, 200

Stone Hill Winery Vignoles, Missouri, 208

St. Supéry Sauvignon Blanc, Napa Valley, 193

Tablas Creek Vineyard Roussanne, Paso Robles, 193

Tasca d'Almerita Leone d'Almerita, Sicily, 100

Tasca d'Almerita Regaleali Bianco, Sicily, 100

Terras Gauda Abadia de San Campio, Rías Baixas, 112

Terras Gauda O Rosal, Rías Baixas, 112

Terrazas de los Andes Reserva Torrontés Unoaked, Mendoza, 243

Trimbach Pinot Blanc, Alsace, 28

Trumpeter Torrontés, Mendoza, 243

Valentín Bianchi Sauvignon Blanc, Mendoza, 243

Vasse Felix Chardonnay, Margaret River, 224

Veramonte Reserva Sauvignon Blanc, Casablanca Valley, 250

Verget Cuvée des 20 Ans, Chablis, 40

Vietti, Roero Arneis, 75

Villa Matilde Tenute di Altavilla, Greco di Tufo, 101

Villa Russiz Friulano, Collio, 81

Villa Russiz Pinot Grigio, Collio, 81

Vincent Girardin Les Vieilles Vignes, Pouilly-Fuissé, 43

Vincent Girardin Rully Vieilles Vignes, Rully, 43

Viu Manent Secreto Sauvignon Blanc, Casablanca Valley, 251

Wairau River Sauvignon Blanc, Marlborough, 235

Warwick Estate Professor Black Sauvignon Blanc, Stellenbosch, 259

Weingut Bründlmayer Kamptaler Terrassen Grüner Veltliner, Kamptal, 146

Weingut Robert Weil Kiedrich Turmberg Riesling Trocken, Rheingau, 139

Weingut Schloss Gobelsburg Lamm Erste Lage Reserve Grüner Veltliner, Kamptal, 145

Wente Vineyards Riva Ranch Chardonnay, Arroyo Seco, 194

Woodward Canyon Chardonnay, Washington State, 206

Woop Woop Chardonnay, South Eastern Australia, 206

Yalumba The Y Series Viognier, South Australia, 225

Zaca Mesa Viognier, Santa Ynez Valley, 194

- **FULL**

Agricola Querciabella Batàr, Tuscany, 91

Alphonse Mellot Génération XIX, Sancerre, 47

Bastianich Plus, Colli Orientali del Friuli, 78

Buena Vista Carneros Ramal Vineyard Chardonnay, Carneros, 163

Château-Fuissé Le Clos, Pouilly-Fuissé, 38

Château-Fuissé Les Combettes, Pouilly-Fuissé, 38

Cuvaison Chardonnay, Carneros, 168

Domaine Albert Mann Schlossberg Grand Cru Riesling, Alsace, 26

Domaine Albert Mann Steingrubler Grand Cru Gewurztraminer, Alsace, 26

Domaine Billaud-Simon Les Blanchots Vieille Vigne, Chablis Grand Cru, 38

Domaine de la Solitude, Châteauneuf-du-Pape, 58

Domaine des Baumard, Savennières, 48

Domaine des Baumard Clos du Papillon, Savennières, 48

Domaine Guffens-Heynen Tri de Chavigne, Mâcon-Pierreclos, 40

Domaine Jacques Prieur Clos de Mazeray, Meursault, 40

Domaine Laroche Les Clos, Chablis Grand Cru, 40

ROSÉ

RED

RED

- **MEDIUM (continued)**

Château Carbonnieux Grand Cru Classé de Graves, Pessac-Léognan, 31

Château de Fieuzal, Pessac-Léognan, 31

Château de Jau, Côtes du Roussillon Villages, 63

Château Fombrauge, St-Émilion Grand Cru, 32

Château Greysac, Médoc, 33

Château La Nerthe, Châteauneuf-du-Pape, 57

Château Pape Clément Grand Cru Classé de Graves, Pessac-Léognan, 34

Chateau Ste. Michelle Canoe Ridge Estate Merlot, Horse Heaven Hills, 202

Chehalem Reserve Pinot Noir, Ribbon Ridge, 196

The Chocolate Block, Western Cape, 256

Christian Moueix, Pomerol, 35

Christian Moueix, St-Estèphe, 35

Chryseia, Douro, 128

Clarendon Hills Clarendon Grenache, Clarendon, 216

Clendenen Family Vineyards Bien Nacido Estate Plantings Petit Verdot, Santa Maria Valley, 161

Cline Ancient Vines Zinfandel, California, 167

Clos de los Siete, Mendoza, 242

Clos du Bois Merlot, North Coast, 167

Cloudy Bay Pinot Noir, Marlborough, 231

Col d'Orcia Banditella, Rosso di Montalcino, 87

Col d'Orcia Riserva, Brunello di Montalcino, 87

Colomé Estate Malbec, Calchaquí Valleys, 240

Columbia Crest Grand Estates Cabernet Sauvignon, Columbia Valley, 203

Columbia Crest H3 Cabernet Sauvignon, Horse Heaven Hills, 203

Condado de Haza, Ribera del Duero, 120

Conde de Valdemar Reserva, Rioja, 107

Contino Viña del Olivo, Rioja Alavesa, 110

Copain Les Voisins Pinot Noir, Anderson Valley, 168

Copain Tous Ensemble Pinot Noir, Anderson Valley, 168

Copain Tous Ensemble Syrah, Mendocino County, 168

Craggy Range Gimblett Gravels Vineyard Sophia, Hawke's Bay, 231

Craggy Range Te Muna Road Vineyard Pinot Noir, Martinborough, 231

Cuvaison Pinot Noir, Carneros, 168

CVNE Imperial Gran Reserva, Rioja Alta, 110

d'Arenberg The Stump Jump Grenache-Shiraz-Mourvèdre, McLaren Vale, 216

Dashe Todd Brothers Ranch Old Vines Zinfandel, Alexander Valley, 169

Delas, Côtes du Ventoux, 53

Delas Saint-Esprit, Côtes-du-Rhône, 53

DeLoach OFS Pinot Noir, Russian River Valley, 169

Descendientes de J. Palacios Pétalos, Bierzo, 121

Descendientes de J. Palacios Villa de Corullón, Bierzo, 121

Di Majo Norante Sangiovese, Terre degli Osci, 98

Domaine Bouchard Père & Fils Beaune du Château, Beaune Premier Cru, 37

Domaine de la Janasse Terre d'Argile, Côtes-du-Rhône Villages, 58

Domaine de la Mordorée La Reine des Bois, Châteauneuf-du-Pape, 58

Domaine Drouhin Oregon Laurène Pinot Noir, Dundee Hills, 197

Domaine Drouhin Oregon Pinot Noir, Willamette Valley, 197

Domaine Dujac Aux Combottes, Gevrey-Chambertin Premier Cru, 39

Domaine du Pégau Cuvée Reservée, Châteauneuf-du-Pape, 59

Domaine Faiveley La Framboisière, Mercurey, 39

Domaine Gerovassiliou Avaton, Epanomi, 152

Domaine La Réméjeanne Les Arbousiers, Côtes-du-Rhône, 59

Domaine Santa Duc, Gigondas, 60

Domaine Santa Duc Les Vieilles Vignes, Côtes-du-Rhône, 60

RED

RED

RED

SPARKLING